Marketing the Author

Marketing the Author

Authorial Personae, Narrative Selves and Self-Fashioning, 1880–1930

Edited by

Marysa Demoor

First published 2004 by
PALGRAVE MACMILLAN
Houndmills, Basingstoke, Hampshire RG21 6XS and
175 Fifth Avenue, New York, N. Y. 10010
Companies and representatives throughout the world

PALGRAVE MACMILLAN is the global academic imprint of the Palgrave
Macmillan division of St. Martin's Press, LLC and of Palgrave Macmillan Ltd.
Macmillan® is a registered trademark in the United States, United Kingdom
and other countries. Palgrave is a registered trademark in the European
Union and other countries.

ISBN 1–4039–3329–4 hardback

This book is printed on paper suitable for recycling and made from fully
managed and sustained forest sources.

A catalogue record for this book is available from the British Library.

Library of Congress Cataloging-in-Publication Data
Marketing the author : authorial personae, narrative selves, and
self-fashioning, 1880–1930 / edited by Marysa Demoor.
    p. cm.
  Includes bibliographical references and index.
  ISBN 1–4039–3329–4
    1. English literature–20th century–History and criticism. 2. Authors in
literature. 3. Authors and readers–Great Britain–History–20th century.
4. Authors and readers–Great Britain–History–19th century. 5. English
literature–19th century–History and criticism.
6. Authorship–Marketing–History–20th century.
7. Authorship–Marketing–History–19th century. 8. American
literature–History and criticism. 9. Authors and readers–United States.
10. Point of view (Literature) 11. Persona (Literature) 12. Narration
(Rhetoric) 13. Self in literature. I. Demoor, Marysa.

PR478.A87M37 2004
820.9'0091–dc22   2003063299

10   9   8   7   6   5   4   3   2   1
13 12 11 10 09 08 07 06 05 04

Transferred to digital printing 2005

To Professor Gillian Beer,
for her ubiquitous presence and support

Contents

List of Illustrations   ix

Notes on the Contributors   x

Acknowledgements   xiii

Introduction   1
  Marysa Demoor

 1 Emilia Dilke: Self-Fashioning and the Nineteenth Century   19
     Elizabeth Mansfield

 2 The Art of Self-Creation: Henry James in the New York
    Edition Prefaces   40
     John H. Pearson

 3 'Who is "We"?' The 'Daily Paper' Projects and the
    Journalism Manifestos of W.T. Stead   54
     Laurel Brake

 4 A Novelist of Character: Becoming Lucas Malet   73
     Talia Shaffer

 5 Irony, Ethics and Self-Fashioning in George Moore's
    Confessions of a Young Man   96
     Annette Federico

 6 Interstitial Identities: Vernon Lee and the Spaces
    In-Between   114
     Hilary Fraser

 7 A Woman Poet Angling for Notice: Rosamund
    Marriott Watson   134
     Linda K. Hughes

 8 Arnold Bennett's Other Selves   156
     Robert Squillace

 9 Perpetuating Joyce   184
     Edward Bishop

10 Making Room for the Woman of Genius: Virginia Woolf, Elizabeth Robins and 'Modernism's Other' as Mother 207
Molly Hite

Index 234

List of Illustrations

1. The launching of the *Daily Paper*, *Review of Reviews*,   69
   January 1904
2. 'Mrs Arthur Tomson', *English Illustrated Magazine*,   141
   April 1894. Reproduced courtesy of the Bodleian Library,
   University of Oxford, Per. 2705 s.223, p. 65

Notes on the Contributors

Laurel Brake is Professor of Literature and Print Culture at Birkbeck, University of London. Her research interests are nineteenth-century print, literature and culture, gender, press and book history, and Walter Pater. *Print in Transition: Studies in Media and Book History* (2001) and *Walter Pater: Transparencies of Desire* (2002), co-edited with Lesley Higgins and Carolyn Williams, are her most recent books; earlier titles include *Subjugated Knowledges* and *Walter Pater* (both 1994) and co-edited collections on nineteenth-century journalism including *Investigating Victorian Journalism* (1990) and *Nineteenth-century Media and the Construction of Identities* (2000). Of the articles, 'On Print Culture: The State We're in', *Journal of Victorian Culture* (Summer 2001) discusses the field(s) of print culture/media history/history of the book.

Edward Bishop is Professor of English at the University of Alberta, Canada. He has published on Joyce and print culture in *Joyce Studies Annual*, written and edited books on Virginia Woolf and the Bloomsbury Group, and won awards for his non-fiction project, 'The Motorcycle and the Archive'.

Marysa Demoor is Professor of English and Gender Studies at the University of Ghent, Belgium and a Life Member of Clare Hall, Cambridge. She has published on Victorian and turn-of-the-century culture. Her most recent book is *Their Fair Share. Women, Power and Criticism in the Athenaeum, from Millicent Garrett Fawcett to Katherine Mansfield, 1870–1920* (2000). Previously she edited correspondences of Andrew Lang and Henry James. She is currently working on the representations of Flemish late medieval and Renaissance art in English and American literature.

Annette R. Federico teaches English at James Madison University, Virginia. Her book *Idol of Suburbia: Marie Corelli and Late-Victorian Literary Culture* was published in 2000.

Hilary Fraser holds the Geoffrey Tillotson Chair in Nineteenth-Centry Studies at Birkbeck College, University of London. Her books include

Beauty and Belief: Aesthetics and Religion in Victorian Literature (1986); *The Victorians and Renaissance Italy* (1992); *English Prose of the Nineteenth Century* (1997, with Daniel Brown); and *Gender and the Victorian Periodical* (2003, with Stephanie Green and Judith Johnston). She is currently working on an AHRB-funded project on women writing art history in the nineteenth century.

Molly Hite is Professor of English at Cornell University, where she teaches twentieth-century literature and theory. She is the author of *Ideas of Order in the Novels of Thomas Pynchon* (1983); and *The Other Side of the Story: Structures and Strategies of Contemporary Feminist Narrative* (1989); and two novels, *Class Porn* (1987); and *Breach of Immunity* (1992). She has written articles on postmodernist and modernist fiction, feminist theory and practice, and academic culture. She is finishing a new book, *Weird Woolf.*

Linda K. Hughes is Addie Levy Professor of Literature at Texas Christian University, Fort Worth, Texas. Author of *The Manyfaced Glass: Tennyson's Dramatic Monologues* and a forthcoming biography of Rosamund Marriott Watson, she is also editor of *New Woman Poets: An Anthology* (2001) and a forthcoming volume of Elizabeth Gaskell's shorter fiction, and co-author, with Michael Lund, of *The Victorian Serial* (1991) and *Victorian Publishing and Mrs. Gaskell's Work* (1999).

Elizabeth Mansfield is Associate Professor and Chair of Art and Art History at the University of the South in Sewanee, Tennessee. She writes on art historiography and has published numerous articles on the Victorian art historian Emilia Dilke. Other publications include the edited volume *Art History and Its Institutions* (2002) to which she contributed an essay on 'Art History and Modernism'. Current projects include an article examining how the College Art Association has shaped the practice of art history in the United States and a book-length study of the modern reception of the antique legend of Zeuxis Selecting Models.

John Pearson is Nell Carlton Professor of English at Stetson University in DeLand, Florida. He is author of *The Prefaces of Henry James: Framing the Modern Reader* (1997); and articles on American literature, autobiography and literary theory. He is currently completing a book on aesthetics in the nineteenth-century American novel.

Talia Schaffer is an Associate Professor at Queens College, CUNY. She is the author of *The Forgotten Female Aesthetes: Literary Culture in Late-Victorian England* and co-editor, with Kathy A. Psomiades, of *Women and British Aestheticism*. She has written many articles on Lucas Malet and other turn-of-the-century women writers, and recently published a new edition of Lucas Malet's 1901 novel, *The History of Sir Richard Calmady*. Other work includes a forthcoming reader, *Literature and Culture at the Fin de Siècle*, and a new book about Victorian women's domestic handicraft.

Robert Squillace is a Master Teacher of Cultural Foundations in the General Studies Program of New York University. His publications on Edwardian literature include *Modernism, Modernity and Arnold Bennett* (1997); 'Self-isolation and Self-advertisement in Arnold Bennett's The Old Wives' Tale', in *Seeing Double: Revisioning Modernist and Edwardian Literature*, ed. Anne Simpson and Carola Kaplan (1996); and 'Bennett, Wells and the Persistence of Realism', in *The Columbia History of the British Novel*, ed. John Richetti (1994). With Edward Mendelson, he edited the Penguin edition of *Riceyman Steps* (1991). He lives in Brooklyn with his wife, the medievalist Angela Jane Weisl.

Acknowledgements

I owe thanks to all the contributors to this volume for their belief in the project and their unflagging enthusiasm, to the editors of Palgrave Macmillan, Emily Rosser and Paula Kennedy, for their kind help, to the University Foundation, Belgium, for their publication subsidy, and to Professor Kate Belsey for convincing me to get on with it.

Permission to reproduce a quotation from Ms. Walpole d. 19, fols. 107–108. In Linda K. Hughes' essay, 'A Woman Angling for Notice: Rosamund Marriott Watson', was kindly granted by the Bodleian Library, Oxford.

... as the model of the integrated private self of the author fades, the rights of the author as a persistent self-identity also become more evanescent, more difficult to define. If the work of the author no longer carries with it definite physical properties as a unique *original*, as a book in a definite form, then the author's rights too grow more tenuous, more indistinct.

(Heim 1999)

it would be worth examining how the author became individualized in a culture like ours, what status he has been given, at what moment studies of authenticity and attribution began, in what kind of system of valorization the author was involved, at what point we began to recount the lives of authors rather than of heroes, and how this fundamental category of 'the-man-and-his-work criticism' began.

(Foucault 1979)

Introduction

Marysa Demoor

The last quarter of the nineteenth century saw a sea change in publishing history. This was the zenith of the Victorian commodity culture, which now reached out to all areas of public life, including that pertaining to authorship and the reading public, in other words, to the production and consumption of the word.[1] More books, newspapers and journals were published than ever before, and some reached a wider readership and made more money than ever before. If *The Times* could boast a circulation of 39,000 in 1851, that was nothing compared to the 500,000 reached by the *Daily Mail* at the end of the century, with sales soaring to over a million in 1900 at the height of the Boer War (Hartley Withers et al. 187). The book market too attained vast proportions. A best-selling author like Marie Corelli sold on average more than 100,000 copies of her books each year at the height of her career (Federico 6).

Publishing had become big business. Merchants and others engaged in commerce realised, almost simultaneously with this development, the extent to which periodicals could boost their trade. Journalism and advertising had been in partnership for some time. Indeed, advertisements had been as vital to periodicals as they are today. Then, in the 1850s, the revenue from advertisements for both the advertising firms and the media they used increased extensively when the tax on advertisements in journals and newspapers was lifted in 1853 followed, two years later, by the abolition of stamp duty. But the history of modern advertising really began in the 1870s and 1880s when crude repetitions of firm names had to make way for more sophisticated displays and illustrations. Only the older papers, such as *The Times*, were to wait until the 1890s before introducing illustrations with their advertisements. It was an era in which independent advertising agencies saw the opportunity to acquire power and money, or vice versa. By the 1880s many of the best-known agencies had been founded and a decade later their own trade paper, significantly called *Fame*, was launched (Hartley Withers et al. 188). Also in the 1880s, advertisers began to replace black and white engravings with photo reproduction and the even more attractive coloured photograph (Anderson 197). They were quick to realise how much coloured photographs could do for their products and how well periodicals could serve their ends.

Forster's Education Act of 1871 added considerably to the expansion of the market. Henceforth every child would be required to attend school until the age of ten and so was expected to learn to read and write. The younger working class, ten years later, were potential readers and perhaps even purchasers of books, journals and newspapers. 'The difference between the nineteenth-century and the twentieth-century mass is literacy,' John Carey declared in a recent book on *The Intellectuals and the Masses* (Carey 5). This new and unknown reading public had to be wooed and lured into buying. Publishers understandably targeted their publications at them. The other condition for a growth in the readership, the lowering of the price of all kinds of publications, had already been fulfilled in the course of the century. The expensive three-deckers, and with them Mudie's circulating library, had become a thing of the past by the 1890s. Paperbacks, which were both inexpensive and light to carry, filled the shelves of the growing number of bookshops. The introduction of such technical innovations as the Fourdrinier paper-making machine, and the Cowper and Applegarth cylinder press literally accelerated the mass production and consumption process by making paper cheaper and faster to produce (Brendon 17).

Concurrent with the rise of a mass readership was a growing unease and a sense of doom on the part of the previously privileged, highly educated classes. The masses were considered a danger and threat by many intellectuals. H.G. Wells observed that 'the great gulf that had divided the world hitherto into the readers and the non-reading mass became little more than a slightly perceptible difference in educational level' (quoted in Carey 6). Wells' remark is interesting because it says more about his perception of the public than about the actual level of education of the general reading public. It was, however, a perception that other turn-of-the-century authors shared, leading them to create works which the general public found increasingly hard to access and to enjoy. Pierre Bourdieu was to label this the 'field of restricted production' (115). With hindsight, therefore, it appears that the 'gulf' between the masses and the intellectuals became even greater, with the result that 'Popular authors' were stigmatised simply for being popular. Joseph Conrad vented his disgust with the species of 'the best-selling writer' in a letter to Aniela Zagórska when he commented that these authors 'are popular because they express the common thought, and the common man is delighted to find himself in accord with people he supposes distinguished' (Conrad 2: 137).[2]

Others thought of the masses as a political force they could influence and manipulate. As early as 1855 Walter Bagehot famously observed that 'modern man must be told what to think – shortly no doubt, but he *must* be told it ...' (quoted in Houghton 7). These social changes and technical innovations coincided with important political developments. Suffrage was extended once again in 1884 in the Third Reform Act. Now the electorate almost trebled to 2.5 million voters.

Yet the development in the book publishing market differed to some extent from that in the periodical market in that new readers would not automatically opt for a book if they could get the same kind of entertainment from a magazine or journal. Furthermore, periodicals could publish the stories the average reader wanted faster and cheaper while covering a greater variety (Ohmann 23). Consequently, while the book market grew in this period, its role within the cultural field underwent an overall decline because of the choice available to the potential consumer of culture.

Performing authorship

As hinted above, authors may have been the first to be aware of socio-political changes. Some of the great Victorian authors had warned in the middle of the century of the power of the press and the threat of commercialising culture. Alfred Tennyson wrote these exalted lines in 1852:

'O you the Press! What good from you might spring!
What power is yours to blast a cause or bless!
I fear for you, as for some youthful king,
Lest you go wrong from power in excess,
Take heed of your wide privileges! we,
The thinking men of England, loathe a tyranny

(Tennyson 852)

Others recognised the new possibilities within a growing cultural market and chose to profit from it. Charles Dickens is a prime example of an author who saw and understood the market forces and thrived in them. Dickens exulted in constructing discursive selves for himself, narrative alter egos in fiction as in life, and loved to perform them. His public responded enthusiastically.

Dickens' talent at selling himself and his books prefigured in many ways the more sophisticated marketing techniques of subsequent generations. These techniques necessarily developed against a background of and in connivance with what has come to be known as 'new journalism' and its practices. 'New journalism' was Matthew Arnold's term for what he called 'the voice of the new voters, the *democracy*, as people are fond of calling them' (quoted in Tucker 55). The high priest of new journalism was W.T. Stead. He wanted to be, and to be perceived as, a prophet; this in turn meant that he was constantly preoccupied with the projection of the right image of himself. His death on the *Titanic* was the grand exit of this arch-performer. The popularity of Stead the journalist, his successful performance as a martyr for the cause of morality, honesty and against hypocrisy caught the eye of many authors and, in the early years of his career, they backed him when he needed it.[3] Interestingly, Stead also took it upon himself and had the power to fashion the image of contemporary celebrities according to his views of them. The personal interview, photographs of the artist at home, autobiographical and even confessional writings were, he thought, what the public unwittingly craved (see McDonald 8). Stead made sure they got it.

As a result of the changes in the publishing world authors knew they had to adapt or die. George Bernard Shaw described this feeling with characteristic gusto:

> The Education Act of 1871 was producing readers who had never before bought books, nor could have read them if they had; and publishers were finding that these people wanted not George Eliot and the excessively literary novice Bernard Shaw, but such crude tales of impossible adventures published in penny numbers only for school boys. The success of Stevenson's Treasure Island and Jekyll and Hyde fairy tale, forced this change on the attention of the publishers; *and I, as belated intellectual, went under completely* ... (Holroyd 1: 79; my emphasis)

Shaw did not go under and had no intention of doing so, but instead decided to sell himself together with his work. In a letter to the playwright and actress Elizabeth Robins, he gave this perspicacious advice as the last (and chief) of a series of points to take into account in dealing with the media: 'Always *interview yourself* if you can' (Shaw 1: 381).[4] The advice reflects his conviction that artists had to remain in control of their public image at all costs. The predicament of the author who did not heed Shaw's advice, or rather who did not think of his writings as a commodity which he had to try to sell, is eloquently described in George Gissing's *New Grub Street*. The character of Harold Biffen reflects Gissing's conviction that money is no consideration of the true artist:

> He worked very slowly. The book would make perhaps two volumes of ordinary novel size, but he had laboured over it for many months, patiently, affectionately, scrupulously. Each sentence was as good as he could make it, harmonious to the ear, with words of precious meaning skilfully set. Before sitting down to a chapter he planned it minutely in his mind; then he wrote a rough draft of it; then he elaborated the thing phrase by phrase. He had no thought of whether such toil would be recompensed in coin of the realm; nay, it was his conviction that, if with difficulty published, it could scarcely bring him money. The work must be significant, that was all he cared for. (Gissing 352)

But the reality was that all artists, however highly motivated, needed money in order to live and the fact of writing a good book was no guarantee of a good income.

Indeed, the changed socio-political circumstances could only fundamentally alter the nature of authorship. Writing became a trade in which it was acceptable for authors to be assisted by a literary agent who had his or her commercial interests at heart. The best-known agents of the period were A.P. Watt (who was the first to establish a literary agency in 1875), J.B. Pinker and Curtis Brown. Another step in the process was the foundation, by Walter Besant, of a Society of Authors in 1884. The Society was meant to protect the interests of authors and, like the advertisers, it had its own paper, the *Author*, which gave voice to the pressing concerns and complaints of the professional author. Gissing joined the Society in 1890 only to find it a 'mere gathering of tradesmen' (Bradbury 135). Yet his financial difficulties (and possibly his lack of commercial talent) forced him to turn to a literary agent a year later to manage his affairs and further his career.[5]

Interestingly, agents increasingly began to sell the authors first, and their books second. The personality of the author, whether real or fictional, was what mattered. Anonymous writing became a thing of the past in journalism as well as in literature since consumers were often moved to buy a book or a journal because they knew and liked a particular writer. 'Certainly, it would be worth examining how the author became individualized in a culture like ours,' said Michel Foucault in his seminal lecture 'What is an Author?', adding that he would be equally interested in finding out 'at what moment studies of authenticity and attribution began, in what kind of valorization the author was involved, at what point we began to recount the lives of authors rather than of heroes' (Foucault 2: 205). Foucault too is puzzled by the fact that whereas anonymous literary texts had been acceptable in previous centuries this had changed radically to the extent that today 'we cannot tolerate literary anonymity' (Foucault 2: 213). This book claims that the moment of change happened in the last decades of the nineteenth century.

The chief aim of the essays collected here is to look at the careers and writings of a selection of authors who started to write in the last decades of the nineteenth century or the first decade of the twentieth century and who each tried to control their public image by creating a self that would help them to do just that. Their reasons for self-invention were the direct result of the social, economic and cultural changes of the era. For this period was an especially dense and complex one, covering the transition from what has come to be called the late Victorian era to a modernist era. All the authors considered here lived and worked after 1870 at the intersection between the Victorian and the modernist cultural scene. Apart from Virginia Woolf and James Joyce, who are now unhesitatingly called modernist, it is difficult to allocate them to a particular, period-bound category of writers. Bennett was relegated to the Georgian camp by his contemporary Virginia Woolf but he seems, like James, Wilde and Shaw, to be a hybrid, a transitional figure with roots in the Victorian age, but looking and working towards a new era (see Woolf 1: 321, Squillace). The same goes for women authors like Emilia Dilke, Vernon Lee, Lucas Malet and Rosamund Marriott Watson. All made the most of the opportunities they were given and the talents they obviously had in a rapidly changing literary world. When emphasising the challenges for the post-1870s writer, the book sides with Raymond Williams who argued that the Victorian period ended in the late 1870s or the early 1880s and then '[s]ocially, culturally, economically, politically, a new phase of our history began' (Williams *English Novel* 121). Indeed, Williams saw the changes in the public media as the preconditions of the modernist movement (*Politics* 33–4).

Hence, the key moment mentioned in Virginia Woolf's celebrated phrase 'in or about December, 1910, human character changed' (Woolf 1: 320) is to be seen as just one of several significant dates in an evolution that had started many years earlier. The claim that 1910, or for that matter any of the other dates suggested by contemporaries of Woolf,[6] signalled a radical break between two generations, has been exploded by a number of cultural and literary historians in recent years as so many attempts at defining themselves as other and new. Most recently Ann Ardis has pleaded for 'a more detailed and more nuanced topographical mapping of the period than modernism's classic "narrative[s] of rupture"' since, as she points out, the 'men of 1914' successfully obliterated the work of competitive aesthetic traditions and, equally successfully, masked the conservative nature of much of their sexual and cultural politics (Ardis 7–8). The essays collected in this volume follow the same line of thought while adding and stressing that the art of self-definition so central to the modernist aesthetic was not its monopoly.[7] The authors discussed here, whether considered modernist or not, explored and exploited the new possibilities offered by the expanding mass media, as well as the new dimensions of the self, the existence of which had been tantalisingly uncovered in Sigmund Freud's controversial writings.

Self-creations and women authors

Not only did the last quarter of the nineteenth century see the emergence and growing power of the mass media, the commodification of culture and profound political changes, it was also the period in which women began to fight for – and in some cases won – the right to vote, to attend university, to obtain university degrees and to pursue professional careers. In what follows, the writings and the careers of five women are examined. Arranged in chronological order they are: Emilia Dilke (1840–1904), Lucas Malet (1852–1931), Vernon Lee (1856–1935), Rosamund Marriott Watson (1860–1911) and Virginia Woolf (1882–1941).

Growing independence gave women authors the strength and the courage to venture into areas which women had not visited before and to conceive narrative personae or authorial identities which transgressed the societal rules women were expected to observe. Women authors' attempts at inventing new, possibly more liberating, selves in this transitional period to improve their social and economic position has drawn the attention of literary scholars before (Federico, Beard,

Demoor). Yet the phenomenon has always been viewed as an individual author's unique adaptation to circumstances. In juxtaposing the career strategies of the authors selected for the present collection it appears that the age required many of them to make that effort. The nineteenth century had seen great women writers who had become literary giants in spite of their sex. Jane Austen, Elizabeth Gaskell and the Brontës did not have to 'play' the successful author in order to be or to continue to be one. The changed economic circumstances at the end of the century and the growing prestige of the novel, however, made it necessary for women to perform selves they had fashioned in order not only to emerge from a crowd of writers, but even to survive (see Tuchman).

Unfortunately, women, even at the time, became overtly associated with mass consumption, the selling of culture and cultural decadence. This highly problematised the position of the aesthetically and intellectually ambitious woman writer (Demoor). Her quandary has been made explicit by Andreas Huyssen in his essay 'Mass Culture as Woman':

> In the age of nascent socialism and the first major women's movement in Europe, the masses knocking at the gate were also women, knocking at the gate of a male-dominated culture. It is indeed striking to observe how the political, psychological, and aesthetic discourse around the turn of the century consistently and obsessively genders mass culture and the masses as feminine, while high culture, whether traditional or modern, clearly remains the privileged realm of male activities. (46)

Even so, as recent feminist scholarship has been at pains to point out, women did not only knock at the door of what later generations of critics and historians came to perceive as a male bastion, they were also inside. In an impressive inclusive study of British aestheticism, for instance, Talia Schaffer has convincingly shown the significance of the participation of women artists to that movement. Yet in spite of the contemporary reputation and the undoubted influence of women authors like Ouida, Lucas Malet and Alice Meynell, their names were erased from literary history.

Until recently, scholars underestimated the height of the hurdles women had to cross as well as the subtle strategies they deployed in doing so. Nor is it the case that the most successful writers were those who later came to be seen as the most meritorious. At one extreme one finds Marie Corelli, a writer whose public (and private) antics are examined in great detail in a recent monograph by Annette Federico. To her envious male contemporaries, Corelli appeared to confirm all the prejudices concerning successful best-selling authors. At the other extreme there are the women who dared to appropriate male encoded cultural positions but who, in order to do so, needed to create new selves. The women discussed here fall into the second category.

Emilia Dilke has had three biographies devoted to her and her unusual life and at least as many novels have recycled her unhappy marriage to the much older Mark Pattison, the Rector of Lincoln College. George Eliot's Dorothea Brooke in *Middlemarch* is probably the best-known fictionalisation of her life. In her essay for this book, however, Elizabeth Mansfield looks at all the ways in which Dilke deliberately tried to make a difference, forging an ever-changing identity suited to the particular moments in her life.

The pitfalls of fashioning a writerly self which one has to abandon in the course of one's career because of real life choices, are also explored in Linda Hughes' essay on Rosamund Marriott Watson (*née* Ball). Watson decided to kill off her first poetic persona, 'Graham R. Tomson', when she eloped with H.B. Marriott Watson, thereby losing, in Bourdieu's terms, the cultural capital she had carefully amassed under that first pseudonym.

And Lucas Malet, in spite of her persistent efforts to discard the burden of being Charles Kingsley's daughter and in spite of the high quality of her work, never successfully fashioned an authorial self that was strong enough to be superimposed on the self the public had created for her. Her almost heroic struggle is depicted in Talia Schaffer's essay.

Similarly, that most brilliant of turn-of-the-century women, Vernon Lee, who in Hilary Fraser's essay is shown almost to personify that moment of transition between the Victorian era and Modernism, failed to create a self which endured. Perhaps hers had been too unstable a persona, always moving between cultures as between sexes, always eluding the binary. She could not be pinned down to one clearly definable subject position by posterity. With the help of Homi Bhabha and Stuart Hall's theoretical reflections, Fraser labels this 'Lee's own interstitial condition, of the hybrid, becoming identity', which she finds to be forever in process.

If one uses the number of articles and books devoted to an author as a means to gauge his or her literary achievement, then it appears that Virginia Woolf has been particularly successful. Woolf was much

younger than the other women writers discussed here and that may
have given her the advantage of learning by hindsight. Woolf, Molly
Hite contends, was at pains to define herself as a woman of genius. In
order to do so, she had to adapt her feminism to suit her purpose and,
in spite of her professed intention to think back 'through our mothers',
she in effect had to dismiss her female predecessors and contemporaries as inferiors. She alone was fit to stand in the category of those
she labelled the Georgians, all of them men.

Apart from fashioning authorial identities in order to inhabit or
perform them, the women discussed in this study also imbued some of
their fictional characters with autobiographical material, thus creating
narrative selves which were sometimes closer to the selfhood of the
authors. In fact they illustrate and endorse Paul Ricoeur's theory about
self-identity and life-stories in that their stories provide a pseudo-
fictional structure to autobiographical data (Ricoeur 138). In truth,
these women authors seem to have experienced a need to construct
different selves: public selves which they performed and which were
apt to change in the course of their lives, and more stable private yet
discursive selves.

None of the women dealt with in this book can be associated with
the cheap, the popular and the so-called low culture, which was the
fate of the Marie Corellis of this world. But apart from Woolf, they
eventually failed to attain immortality. At best, they were granted the
respect of their peers. Yet for some, still largely inexplicable, reason all
the selves they fashioned collapsed once the authors themselves died.

Self-fashioning strategies of male authors

Most of the men in this book fared much better. The first two have
achieved a canonical position as the inventors of modernity. Indeed,
Henry James (1843–1916) and James Joyce (1882–1941) seem to be
growing in popularity, thanks to the film industry and some influential
academic groups. The work of George Moore (1852–1933) does quite
well too, if one lists the academic articles it has spawned. Arnold
Bennett (1867–1931), however, lags a little, although interest in his
oeuvre has picked up in recent years. W.T. Stead (1849–1912) is the
great unknown compared to those authors whose careers he sometimes
influenced and sometimes helped to shape.[8] Interestingly, James, Joyce
and Moore were 'outsiders', not English (Williams *English Novel* 123).
Perhaps, like the women authors we have considered, they felt the
need to deploy certain marketing strategies and tried harder to be suc-

cessful than their English colleagues. But they were certainly much better at selling themselves, eventually, than their female colleagues. And, more surprising still, two of them gave the impression of not being interested in the sales or the critical reception of their writings.[9] They were eventually the most successful.

This book covers the work and sometimes the lives of those whom Peter McDonald in a recent work on British culture and publishing practice would have labelled the 'profiteers', those who wanted to and succeeded in achieving a best-selling career, or, again in McDonald's words, those who 'value only the most fungible goods of all, namely money' (Arnold Bennett and George Moore). But, contrary to what McDonald might expect, this categorisation does not exclude Henry James and James Joyce whom he would undoubtedly have dubbed 'purists', those for whom 'the literary field exists in and for itself' (14). Indeed, both James and Joyce are included in this book since both were demonstrably engaged in self-mythologising in order to seduce a consumerist public.

James's initial despair at the poor sales of his books did not paralyse him as it did Reardon in Gissing's *Grub Street*; rather, it spurred him on to seek and follow a different route which would not have him diminish the quality of his writings. James's attempts at negotiating a position between that of the commercially inclined writer and the aloof aesthete or the elitist modernist were revealed first by Michael Anesko in his book *'Friction with the Market': Henry James and the Profession of Authorship*.[10] In his essay for the present collection John Pearson has examined the ways in which James used the prefaces to the New York Edition of his works to produce a self which was to bridge the gap between the text and the uninitiated (and for James at the time elusive) reader. Pearson pays homage to and uses Judith Butler's theory on performance when he unravels James's intricate spinning of different metaphors for the writer which, taken together, produce a performing subject.

James, Pearson concludes, worried that the writerly self he had conjured up would lead its own life, like the broom brought to life by the sorcerer's apprentice in the Disney *Fantasia*, and perhaps that is just what happened. But James's main purpose – that is, if we are allowed to reconstruct a writer's intention when analysing the prefaces to his collected work – was 'to fix his place in the literary world' and 'to receive remuneration for his work'. That he undoubtedly achieved.

Things are somewhat different with Arnold Bennett, since his resurrection as a writer of some note has only just begun. Bennett seems to have believed that he could have become anything he wanted if only he had set his mind to it: 'I am a writer, just as I might be a hotel-keeper...' (Bradbury 157). True to this axiom he wrote a series of self-help books which made others believe that they too, if they only persevered, might achieve their most cherished goals in life. You could fashion, form and improve yourself if you only followed his advice in *How to Live on 24 Hours a Day*. Yet, as Robert Squillace points out, there is an intriguing contradiction between Bennett's confident belief in the formation of one's self in his self-help books and the self emerging in his novels, where it remains a largely unknowable and unpredictable depiction of the authorial self.

Bennett is to some extent comparable to W.T. Stead, the one other Englishman discussed below, in that, like Stead, Bennett started his career as a journalist. But his boundless belief in what a person could achieve if he only tried hard enough soon set him to write successful novels. Stead's career took a less propitious turn. From Laurel Brake's essay it appears that Stead's career initially seemed promising enough, but by the age of forty he had had to leave daily journalism and was to spend the rest of his life dreaming of a return to the business he believed he alone could reform. Ousted from his post on the *Pall Mall Gazette*, he never regained a position on a daily newspaper. On two occasions, however, Stead tried to relaunch himself as a journalist with a newspaper that was to be an extension or a refashioning of himself. Stead wrote about journalism all his life, defining it in terms of commerce, politics and religion. His ideal journalist, the self he wanted to embody, was a cross between 'two types of minister, the minister of religion and the Prime Minister of party and government'. His stint as editor of the *Pall Mall Gazette* was the one chance he had of achieving this. Stead differs from the others writers discussed here in that he never authored any *fiction* in the true sense of the word. Yet it is his crucial position within the turn-of-the-century culture of (self-)mythologising, the paradoxical combination of his moral and commerce interests, and his immense influence on writers like Joyce which warrant his inclusion here.

With Annette Federico's essay on George Moore yet another aspect of late century self-fashioning emerges. Drawing on the work of Jill Larson and Richard Rorty, Federico considers George Moore's need to self-invent as an ethical position. In fact, Moore's entire life was dedicated to the process of creating his own self and most of that was done in public. Federico focuses on the way he invented and described himself in the autobiographical *Confessions of a Young Man* (1888). In this satirical as well as moralistic work, Moore creates an 'ideal George Moore'. Indeed, his stress on the contingency of selfhood and the claim that he might 'equally have been a pharaoh, an ostler, a pimp, an archbishop' at once echoes as well contradicts Bennett. Moore's *Confessions* has been viewed as an activist piece of writing which encouraged social change with the help of the aesthetic movement. But it was also, Federico argues, a 'playful self-construction as a legitimate ethical and even political position'.

With James Joyce we come to the last, possibly the most creative, certainly the most successful of self-creators. Joyce thrived in the artistically liberal climate of the turn of the century and quickly saw (and chose) the ways in which to sell his writerly persona together with his work. He started to invent himself at an impossibly early age. Edward Bishop follows the artist as a young man in his exchanges with Henrik Ibsen and Lady Gregory. He points out how expertly Joyce later succeeded in acquiring both cultural and real capital, using people, language and the construction of his self. To date, Bishop concludes, and in spite of all the painstaking research on Joyce, the myths created by Joyce have persisted. Bishop explains this as a 'lock-in': 'something like lock-in occurs with an influential critical work'. Joyce, Bishop writes, 'was writing to posterity' and 'posterity listened'.

The conclusion seems to be that these authors succeeded in controlling the reception of their work to a much larger extent than was contended by Bourdieu when he wrote that

> writers' efforts to control the reception of their own works are always partially doomed to failure ... if only because the very effect of their work may transform the conditions of its reception and because they would not have had to write many things they did write and write them as they did ... if they had been granted from the outset what they are granted retrospectively. (31)

Self-fashioning with a difference

When including the term 'self-fashioning' in the subtitle of this book, I realised that some readers would expect the critical approach of the contributions to be a further illustration of the new historicist method applied with such brilliance in Stephen Greenblatt's *Renaissance Self-Fashioning*. And, certainly, the idea for the volume was to some extent constructed along Greenblatt's lines in that the self-fashioning explored in this volume functions without regard for 'a sharp distinction between literature and social life'; and the term itself, for many of the authors discussed here, retains the original meaning of consciously constructing and improving the self. But it needs to be said too that the term has now entered critical jargon with respect to any period in which individual artists choose to self-mythologise, to, that is, construct an identity in and through language and represent it 'before an audience' (Greenblatt 245, Pieters 51).[11] The theatricality involved in the latter aspect of self-fashioning, as well as the stress on the role of language in the process, provides an immediate link with Judith Butler's concept of performativity. Given the turn-of-the-century's developments within the field of psychology and psychiatry and the subsequent influence of Freud's theory with its stress on the conscious (or constructed) and unconscious dimensions of the self, the significant use of 'self-fashioning' as a practice among early twentieth-century authors seems logical. The association with performance as well as psychoanalysis may have contributed to the fact that the practice of self-fashioning is associated in the first place with the emergence of modernist art. In *Institutions of Modernism*, Laurence Rainey points out how 'new strategies for reputation building – involving theatricality, spectacle, publicity, and novel modes of cultural marketing and media manipulation – responded to increasingly international cultural interchanges, the growing prominence of the early mass media, the rising pressure of advertising, the unprecedented fusion of information and entertainment, and arenas in which to speak to an increasingly fragmented public' (4). In what follows, it will be shown that authorial self-invention was not a purely modernist strategy, though the modernist authors discussed in this volume were particularly good at it.

The contributors to this volume, then, have been invited to look at the ways in which turn-of-the-century authors chose to fashion identities for themselves through and in their writings as well as in the media of the time. They examine the different manipulative processes, the deception effected on the public through the fashioning of 'fictional' public selves and in some cases they have addressed the question as to why these behavioural styles were successful or why they failed.

Some of the essays included here, such as Elizabeth Mansfield's on Emilia Dilke, were patently influenced by Greenblatt's theory and his new historicist practice. Other contributors relied on theoretical approaches in tune with the new historicist interest in the cultural poetics of an age, the ways in which all sorts of texts talked to one another, giving expression to as well as reflecting contemporary thought, ideology, ambitions and power structures.

In '*fashion*ing', however, one detects an additional meaning, which one might have thought equally applies to the group of authors under scrutiny here. What this book seeks to show is that this practice of self-mythologising was far from being an isolated phenomenon at the time and authors of both genders, sometimes adapting to different market exigencies, developed and excelled at it. It was fashionable to create and perform a well-designed writerly identity but there seems to be little evidence to conclude that authors followed each other's example or copied certain styles from one another.

Finally, although the reclusive author often reluctantly engaged upon the construction of such a public self-image, (s)he might come to the surprising conclusion that the newly fashioned persona, apart from drawing the public to their work, paradoxically protected their their innermost thoughts and beliefs from public scrutiny. Yet, once a 'persona' was created, it was all but impossible to change or replace it.

It is my belief that the importance of authorship grew in the course of the nineteenth century until, at the end of that century and the beginning of the twentieth, its importance even preceded the text. Whereas books by anonymous authors (by 'A Lady', for instance) still sold well at the beginning of the century and, indeed, anonymous books continued to be published and sold throughout the nineteenth century, the name of the author and the identity of the author attached to that name had become the foremost marketing strategy by 1900. Although evolving models of selfhood were developing as a result of psychology, psychiatry, and an embrace of syncopated rather than stable life rhythms, in authorship the implications were that identity had become proleptic, containing the promise of the work to come.

Notes

1 Pierre Bourdieu links the emergence of the mass production of texts, which he calls 'a veritable cultural industry', with the movement towards 'artistic autonomy'. Yet he situates this at the end of the eighteenth, the beginning of the nineteenth century (113).
2 In a vitriolic attack on John Carey's book on the masses, Roger Kimball rightly points out that intellectuals had always been frightened of 'the masses', but I believe he may have underestimated their conviction that the danger now seemed to affect their own living and writing standards much

more directly. Writers such as Conrad believed the economic value they stood for might dictate (read 'lower') the quality of the cultural production.

3 George Bernard Shaw, for instance, supported Stead in his campaign against child prostitution, the 'Maiden Tribute of Modern Babylon' debate, and later continued to observe him only to be disappointed. Stead's created self, so seductive to some, proved too predictable for Shaw.

4 Shaw's self-fashioning has been dealt with at length by John A. Bertolini.

5 It was J.B. Pinker who was eventually successful at it. See Bradbury 157.

6 D.H. Lawrence thought that 1915 was the year the old world changed, whereas Henry Adams argued for 1900 (Bradbury and McFarlane 51).

7 Although therefore partly endorsing the central theses of Dettmar and Watt's *Marketing Modernisms* it also fundamentally deviates from it by not linking the new selling strategies to modernist writers only.

8 I am not only basing these statements on my possibly subjective perception as an academic, but also on the comparable figures of publications on these writers listed in ABELL and the MLA bibliography. I will list the names of the writers and the number of publications below with the search results in ABELL first, in the MLA second and starting with the most popular authors. James Joyce (7808/6934), Henry James (6739/4556), Virginia Woolf (3767/3089), George Moore (584/258), Arnold Bennett (533/149), Vernon Lee (52/36), W.T. Stead (7/47), Lucas Malet (5/4), Rosamund Watson (4/6) and Emilia Dilke (1/6).

9 It is well known that Henry James, for instance, refused to read reviews of his books and constantly complained about their poor sales. No wonder then that his nephew, Harry James, was somewhat embarrassed when finding, after James's death, that his uncle's financial affairs were not as bad as the latter had claimed them to be.

10 Since then others have been looking at James's response to the changes within the literary market. Richard Salmon has possibly written the most exhaustive analysis of James's ambivalent relation to the culture of publicity.

11 Talia Schaffer and Kathy Psomiades use the term unhesitatingly in their introduction (17).

Works cited

Anderson, Patricia, The *Printed Image and the Transformation of Popular Culture 1790–1860*. Oxford: Clarendon, 1991.

Ardis, Ann L., *Modernism and Cultural Conflict, 1880–1922*. Cambridge: Cambridge University Press, 2002.

Beard, Mary, *The Invention of Jane Harrison*. Cambridge, Mass.: Harvard University Press, 2000.

Bertolini, John A., *The Playwrighting Self of Bernard Shaw*. Carbondale: Southern Illinois University Press, 1991.

Bradbury, Malcolm, *The Social Context of Modern English Literature*. Oxford: Blackwell, 1971.

Bradbury, Malcolm and James McFarlane, eds., *Modernism 1890–1930*. Harmondsworth: Penguin, 1976.

Bourdieu, Pierre, *The Field of Cultural Production. Essays on Art and Literature*. Ed. Randal Johnson. Cambridge: Polity Press, 1993.

Brendon, Pierce, *The Life and Death of the Press Barons*. London: Secker & Warburg, 1982.

Carey, John, *The Intellectuals and the Masses. Pride and Prejudice among the Literary Intelligentsia, 1880–1939*. London: Faber and Faber, 1992.

Conrad, Joseph, *The Collected Letters of Joseph Conrad. Volume 2 1898–1902*. General editor, Frederick R. Karl. Cambridge: Cambridge University Press, 1986.

Demoor, Marysa, ''Not with a bang but a whimper': Lucy Clifford's Letters, 1919–1929'. *Cambridge Quarterly* 30 (2001): 233–56.

Dettmar, Kevin J.H. and Stephen Watt, *Marketing Modernisms. Self-Promotion, Canonization, and Rereading*. Ann Arbor: University of Michigan Press, 1996.

Federico, Annette R., *Idol of Suburbia. Marie Corelli and Late-Victorian Literary Culture*. Charlottesville and London: University of Virginia, 2000.

Foucault, Michel, 'What is an Author?'. *Aesthetics, Method, and Epistemology*. 3 vols. Ed. James Faubion. Harmondsworth: Penguin, 1994.

Gissing, George, *New Grub Street*. 1891. Boston: Houghton, 1962.

Greenblatt, Stephen, *Renaissance Self-Fashioning. From More to Shakespeare*, Chicago and London: University of Chicago Press, 1980.

Heim, Michael, *Electric Language: A Philosophical Study of Word Processing*. New Haven: Yale University Press, 1999.

Holroyd, Michael, *Bernard Shaw. 'The Search for Love. 1856–1898'*. Volume 1. London: Chatto & Windus: 1988.

Houghton, Walter, 'Periodical literature and the articulate classes'. *The Victorian Periodical Press: Samplings and Soundings*. Eds. Joanne Shattock and Michael Wolff. Leicester: Leicester University Press, 1982.

Huyssen, Andreas, *After the Great Divide. Modernism, Mass Culture and Postmodernism*. Basingstoke: Macmillan, 1986.

Israel, Kali, 'Writing inside the Kaleidoscope: Re-representing Victorian Women Public Figures'. *Gender and History* 1 (1990): 40–8.

Larson, Jill, *Ethics and Narratve in the English Novel, 1880–1914*. Cambridge: Cambridge University Press, 2001.

Lloyd, Geneviève, 'Maleness, Metaphor, and the "Crisis" of Reason'. *A Mind of One's Own*. Eds. Louise Antony and Charlotte Witt. Boulder: Westview Press, 1992, pp. 69–84.

McDonald, Peter D., *British Literary Culture and Publishing Practice 1880–1940*. Cambridge: Cambridge University Press, 1997.

Meyers, Diana, 'Feminist Perspectives on the Self'. *The Stanford Encyclopedia of Philosophy (Summer 2000 Edition)*, (ed.), <http://plato.stanford.edu/archives/sum2000/entries/feminism-self/>.

Pieters, Jürgen, *Moments of Negotiation. The New Historicism of Stephen Greenblatt*. Amsterdam: Amsterdam University Press, 2001.

Ohmann, Richard, *Selling Culture. Magazines, Markets, and Class at the Turn of the Century*. London: Verso, 1996.

Rainey, Laurence, *Institutions of Modernism. Literary Elits and Public Culture*. New Haven and London: Yale University Press, 1998.

Ricoeur, Paul, *Soi-même comme un autre*. Paris: Editions du Seuil, 1990.

Robertson Scott, J.W., *The Life and Death of a Newspaper*. London: Methuen, 1952.

Ryan, Kiernan, *New Historicism and Cultural Materialism. A Reader.* London: Arnold, 1996.

Schaffer, Talia and Kathy Alexis Psomiades, *Women and British Aestheticism.* London and Charlottesville: University Press of Virginia, 1999.

Shaw, George Bernard, *Bernard Shaw. Collected Letters, 1874–1897.* Ed. Dan H. Laurence. 4 vols. London: Max Reinhardt, 1965.

Squillace, Robert, *Modernism, Modernity and Arnold Bennett.* Cranbury, NJ: Bucknell University Press, 1997.

Tucker, Herbert F., ed., *A Companion to Victorian Literature and Culture.* Oxford: Blackwell, 1999.

Tennyson, Alfred, *Tennyson. Poems and Plays.* Ed. T. Herbert Warren. London: Oxford University Press, 1971.

Tuchman, Gaye with Nina E. Fortin, *Edging Women Out. Victorian Novelists, Publishers and Social Change.* London: Routledge, 1989.

Williams, Raymond, *The English Novel from Dickens to Lawrence.* London: Hogarth Press, 1984.

—— *The Politics of Modernism: Against the New Conformists.* London: Verso, 1989.

Withers, Hartley et al., *A Newspaper History, 1785–1935.* London: Times Publishing Company, 1935.

Woolf, Virginia, 'Mr Bennett and Mrs Brown'. *The Collected Works of Virginia Woolf.* 4 vols. London: Hogarth Press, 1966.

1

Emilia Dilke: Self-Fashioning and the Nineteenth Century

Elizabeth Mansfield

Self-fashioning is always, but not exclusively, in language.

When Stephen Greenblatt introduced self-fashioning into the lexicon of cultural studies, he cast the term historically. Renaissance England presented compelling instances of the social phenomena he labelled self-fashioning. This is not to say that Greenblatt withheld from earlier cultures a 'self-consciousness about the fashioning of human identity as a manipulable, artful process' (Greenblatt 2). On the contrary, he observed that 'Such self-consciousness had been wide-spread among the elite in the classical world'. But the Renaissance marks the beginning of the *modern* manifestation of this notion of self. According to Greenblatt, Renaissance self-fashioning developed in opposition to a medieval concept of self as formed and formable only by God. The persistent and unresolved tension between the medieval and Renaissance models of selfhood continues, Greenblatt suggests in the final pages of *Renaissance Self-Fashioning*, to contribute to our own uneasy comprehension of personal identity.[1]

By locating self-fashioning in the Renaissance, Greenblatt makes the concept especially intriguing for students of the nineteenth century. The Renaissance he addresses coincides largely with the Renaissance described and codified by nineteenth-century scholars. Individual autonomy and self-knowledge – essential for self-fashioning – were among the chief characteristics ascribed to the Renaissance by Burckhardt, Michelet and Symonds, among others. Even the dialectic in which Greenblatt casts the Middle Ages and the Renaissance appears in nineteenth-century accounts (Mansfield). That the Renaissance defined by nineteenth-century historians mirrors the concerns of their own age has been observed (Houghton 324–5). And from this observation comes the realisation that a *historiography* of the Renaissance remains intimately – and often imperceptibly – entwined with nineteenth-century *history*. From this tangle of history, historicity and historiography I wish to pursue a single line: the possibility that self-fashioning is a concept whose fulcrum rests in the nineteenth century. In other words, the axis of self-fashioning runs through the nineteenth century, mediating our understanding of the Renaissance as it colours our notions of selfhood.

This historiographic nexus is illustrated by the life and career of Emilia Dilke (1840–1906). One of Victorian Britain's most prominent scholars of Renaissance culture, she was also a remarkable practitioner of self-fashioning. In this essay, I will treat these as interdependent interests. Like so many of her colleagues, Dilke attributed to the Renaissance the very ideals she championed in her own age: the individual's capacity for self-improvement, social mobility and self-government. What is more, she dedicated herself to realising these ideals personally and politically.

Emilia Dilke's rise to intellectual and popular fame occurred simultaneously. In 1871 – Dilke's thirty-first year – her first series of essays on Renaissance culture appeared in the art journal *Portfolio*. That same year, a fictionalised version of her life unfolded in George Eliot's popular new serial, *Middlemarch*.[2] At her death in 1906, obituaries celebrating her various roles as union activist, suffragist, fiction writer, scholar and socialite appeared in newspapers throughout Europe and North America. The strategies that Dilke used to propel herself to such celebrity bear a suggestive resemblance to Greenblatt's account of self-fashioning.

Emily Francis Strong grew up in Oxfordshire where her father earned his living as a banker.[3] Called 'Francis'[4] by her family, details of her youth are scant due to her later enthusiasm for editing – with scissors or penknife – her personal papers. References to her mother, Emily Weedon Strong, seldom appear in her namesake's extant correspondence, obscuring almost entirely their relationship. Because no evidence of a serious rift between mother and daughter exists, Mrs Strong's invisibility suggests personal interest rather than familial discord (Askwith 7, Dilke *Book of Spiritual Life* 4).[5] Perhaps, like many ambitious Victorian women, Francis Strong found her mother's conventional life incompatible with her own goals and, in order to overcome this antithetic influence, evacuated her from her autobiography. The phenomenon of the missing (dead or estranged) mother in fictional and autobiographical literature by Victorian women writers deserves notice here and may shed some light on the erasure of Emily Weedon Strong.

A common literary device, the missing mother serves two ends. First, it forces the daughter-heroine to leave home due to desperate financial or emotional circumstances. Second, the device allows her to defy social expectations, since she has no proper domesticating influence. Ultimately, the heroine's inevitable transgressions against patriarchal society lead to her salvation and her eventual re-entry into society on her own terms (see MacDonald and Zimmerman). This model may help explain Francis Strong's inclination to edit her mother out of her own life story: the younger woman's rejection of traditional gender roles made it easier to refashion herself motherless than to reconcile her mother's apparently placid acceptance of conventional femininity.[6]

Francis Strong's education followed lines conventional for middle-class Victorian girls, with the exception of her study of classical languages. Her father, an enthusiastic amateur painter, also encouraged her artistic abilities. Francis's student drawings suggested enough promise that several of them were shown to the eminent art critic John Ruskin. To Francis's delight, he recommended that she attend the South Kensington Art Schools for further training. Thus, despite her mother's apparent misgivings, Francis Strong left home for London in 1858 at the age of eighteen.[7]

At South Kensington, Francis Strong became 'Francisca'. The nickname was conferred by one of her painting teachers, George Frederick Watts, whom Strong called 'Signor'. No doubt their shared admiration for fifteenth-century Italian art underlay these pet names. But her pursuit of a new persona – more passionate and exotic than an Oxfordshire banker's daughter – led her also to adopt unconventional dress. Colourful, flowing skirts and shawls based loosely on eighteenth-century French fashions became her hallmark. One acquaintance would remember her as 'the best dressed Englishwoman I have ever known. In her attire she seemed to impart a reminiscence of the canvases of Boucher and Van Loo...' (J.E.C. Bodley to Sir Charles Dilke as recorded in Dilke *Book of Spiritual Life* 120). Her frequent practical jokes and occasional run-ins with the South Kensington administration further distinguished her from her female classmates. She notoriously demanded – and eventually received – permission to study and draw the nude model, a practice previously withheld from women students.

Strong's transformation at South Kensington also manifested itself in a new religious regime. The Strong family practised High Church

Anglicanism, though Francis had long gravitated toward Roman Catholicism. She regularly translated and memorised passages from the Latin of the Church Fathers and Thomas à Kempis' *Imitatio Christi*. Once away from her family, her devotion assumed greater physical expression. She often would endure severe self-imposed penance for seemingly minor transgressions. This behaviour, while characterised as bizarre by her art school colleagues, points to Strong's attempt initially to fashion herself after what Greenblatt describes as 'the ultimate model' (Greenblatt 3). Like the medieval mode of self-fashioning that Greenblatt links with the imitation of Christ, Francis Strong's early exercises in self-fashioning rely mainly on mortification. Later in life, she would rely almost exclusively on representation, especially language, as a means for self-fashioning.

It is not entirely clear why Strong abandoned her formal art training. But in 1861, after nearly three years in London, she put aside her life as the passionate art student Francisca and returned to Iffley to marry a man she barely knew. Mark Pattison was a prominent Oxford theologian and education reformer. He had recently been named rector of Lincoln College, finally making him eligible – at the age of forty-eight – to marry.[8] By the time he wed Francis Strong, Pattison had spent almost thirty years at Oxford. He had arrived at Oriel College in 1832 with neither the financial resources nor the social standing essential for college society. Alienated from his peers, Pattison sought refuge in his studies and in the teachings of John Newman. Newman's influence had shaped Pattison's convictions and his work. But by the time Pattison accepted a fellowship at Lincoln College, his association with Newman had branded him a radical. With too few social graces and too many ties to Tractarianism, Pattison's first attempt to obtain the rectorate in 1851 was thwarted by his colleagues. This was an unexpected and demoralising blow. His eventual appointment to the coveted office in 1861 restored some of his confidence. But the preceding years of conflict and penury left him a bitter and wary man.[9] His decision to marry an eccentric twenty-one-year-old art student struck friends and relatives as precipitate. They were right. Pattison would later refer to the anniversary of his wedding as the date 'which depresses me to the lowest depths of misery'.[10]

Francis Pattison shared her husband's disappointment. Wholly unprepared for life as the wife of a cantankerous Oxford don, she seems to have at least attempted to fulfil this role for the first few years of their union. Mark Pattison's intellectual generosity remained, for his wife, the only consistently positive consequence of their union. He oversaw her continuing education and encouraged her to embark on a scholarly career. As Mrs Mark Pattison – a by-line still familiar to art historians – she established herself during the course of their marriage as *the* living authority on the French Renaissance. The culmination of this endeavour was the publication in 1879 of her first book, *The Renaissance of Art in France*.

The book itself serves as another venue for Pattison's self-rehearsal. Her discussions of artists' spiritual quests, their desire for forbidden knowledge, their unappreciated genius and their unsympathetic spouses reveal an autobiographical strain. But her emphasis of these themes also made the French Renaissance more accessible to her nineteenth-century audience. Her account links Renaissance art to social forces such as religious dissent, new approaches to manufacturing and changing notions of national identity. Such concerns undoubtedly resonated with her Victorian readers.

The success of *The Renaissance of Art in France* did not, however, herald an improvement in the Pattisons' marriage. Their day-to-day life together remained difficult even as it became intellectually more vigorous. Francis Pattison's correspondence conveys her frustrations with Oxford's conservative customs and her husband's fiscal and emotional miserliness. At first she sought relief in the cultivation of an Oxford salon. Then she turned to scholarship for refuge. Only through illness, though, did she finally escape Mark Pattison and her unhappy life at Oxford.

Beginning in 1867, upon the advice of her doctors, Francis Pattison spent most of her winters away from Oxford. Thus separated from friends and family, her letters from this period are uncharacteristically intimate, revealing the precarious state of her health and marriage. Her first prolonged illness seems to have involved a nervous breakdown as well as a gynaecological disorder. She explains the situation to her sister Rosa Tuckwell in a letter from Iffley dated February 1868:

> You will see that I am staying with mother ... as it is still considered that for some months to come I am better out of Oxford and the cares, and occupations, it entails on me. At present (which is just what dearest mother fails to comprehend) I am still a 'nervous invalid' and this they say would have been just the same, even had there been no local derangement. I used to tremble for half an hour if I heard a bell ring and now I still cannot suffer much external distractions. A stranger or acquaintance is torture to me and if I force

myself to meet the terror, the reaction is serious ... In other respects, I am still not out of the doctor's hands, that is to say that the last instrument inserted remains until the end of summer or autumn. All this makes return home somewhat of a trial, I am told I can manage myself in relation to the 'nervous state' as well as any doctor but progress is very slow, and little things which I would meet bravely at any other time are often a heavy trouble.[11]

Despite the mention of an 'instrument inserted', the precise nature of her physical ailment remains unclear (Askwith 53–4). Her concurrent condition as a 'nervous invalid', although possibly coincidental, raises questions not only about the relationship between her physical and mental health, but the role these matters played in the lives of Victorian women.

Francis Pattison's physical and psychological deterioration began shortly after her marriage to the rector and ceased at his death, a period of approximately twenty years. She suffered from a number of ailments, including rheumatoid arthritis, recurring abscesses and spinal neuralgia in addition to the aforementioned complaints. These maladies, while painful and often debilitating, had the effect of removing her from Oxford and her husband's company. It is worth noting that she enjoyed generally good health during the last twenty years of her life.

The relationship between Victorian medical practice and its female patients has come under scrutiny by feminist scholars.[12] Most contend that the medical establishment served to maintain the patriarchal status quo by inflicting deleterious or restrictive 'cures' on 'rebellious' female patients. In particular, nervous disorders among intelligent or ambitious women became more widespread and the treatment more severe as women's demands for economic and political emancipation rose. Undoubtedly, much of Victorian medical practice contributed to the suppression of women's enfranchisement. On the other hand, I propose that many women, including Francis Pattison, found illness a powerful vehicle for greater personal freedom and control. Whether or not these women consciously or deliberately manipulated medical practice remains less important than their ability to gain sanction and assistance for their escape from unpleasant, oppressive or dangerous personal relationships. In particular, the treatments prescribed prior to the introduction of S. Weir Mitchell's rest cure in the 1870s could provide women with a much needed, if only temporary, leave from difficult lives. Victorian society, not unlike our own, vested tremendous authority in the (male) doctor. His opinions and suggestions were accepted without question and the pronouncement 'doctor's orders' could liberate as easily as it could confine.

Francis Pattison's letter to her sister points to this emancipative possibility. As she reports, 'it is still considered that for some months to come I am better out of Oxford and the cares, and occupations, it entails on me'. Two important points can be inferred from this comment. First, she did not assume responsibility for her decision to quit Oxford; rather this recommendation came from an outside authority – her doctor. Second, life with Mark Pattison had become too burdensome. She even appealed to her physical and psychological condition as cause for ceasing sexual relations after a decade of marriage. Writing to her husband in 1876 during her annual convalescence in Nice, she forestalled any renewal of physical intimacy:

> you cannot forget that from the first I expressed the strongest aversion to that side of the common life, during '73–'74 this became almost insufferable, but I tried to conceal it hoping that it might settle itself. You had told me constantly all along that it would soon cease and when I thought it had by [Dr] Acland's directions I rejoiced ... anyway anything of the sort in my state of health must be impossible for a long time to come.[13]

The revelation of her revulsion at physical contact with her husband made emotional reconciliation impossible. He attempted to arrange a separation from his wife, but she refused to acquiesce. She insisted that their intellectual compatibility could sustain the union. Her condition as an invalid did not, in her view, conflict with her role as devoted wife. Mark Pattison craved affection, however, eloquently expressing his desperation in his letters to John Ruskin.[14] The correspondence between these two aged and forlorn scholars testifies poignantly to the rector's distress. Ultimately, he would forgive his wife during his final illness through which she dutifully nursed him.

Pattison's fictional works, though published after her final departure from Oxford, bear introduction here for their relevance to her ability to manage her sense of self – physical, intellectual and emotional – via representation. The autobiographical impulse underlying the gothic tales collected in *The Shrine of Death* and *The Shrine of Love* emerges plainly in the almost obsessive repetition of a single theme: the plight of a dutiful heroine who cannot escape from a brilliant but evil older man. The author herself acknowledged that each story is a 'record of the essential facts of some situation which I have known in real life' (*Shrine of Love* Preface).

These volumes received little public notice during her lifetime and remain less interesting for their literary merit than their autobiographical content. For example, her opinion of Oxford surfaces in 'A Vision of Learning' (*Shrine of Death* 57–76) in which a young man eagerly embarks on a life of study and contemplation in a cold and foggy 'city of learning'. Growing frustrated at his inability to learn anything meaningful, he visits a graveyard one night and finds his professors resting in open graves and laughing at him. The young man then goes insane and is committed to an asylum. There he meets a kind young woman named Love, who restores his sanity.

In addition to such heavy-handed attacks on Oxford, her stories portray the contradictions and frustrations confronted by a Victorian woman intellectual. Largely populated by misunderstood women whose desire for knowledge results in death, these stories illustrate the emotional cost of an unconventional life. The boundary between complacency and ecstasy, ignorance and knowledge, life and death recurs in the form of a river, or wall or other threshold. Once the heroine has transgressed the boundary, return is impossible and her inevitable destruction takes place.

Perhaps the most illustrative of these stories is 'The Shrine of Death' (*Shrine of Death* 9–24). In this tale, a young woman seeks to decipher her mother's dying words: 'Ah! Life has many secrets!' Ignoring the townspeople who entreat her to marry one of her suitors, the heroine instead follows the advice of a witch who tells her: 'Marry Death, fair child; and you will know.' Drawn by a light emanating from the church crypt, she persuades her family to dress her as a bride and leave her there. Death is waiting for her. Seated at an enormous table, he holds open a large book. Death points to a place in the book for her to read, but she cannot. The characters and symbols continually shift and disappear before her eyes. Finally, exhausted and frightened after hours of struggling with the text, she tries to run away only to be stopped by ghouls who emerge from the tombs. The next morning the villagers arrive to find her dead, her eyes wide open with terror. This overwrought story hardly needs interpretation. Death's promise of enlightenment to a young woman depends first upon her submission to social expectations (marriage), then upon her physical and psychical degeneration (death). The price paid, enlightenment comes and her eyes are opened.

The temptation to read these tales as metaphors for Francis Pattison's own life becomes even stronger in light of the circumstances of their production. Unlike her scholarly work, which she wrote alone in her study, her stories were composed while she engaged in other activities. In his biography of her, Charles Dilke describes how she drafted her stories while conversing with him or other friends in addition to sketching or mending damaged books. At these times, she would write without losing track of conversation or her handiwork, which she would alternate with pen and notebook (*Book of Spiritual Life* 92–3). This form of writing, in contrast to her intellectual work, resulted in self-revelations at odds with her carefully constructed public personas. The allegorical nature of the stories, her method of writing them and her admission that they functioned as an emotional 'safety-valve' leave little doubt that her fiction exposes a suggestive literary unconscious.

Her final phase of self-fashioning transformed her from Mrs Mark Pattison into Emilia, Lady Dilke. She had met Sir Charles Wentworth Dilke at South Kensington, where he too studied for a time. Dilke retains some notoriety as 'the lost prime minister': a successful Liberal MP whose involvement in a highly publicised sex scandal curtailed a promising career.[15] Although their extant correspondence begins in 1875, Francis Pattison and Charles Dilke had maintained a quiet acquaintance for many years. Filled with discussions of politics and the arts as well as a good bit of gossip, their notes to each other shift easily from earnest to playful.[16] A deepening intimacy is clearly evident.

Among the issues addressed in their letters was the need for reform at that Royal Academy of Arts. In particular, Francis Pattison voiced her belief that the Academy should provide equal access and support to female students. She attempted to bring about the changes herself in 1885. In this year, she offered a portion of Mark Pattison's estate to endow a scholarship fund for Royal Academy students.[17] Her terms, which dictated that the anonymous award be available to female as well as male students, drew this response from Academy president Frederick Leighton:

I would be glad to help you in carrying out your present desire in any way in my power tho' I do not see from your letter ... how the scheme is feasible. If the scholarships are to include drawings from the nude amongst ... qualifications they cannot go to the Royal Academy female students as the nude is not open to them. What is the fundamental postulate, so to speak, of the bequest?[18]

Not giving up the fight, she elicits a more forceful letter from her old friend:

> I fully appreciate your motives in regard to the proposed scholarships as to which I fear there is an implacable difficulty. The [prizes] and scholarships of the R.A. are or have been open to all ... and there are always a good many young ladies among the final winners – but the nude does not form part of their study and a discussion in the assembly last year in which certain members advocated its introduction was negatived by a considerable majority; your interpretation is therefore fatal.[19]

The debate ended there and Francis Pattison withdrew the gift.

The most obvious vehicle for Pattison's advocacy of women artists was her writing. She had been an art critic since the late 1860s. Her reviews of British and Continental exhibitions appeared regularly in popular journals like the *Saturday Review, Westminster Review*, and *Athenaeum*.[20] But she rarely commented on the status of women artists, and then only in reviews of the Society of Female Artists. In these notices, she never failed to admonish members of the Society for their self-segregating policies, encouraging them to exhibit their work alongside that of men.[21] Her relative reticence on the subject of women artists in her published writing is puzzling, since she was a familiar advocate of women's suffrage – a much more volatile issue.[22] What is more, her private correspondence contains references to her support for contemporary women artists as well as her interest in women artists of the seventeenth and eighteenth centuries. Why she failed to align herself publicly with the advancement of women artists deserves examination.

Francis Pattison's meticulous construction of various independent, and occasionally antithetical, personas offers a clue to this unexpected behaviour. To affiliate herself with women artists specifically could have undermined her credibility as a critic of artists generally. Thus marginalised through association, her opinions would have become those of 'a woman' rather than an experienced and incisive art critic. Pattison's own (always unsigned) advice to women artists to dispense with segregated exhibitions – because they invite a critical distinction between men's and women's work – applies equally to critics.[23] In other words, had she distinguished herself as an advocate of women artists, her views would have been set in opposition to those of her male colleagues. In venues other than her art publications, she did not shy away from taking controversial stands on behalf of women's economic and political rights. By the 1870s she was a regular participant in meetings for women's labour unions and suffrage. Her sustained involvement with the Women's Trade Union League (originally the Women's Protective and Provident League) culminated in her assumption of the organisation's presidency in 1886 (Israel 226). But her determination to keep her role as a political activist distinct from her identity as a critic and scholar became more difficult after her marriage to Sir Charles Dilke MP.[24]

The formidable political and social union between Francis Pattison and Charles Dilke finally evolved into marriage following Mark Pattison's death. Although they seem not to have shared their intention to marry with anyone, hints of this plan surface in their letters to each other as early as January 1884, six months before the rector's death.[25] One intimation of her change in marital as well as social status came in her assumption of the name 'Emilia' among Charles Dilke's friends.

She had begun to sign herself as Emilia in letters to her friend Pauline, Lady Trevelyan in 1865. During the 1870s, Emilia increasingly served as her alter ego, a persona that would eventually eclipse the more mundane Francis. Among family and her Oxford friends she remained Francis, while she introduced herself as Emilia to well-placed London and Paris acquaintances. By the late 1870s, the distinction became even clearer as she entered the circle of socialites and politicians around Charles Dilke. Finally, upon marrying Dilke, she shed the earlier identity entirely. Professionally as well as socially, she became Emilia, Lady Dilke. No doubt her desire to assimilate into Dilke's world partly motivated this change, but her own social ambitions and professional aspirations cannot be discounted. Self-consciousness over her changing social status shows up in her correspondence with Charles Dilke during the spring of 1885, several months before their planned wedding. In these letters she expressed doubts about her suitability to be the wife of a titled and famous MP. But by that summer, she had reconciled herself to her new status. In a note discussing a future trip to Oxford together, she wrote, 'if I did go down with you I had much rather go to an Inn. You know how I loathe other people's houses especially of the middle-class because in them you're least free.'[26] Her transformation from a provincial banker's daughter into a prominent member of London's elite was complete.

Francis Strong's literary persona underwent a similar metamorphosis. Her career as an influential critic and historian of art – whether under the name E.F.S. Pattison, Mrs Mark Pattison or Lady Dilke – succeeded in part through her ability to fashion for herself a voice of intellectual authority. The formation of this voice can be traced in her initial periodical publications. Through a series of rhetorical manoeuvres enacted in her early art writings, she assumed an agency and authority usually reserved for men. Her literary reviews reveal an awareness of the conventions that militated against women intellectuals as they divulge her strategies for overcoming them. She recognised that the assumption of literary authority depended on her ability to subvert Victorian norms without appearing to challenge them. A policy of infiltration as opposed to insurrection – which characterises her advocacy of women's economic and political rights – finds its rhetorical counterpart in her early writings on art and literature.

She started reviewing books and exhibitions for the *Saturday Review* in 1863. Her decision to contribute to this rancorous journal derived from financial as well as intellectual aspirations. Charles Dilke records that 'in order to increase her personal income, she began to write much for publication, and was indeed a considerable contributor to the *Saturday Review*' (*Book of Spiritual Life* 19). Her first husband had kept the purse strings tightly closed. Despite the comfortable living afforded by his appointment at Lincoln College, Mark Pattison haggled incessantly with his wife over her modest household 'allowance'. The fees she received for her writing, ranging from two to three pounds per article, provided a degree of financial independence from her husband.[27] More important, perhaps, was their value as a symbol of her professional status.

In her later years, Emilia Dilke recalled that professional rather than financial goals motivated her initial foray into journalism. In a letter to her niece, who was contemplating a literary career, Dilke made explicit her pursuit of a professional identity. That she deliberately formulated a strategy of professional self-fashioning cannot be doubted:

> when I began it was put before me that if I wished to make <u>a position</u> and command <u>respect</u> I must make myself **the** authority on some one subject which interested me. I was told and I believe it was good counsel to reject even well paid things that would head me off this track ... Some day I will show you my list of articles and 'works' and explain how it all developed and how you might develop yourself on similar lines.[28]

Self-fashioning – physical, spiritual, emotional, nominal, and rhetorical – was the means through which Dilke achieved 'a position,' 'respect' and 'authority'.

Occasionally, she assumed this authority at the expense of her colleagues and mentors. John Ruskin, whose early encouragement had led her to study art and art history, was among those injured. An attempt at reconciliation with her old teacher elicited this reply:

> I'm entirely delighted but more astonished than ever I was in my life by your pretty letter and profession of discipleship. Why, I thought you always one of my terriblest, unconquerablest, antagonisticest, Philistine, Delilah powers! I thought you at Kensington the sauciest of girls – at Oxford the dangerousest of Don-nas.[29]

With this, John Ruskin recalled more than his frustration with a rebellious disciple. Associating Emilia Dilke with a woman who seduces then steals masculine power and authority, Ruskin compared himself with the shorn and helpless Samson. The analogy may not be as fanciful as it first appears. Written in 1886, this gently chiding characterisation probably refers to her much earlier review of one of his books. Emilia Dilke's years of study with Ruskin, first at South Kensington and later at Oxford, had endowed her with a lethal authority on his work. This authority – both as a knowledgeable critic of Ruskin and as a new but confident voice within late Victorian criticism – resounds clearly in her 1870 review of Ruskin's *Lectures on Art*.

The review begins conventionally enough, recapitulating Ruskin's leading argument that art serves only to raise the religious, moral and physical well-being of humanity. Having outlined his argument, she allows that 'It is an *ungracious* task to controvert the propositions on which Mr Ruskin has based his scheme of the arts' ('Notes' 305, emphasis mine). Such a warning of an impending breach of propriety occurs frequently in Victorian reviews. It appears, however, almost exclusively in reviews that address books written by women.

Upon invoking this familiar rhetoric, Dilke begins a subtle transformation whereby her critical voice becomes masculinised and, therefore, authoritative. In order to complete this process, she needs to counterpoise an authorial masculinity against the femininity ascribed to Ruskin's text. Toward this end, she concludes her dismissal of Ruskin's methodology with supreme condescension, allowing that 'Strong feelings are the natural accompaniment of keen sensibilities, they may deepen the force of emotion, but they do not deepen the force of reason' ('Notes' 306). The deeply rooted cultural association between feminine emotion and masculine intellect percolates easily through this statement. Through a simple but effective manipulation of social stereotypes (reason is masculine, emotion is feminine), Dilke constructs an opposition between her reasonable, hence masculine, authority, and Ruskin's emotional, hence feminine, lack of authority.

The notion of rhetorical cross-dressing, while hardly new to the nineteenth century, was brought to the fore by George Eliot. Both her adoption of a masculine pseudonym and her investigation of themes beyond drawing-room intrigues made Eliot less a threat than an anomaly. As one essayist explained, 'If there is another woman who has ever shown original humour in print, we cannot recall her to mind.' The anonymous author continued, '*Romola* also makes it clear that [Eliot] can view the range of spiritual facts with a breadth, a calmness, and an insight that we should, but for her, have considered exclusively masculine.'[30]

These comments prelude an essay titled 'Authoresses', published anonymously in the *Saturday Review* in 1863, the year of Dilke's debut as a contributor. After admitting that an exceptional woman can write literature, the author determines that criticism is another matter. Women 'pour out their whole souls in loving rapture, and think every decent bit of poetry or prose sublime, beautiful, and thrilling'. Therefore, 'No one expects balanced and cold criticism from them', for in order to do so 'she has to judge and write as a man' (484). As 'authoresses' attests, conventions regarding the relationship between gender and authority remained stable while the link between gender and sex showed some flexibility, at least in the realm of intellectual pursuit. In other words, regardless of their biological sex, Victorian women could modify their intellectual or rhetorical gender. That Dilke would have been aware of this essay is likely, but remains less important than the piece's articulation of contemporary conventions and expectations surrounding women reviewers.

Dilke's review of Ruskin marks her first sustained assumption of a masculine critical voice. Finally and irreparably breaking with Ruskin's doctrine, she proclaims:

> Art itself is neither religious, nor irreligious; moral nor immoral; useful nor useless; if she is interpreted in any one of these senses by the beholder, is she to bear the blame? Not one of these qualities are essential to fine art, and as to perfecting the ethical state, that by means of art comes to pass, not by 'direction of purpose,' but by her constant presence indirectly refining our perceptions, and rendering them more delicate and susceptible. (306)

This pronouncement condemns Ruskin's philosophy in favour of the art for art's sake doctrine promoted most forcefully in England by Walter Pater and his Oxford coterie. Her decision to announce her shifting intellectual loyalties within the framework of a hostile and psychologically charged review invites consideration of her motives.

Dilke's desire to supersede Ruskin's approach led to a personal as well as intellectual break with her former mentor. Rather than shrink from such a task, Dilke devised a way to misrepresent the import of Ruskin's influence on her. In a gesture similar to the 'anxiety of influence' described by Harold Bloom, Dilke metaphorically killed her intellectual father in order to seize authority for herself. Her life-long denial of any conflict with her teacher puzzled the wounded Ruskin, but confirms the psychically and professionally expedient (as opposed to malicious) nature of her review.[31] Bloom's theory, however, does not account for women's authorship, and subsequent feminist critics have hesitated to ascribe the same impulse to women, preferring instead to focus on the productive rather than critical means through which women have achieved authority. In the case of Dilke, however, I believe that her assumption of stereotypical masculine rhetoric allowed her to partici-pate in a metaphorical act of intellectual patricide.

By stereotypical masculine rhetoric, I mean to distinguish between her use of standard nineteenth-century critical vocabulary and her invocation of a rhetoric of gendered oppositions through which she characterised the subject of her review as feminine in contrast to her masculine position. Following her review of Ruskin, the next essay in which she employed this rhetoric is her notice of Walter Pater's *Studies in the History of the Renaissance*. Dilke counted Pater, like Ruskin, among her exclusive circle of Oxford friends and colleagues. United by their interests in the aesthetic implications of the Renaissance as well as their shared distaste for Oxford conventionality, she and Pater met often to discuss art and philosophy.

Dilke disagreed with Pater on a crucial point regarding aestheticism: for her, aestheticism's divestiture of historical conditions from artistic meaning provided a means rather than an end to aesthetic analysis. The integration of artistic meaning with social, economic and political circumstances struck Dilke as incontestable. Her review, which appeared in the April 1873 issue of the *Westminster Review*, immedi-ately establishes what is at stake:

The title is misleading. The historical element is precisely that which is wanting, and its absence makes the weak place of the whole book ... the work is in no wise a contribution to the history of the Renaissance. ('Contemporary Literature' 639)

Dilke then goes on to discuss Pater's methodology, or lack of one, as she sees it

instead of approaching his subject ... by the true scientific method, through the life of the time of which it was an outcome, Mr. Pater prefers in each instance to detach it from its surroundings, to suspend it isolated before him, as if it were indeed a kind of air-plant independent of the ordinary sources of nourishment. The consequence is that he loses a great deal of the meaning of the very objects which he regards most intently. ('Contemporary Literature' 640)

Pater's failure to deliver an accurate account of Renaissance culture results, according to her review, from his refusal to approach his subject 'scientifically'.[32] Instead, Pater 'writes of the Renaissance as if it were a kind of sentimental revolution'. Dilke repeatedly cites his 'sentimentality', 'delicacy' and 'charm', ultimately declaring that his 'sentiment is so pregnant for us with weighty meaning'. As in her review of Ruskin, Dilke uses language that distinguishes her search for a 'vital', 'scientific' and 'historical reality' from his interest in 'unsubstantial dreams' put forth in a 'charming book'. This charged discourse concludes with a recognition of Pater's 'touch of genius', which allows him to

detect with singular subtlety the shades of tremulous variation which have been embodied in throbbing pulsations of colour, in doubtful turns of line, in veiled words; he can not only do this, but he can match them for us in words, in the choice of which he is often so brilliantly accurate that they gleam upon the paper with the radiance of jewels. ('Contemporary Literature' 640)

Dilke's characterisation of Pater as the Scheherazade of art historians came at an important moment in her own career. Her new position as arts editor at the *Academy* as well as her recent publication of several signed articles on the French Renaissance confirmed her status as a serious scholar in the field. Deep into research for her forthcoming book on the subject, Dilke had chosen the French Renaissance as the 'one subject' in which she would become '**the** authority'. Pater's encroachment upon the field – *Studies in the History of the Renaissance* addresses the French as well as the Italian Renaissance – threatened this aspiration. Her attempt to deflect this threat by rhetorically feminising Pater's language and method reveals her manipulation, however subli-mated, of the link between authority and masculinity in Victorian scholarship. This strategy worked. Emilia Dilke assumed her position as the undisputed British authority on French Renaissance culture.

Rhetoric was only the most abstract and sophisticated of Emilia Dilke's many strategies for self-fashioning. Her clothes, her name, her social status, her body, her fiction and her prose all serve as signs of her own carefully wrought identity. That she displayed the same wilful self-styling that she attributed to the artists and patrons of sixteenth-century France tells us not only a great deal about this Victorian scholar, but also about the conceptual trajectory of self-fashioning. Dilke shares Greenblatt's 'need to sustain the illusion that I am the principal maker of my own destiny'. For Greenblatt, this need manifests itself in his pursuit of a history of self-fashioning. Just as he finds reassuring reflections of his own concerns in the writings of More and Shakespeare, Dilke located similarly empowering examples among sixteenth-century Huguenot artists. The Huguenots' resistance – willing martyrdom, really – thematises Greenblatt's conclusion that 'to abandon self-fashioning is to abandon the craving for freedom, and to let go of one's stubborn hold upon selfhood, even selfhood conceived as a fiction, is to die' (Greenblatt 257).[33] With this Greenblatt professes faith in the same Renaissance that so captivated nineteenth-century Britain, a Renaissance we continue to fashion after ourselves today.

Notes

This essay expands upon and revises arguments first presented in 'Articulating Authority: Emilia Dilke's Early Reviews', which appeared in the spring 1998 issue of *Victorian Periodicals Review*.

1 In the Epilogue to *Renaissance Self-Fashioning*, Greenblatt recounts his inability to mouth the phrase 'I want to die' when asked to do so by a stranger preparing to see his paralysed and terminally ill son. Greenblatt's unwillingness even to feign this utterance shows, he explains, how our modern sense of self remains inflected by the more superstitious medieval model of self-awareness. Indeed, Greenblatt's oscillation between historical particularity and contemporary relevance in his discussion of self-fashion-ing allows the book to enact precisely the uncertain subjectivity it describes.

2 On Eliot's use of Emilia Dilke as a model for Dorothea Brooke, see Charles Dilke's 'Memoir' of Lady Dilke, which prefaces her posthumous *Book of*

Spiritual Life (London: John Murray, 1905) esp. pp. 16–17. Betty Askwith, *Lady Dilke: A Biography* (London: Chatto and Windus, 1969) pp. 10–17; R.J. Harris, 'Emilia Francis Strong: Portraits of a Lady', *Nineteenth-Century Fiction* 8 (September 1953), 81–93; and John Glucker, 'The Case for Edward Casaubon', *Pegasus* (November 1967), 7–21. Fictional portrayals of Dilke also appear in Mrs. Humphry Ward's hugely successful novel *Robert Elsmere*, Rhoda Broughton's *Belinda*, William H. Mallock's *The New Republic*, and in *Vices français* by Hector Malot, with whom Emilia Dilke privately collaborated.

3   The best sources for biographical information on Emilia Dilke are Kali Israel, *Names and Stories: Emilia Dilke and Victorian Culture* (New York: Oxford University Press, 1999); Askwith and Charles Dilke.

4   The unconventional spelling of her name derived, in fact, from her father's decision to name his daughter after an officer with whom he had served in the British Indian Army. Kali Israel gives sustained attention to the significance of her various and changing names.

5   One extant letter suggests not only that Francis Strong and her mother enjoyed a close personal bond, but that their correspondence dealt with professional as well as personal matters. Writing after the death of their mother, she asks one of her sisters for assistance in compiling a bibliography of her publications: 'I think we decided to burn all my letters to mother but if not and you have any I should be glad if you would send them; they might be helpful,' Francis Pattison to Henrietta Strong, 4 January 1884, Pattison Papers, Bodleian Library, Oxford University, Oxford, MS 140 ff. 57–59.

6   Strong's disavowal of maternal influence extends beyond the confines of family history and into the formation of her intellectual life. Francis Strong pursued few close personal or professional bonds with women, choosing instead to adopt male role models and intellectual companions.

7   This rare reference to her mother comes via Francis Strong's sister, Rosa Tuckwell, who recalled that their mother allowed Francis to study in London under the condition that she live with another female student and have an escort during her transit to and from school.

8   At this time, Oxford fellows, with the exception of the rector, were not permitted to marry.

9   Mark Pattison's autobiography provides the most poignant and unblinking account of his character and circumstances: *Memoirs of an Oxford Don* (Vivian H.H. Green, ed. London: Cassell, 1988 [orig. 1885]). See also Vivian H.H. Green, *Oxford Common Room* (London: Edward Arnold, 1957) and *Love in a Cool Climate: The Letters of Mark Pattison and Meta Bradley, 1879–1884* (Oxford: Clarendon Press, 1985); and John Sparrow, *Mark Pattison and the Idea of a University* (Cambridge: Cambridge University Press, 1967).

10 Mark Pattison to Meta Bradley, PP, MS 119; cited in Askwith, 1. Henry James recorded his impressions of the Pattison *ménage* after dining at Lincoln in 1869. In a letter to his brother William dated 26 April 1869, he writes: 'The Rector is a desiccated old scholar, torpid even to incivility with too much learning; but his wife is of quite another fashion – very young (about 28) very pretty, very clever, very charming and very conscious of it all. She is I believe highly emancipated and I defy an English woman to be

emancipated except coldly and wantonly. As a spectacle the thing had its points: the dark rich, scholastic old dining room in the college court – the languid old rector and his pretty little wife in a riding-habit, talking slang.' In Henry James, *Selected Letters*, ed. Leon Edel (Cambridge, Mass. and London: The Belknap Press of Harvard University Press, 1987) p. 30.

11 Francis Pattison to Rosa Tuckwell, 19 February 1868, Pattison Papers, MS 140 ff. 6–9.

12 Elaine Showalter, *The Female Malady: Women, Madness and English Culture, 1830–1980* (New York: Pantheon, 1985); Vieda Skultans, *Madness and Morals: Ideas on Insanity in the Nineteenth Century* (London and Boston: Routledge and Kegan Paul, 1975); Barbara Ehrenreich and Deidre English, *Complaints and Disorders: The Sexual Politics of Sickness* (Old Westbury: The Feminist Press, 1973).

13 Francis Pattison to Mark Pattison, n.d. (ca. 1877), Pattison Papers, MS 60 ff. 128–29.

14 These letters are among the Pattison Papers MS 57.

15 An excellent recent biography of Charles Dilke is David Nicholls, *The Lost Prime Minister: A Life of Sir Charles Dilke* (London: Hambledon Press, 1995).

16 Dilke's first wife died during childbirth in 1874 after two years of marriage. This change in his personal circumstances would account for the renewed acquaintance or the preservation of correspondence following his bereavement, or both. The exact circumstances of their relationship prior to the mid-1870s remains vague. Whatever these circumstances, there exists a vast archive of correspondence: by the late 1870s and through the early 1880s, they were writing to each other at least once a week.

17 She had received a legacy of £50,000 from the estate of her late husband.

18 Frederick Leighton to Francis Pattison, n.d., Dilke Papers, MS 43,903 f. 143.

19 Frederick Leighton to Francis Pattison, 3 July 1885, Dilke Papers, MS 43,903 ff. 144–45. Several of Leighton's letters to her are cited by Leonée and Richard Ormond in *Lord Leighton* (New Haven and London: Yale University Press, 1975), which discusses their friendship at some length.

20 On her career with the *Athenaeum*, see Marysa Demoor, *Their Fair Share: Women, Power and Criticism in the* Athenaeum, *from Millicent Garrett Fawcett to Katherine Mansfield* (Aldershot: Ashgate, 2000), pp. 64–75.

21 'Society of Female Artists'. *Westminster Review* 35 (April 1869), 597; and 'The British Institution and the Female Artists' Exhibitions'. *Saturday Review* 13 (1 February 1862), 134–5.

22 She maintained a high profile on behalf of women's enfranchisement. For instance, she is pictured in a popular suffrage meeting seated next to Millicent Fawcett in the popular newspaper *The Graphic*, 25 May 1872.

23 See, for example, the discussion of the Society of Female Artists in 'The Spring Exhibitions'. *Saturday Review* 19 (4 March 1865), 256–7. I attribute this anonymous review to Francis Pattison based on the date of the piece – which coincides with her tenure at the *Saturday Review* – as well as on similarity of the views expressed with a later review in *Westminster Review* (April 1869) which *The Wellesley Index to Victorian Literature* attributes, I believe correctly, to her.

24 I discuss the effects of her marriage to Dilke on her scholarly career at greater length in 'The Victorian *Grand Siècle*: Ideology as Art History'.

25 Dilke Papers, MS 43,906.
26 Francis Pattison to Charles Dilke, 11 June 1885, Dilke Papers, MS 43,906.
27 I estimate that her annual income from fees for articles would have ranged from £20 to nearly £100.
28 Emilia Dilke to Gertrude Tuckwell, 16 November [1885 or 1886] Pattison Papers, MS 140 f.87.
29 John Ruskin to Emilia Dilke, 28 January 1886, Dilke Papers, MS 43,908 f. 110.
30 It is not coincidental that Eliot received this notice for a novel set in Renaissance Italy, the standard against which Victorian cultural achievement was often measured.
31 Letters exchanged between them in 1886 and 1887 show their antithetic views of their relationship. This round of correspondence began when Emilia Dilke sent Ruskin a copy of her latest book *Claude Lorrain, sa vie et ses oeuvres* (1884). She asked him to inscribe the book for her, calling herself one of his disciples. He responded with the quote presented earlier in this essay. When Ruskin failed to return the book after a year, Dilke sent another note in which she addressed him as 'Dear Master' and tried to justify her claim to discipleship: 'Surely to live as simply as possible for truth in all things and to try to deal with all people in love and justice, if not done quite in "your way" is yet doing "as you bid".' This elicits a final communiqué from Ruskin, reading in part 'What have I to do with justice? or truth? or simplicity? ...To obey me is to love Turner and hate Raphael – to love Gothic and hate Renaissance – to love sunshine and hate smoke, and to live anywhere rather than Sloane Street.' Given that the Dilkes resided at 76 Sloane Street, it is not surprising that this note marks the end of their correspondence. Dilke Papers, MS 43,908 ff. 110–132.
32 The coding of positivist discourse as masculine during the nineteenth century has been investigated in relation to art history and criticism by Norman Broude in *Impressionism: A Feminist Reading. The Gendering of Art, Science, and Nature in the Nineteenth Century* (New York: Rizzoli, 1991). Broude describes a phenomenon in which succeeding cultural, scientific and historic discourses invoke a rhetoric that characterises preceding movements as feminine in opposition to their own masculine enterprise. In the nineteenth century, 'scientific' methods, i.e. those that relied upon direct observation and classifiable data, assumed a masculine valence in opposition to earlier, especially Romantic systems.
33 Significantly, the Huguenots had a particular hold on the Victorian imagination. Perhaps the struggle between the Huguenots and the Catholics served as historical prefiguration of their own religious difficulties and doubts. Victorian representations of the religious wars in France – whether fiction or non-fiction – generally describe Huguenots as modernising intellectuals.

Works cited

Anon., 'Authoresses'. *Saturday Review* 16 (10 October 1863), 483.
Askwith, Betty, *Lady Dilke: A Biography*. London: Chatto and Windus, 1969.

Bloom, Harold, *The Anxiety of Influence: A Theory of Poetry*. New York: Oxford University Press, 1970.

Dilke, Emilia, *Book of Spiritual Life*. London: John Murray, 1905.

—— [as E.F.S. Pattison], 'Contemporary Literature: Art'. *Westminster Review* 43 (April 1873), 639–40.

—— [as E.F.S. Pattison], 'Notes and News'. Review of *Lectures on Art* by John Ruskin. *Academy* 1, no. 12 (10 September 1870), 305.

—— *The Shrine of Death and Other Stories*. London: George Routledge, 1886.

—— *The Shrine of Love and Other Stories*. London: George Routledge, 1891.

Greenblatt, Stephen, *Renaissance Self-Fashioning: From More to Shakespeare*. Chicago and London: University of Chicago Press, 1980.

Houghton, Walter, *The Victorian Frame of Mind*. New Haven and London: Yale University Press, 1957, pp. 324–5.

MacDonald, Susan Peck, 'Jane Austen and the Tradition of the Absent Mother'. *The Lost Tradition: Mothers and Daughters in Literature*. Ed. Cathy N. Davidson and E.M. Broner. New York: Ungar, 1980, pp. 58–69.

Mansfield, Elizabeth. 'The Victorian *Grand Siècle*: Ideology as Art History'. *Victorian Literature and Culture* (spring 2000), 133–47.

Zimmerman, Bonnie, '"The Mother History" in George Eliot's Life, Literature and Political Ideology'. *The Lost Tradition: Mothers and Daughters in Literature*. Ed. Cathy N. Davidson and E.M. Broner. New York: Ungar, 1980, pp. 81–94.

2
The Art of Self-Creation: Henry James in the New York Edition Prefaces

John H. Pearson

Many have tried to relieve Henry James of the burden encumbered by the title 'Master' that James sought for himself and that Leon Edel ultimately bestowed on him. As John Carlos Rowe notes, several recent studies, including his own book, *The Other Henry James*, transform 'the pompous figure of James as master of the novel ... into the vulnerable, sexually anxious, and lonely writer struggling with the new modern art and new age he had helped make possible' (ix), by engaging James's work in 'the cultural diversification of literary study, its interdisciplinary connections with social sciences and history, and the globalization of literature as a field' (6). The Edition, which James called his marble 'mosaic sarcophagus', was to stand as a monument to the mastery that many now view as an invention (quoted in Edel 321). For generations, the Edition, with its twenty-four plum-coloured volumes and eighteen prefaces, was considered the pinnacle of American literary practice; the prefaces were separated and collected by R.P. Blackmur into a volume entitled *The Art of the Novel* (1934), and indeed these explanations of James's literary art are rarely questioned but often quoted. David McWhirter argues that 'Part of the problem with traditional readings of the Edition ... is that they enshrine not only Henry James but a conception of authorship – the author as an autonomous, unitary, originating and decidedly masculine genius – that seems increasingly untenable in the wake of poststructuralism, and more than a little suspect in the context of recent historicist, cultural, and gender criticism' (2–3). The decidedly problematic traditional readings of the Edition are James's wish: the prefaces present an idealised reading of the novels and tales they precede, modelled and authorised by James (see Pearson). They further construct an identity for the author based upon a well-wrought history of his authorship. This identity is more complex than the monolithic Master, but no less iconic. In the prefaces, James grows from a youthful writer alive to the possibilities of an undiscovered world into the reflective master painter giving with explanation his art to a world he now knows only by visions and revisions of memory. From naïve explorer and would-be circumnavigator to embroiderer and painter, James ages through a series of graceful metaphors that leave him in the prefaces welcoming his readers to his house of fiction. This version of the self, carefully crafted and consonant with James's literary aesthetic, was largely conceived out of a desire for discrimination, appreciation and profit.

Both the young and the old Henry James in the prefaces are creations of a writer anxious to fix his place in the literary world, and especially anxious to receive remuneration for his work. As Michael Anesko explains, from 1895 to 1905, while James was writing his last great novels, he found it almost impossible 'to serialize his work and to find publishers who would take the risk of issuing his books' (142). The copyright agreement of 1891 between England and the United States resulted in a vastly expanded commercial market and, as a result, the profession of literary agent was born to help writers publish transnationally. James was among the first to hire one of the new breed, suggesting both his business acumen and his commitment to personal profitability (Anesko 142, Jakobson). This same commitment led him to consider the Edition not only as the great work (his *vade mecum*) to represent him in the canon, but also as a commercial enterprise that required dedication and compromise. While much has been written about the Edition architecture – the selection and placement of the literary texts – few scholars have considered the rhetorical decisions, both large and small, that James made in the prefaces in response to the same necessities that guided some major decisions about the construction of the Edition as a whole.[1] Yet the prefaces themselves are in large part a result of such exigencies. James understood that authorship was increasingly a public affair supporting a privately conducted craft. In the story 'The Private Life', Henry James dramatises the predicament of writers like himself who long to keep the public and private sectors and selves utterly distinct. Clare Vawdrey, 'the greatest (in the opinion of many) of our literary glories', is a writer with two selves. One self remains alone in the study, without passions but teeming with art. He writes great drama while his other self moves about in society, attending openings and making social contacts, exuding warmth and business acumen. These selves, one isolated and the other social, are 'members of a firm, and one of them would never be able to carry on the business without the other. Moreover mere survival would be dreadful for either' (17: 250). The successful partnership of these selves depends upon the illusion that each is singular. They come to ruin when a suspicious actress shatters the illusion, exposing the isolated writer in his studio while her cohorts detain his social other. Exposing the truth that the author they know is only half a man renders the social self ineffective, and leaves the isolated self unable to write. More alarming to an especially private man like Henry James, it enables a biographical relation of the man and his art that readers adore and that James loathed. As 'The Private Life' suggests, James detested the public's desire that writers serve up their personal life for public fodder; his incineration of personal letters and papers clearly attests to this. It also bespeaks a tremendous desire to control his public persona. Indeed, James writes in the preface to volume 15 of the Edition: 'Living as we do under permanent visitation of the deadly epidemic of publicity, any rash word, any light thought that chances to escape us, may instantly, by that accident, find itself propagated and perverted, multiplied and diffused, after a fashion poisonous, practically, and speedily fatal, to its subject' (*AN* 284). Yet James realised that publicity is necessary to sell books, and as Richard Salmon argues, 'James was aware that the private life of the artist was not ... easily defended' (91). He also realised that a relation between the author's personal life and his art is precisely what readers expected from the prefaces to the New York Edition. The encouragements were clear: let your readers know the man, the writer, the literary lion, and they will buy your books. William Dean Howells was disappointed in the apparent didactic nature of the first prefaces, in fact, and, wishing for something more intimate, he wrote and told James so. Yet James could only do what his aesthetic and sense of propriety would allow, even when exposing himself to public scrutiny. James's understanding of character and identity produced an image of the self quite unlike Howells' more typically realist portraits, yet James believed the prefaces did portray him and offer him up for judgement as the maker of the literary texts they frame. His means of self-exposure, however, are typically Jamesian. The self-image that James constructs in the prefaces is 'the continuity of an artist's endeavour, the growth of his whole operative consciousness'; the prefaces offer up 'his whole unfolding ... for a thrilling tale' (*AN* 4).[2] He fashions a past and present self out of the fabric of authorial consciousness following a formula – though upstream – articulated in the preface to *The Portrait of a Lady*: 'Tell me what the artist is, and I will tell you of what he has *been* conscious' (*AN* 46). In these prefatory acts of self-creation, James tells us of what he is and has been aware, and thereby he tells us who he is.

The prefaces of the New York Edition offer an unusual opportunity to study self-creation through the enactment of a writer's literary aesthetic. The character of this self-construction is immanent in James's selection of novels and tales for the Edition, and equally so in his omission of others. It is most evident, however, in the prefaces, where James weaves literary criticism and theory, autobiography and creative non-fiction into a narrative of a writer's compositional challenges with an equally compelling narrative of his struggles with memory and the Edition. James fashions himself just as he has created characters in his novels and tales, by forming a central consciousness upon which the world is reflected and then revealed to the reader. The reflected world in this case is made up of the author and his art, but it includes the reader and other writers, other texts and other concerns too. We find reflected there an image of the author, often his younger self engaged with the challenges of writing and of the business end of authorship. James's work on the Edition and the many challenges he faced are also reflected there. The self, past and present, is fashioned into a complex authorial identity. James creates an identity in the prefaces, that is, just as he creates the monumental Edition: he edits and revises the past and selectively builds a unified self-image that both belies and gestures toward its artfulness. James makes himself into his own greatest lucid reflector, a consciousness keen and broad enough to encompass past and present, writer and reader, text and prefatory meta-text.

Yet even the most recent studies of authorship and the New York Edition leave the prefaces largely unexamined as the locus for James's construction of Self. While David McWhirter makes the compelling argument in his Introduction to *Henry James and the New York Edition: The Construction of Authorship* (1995) that the prefaces were written by James on the premise of the author as a living, 'active, responsible agent', and it is this self James seeks to create on the threshold of his fiction, the essays that follow examine the complex philosophical, psychological and cultural underpinnings of the Edition as a whole. Ross Posnock and Stuart Culver both argue that James seeks a fuller sense of self at the expense of any aura of mastery. Posnock contends that the New York Edition and its prefaces 'at once memorialise and explode his mastery ... [in a] self-interrogating act of authority' (38). Culver explains why this is so:

> James suggests that the artist may well benefit from the ruin of his own grandiose ambitions. This notion of a literary mastery

grounded in failure complicates the project of publishing a collected edition: on the one hand, the collection is bound to expose the limits of the master's authority; on the other, such an ambitious venture provides a capital opportunity for the mocking hand of the servant who would expose the fallibility of his master. (40)

Paul B. Armstrong, in the most protracted consideration of James's self-representation in the prefaces, extends the argument to include the reader, contending that the prefaces 'help provide the reader with a hermeneutic education that simulates modes of understanding appropriate for construing' James's fiction (126). They force the reader to look forward and back in time. Armstrong explains that 'These elaborate temporal doublings of James's prefaces also seem uniquely a product of his fascination with the epistemology of consciousness and self-consciousness' (131). This 'temporally double structure' of the reader's consciousness that Armstrong describes is complemented perfectly by the double structure of authorial selfhood in the prefaces. The remaining essays in the collection provide a comprehensive historical context for the Edition, unearthing motives and connections that James would leave buried. Carol Holly, Eve Sedgwick and Alfred Habegger speak to the issue of James's sense of failure and shame that motivated him to produce the Edition. The image of James as Master, they contend, is a palliative for James's wounded ego, and a forceful attempt to put his stamp on the present and future of the novel.

Mastery is rife in the rhetoric of the prefaces. James sought to create a self that is at once disarmingly familiar and abundantly masterful. Thinking back to writing *Roderick Hudson*, James admits that 'it must even then have begun for me too, the ache of fear, that was to become so familiar, of being duly tempted and led on by "developments"' (*AN* 4). This glimpse of the young, shy writer fearful and excited by the possibilities of his tale may warm the reader to James, but soon thereafter James adopts a different tone. As if chastising himself for thinking that composition would somehow take care of itself, he writes in a tone that is distinctly older, wiser and more secure: 'Art would be easy indeed if, by a fond power disposed to "patronise" it, such conveniences [of a natural, convenient stopping place for the tale], such simplifications, had been provided. We have, as the case stands, to invent and establish them, to arrive at them by a difficult, dire process of selection and comparison, of surrender and sacrifice' (*AN* 6). While the young James is awed by the seemingly limitless array of compositional possibilities, the seasoned author preaches hard work and sacrifice. He is no less directive when discussing the work of authorship in general, and he states principles clearly:

> there can be for him [the novelist] only one truth and one direction – the quarter in which his subject most completely expresses itself. The careful ascertainment of how it shall do so, and the art of guiding it with consequent authority – since this sense of 'authority' is for the master-builder the treasure of treasures, or at least the joy of joys – renews in the modern alchemist something like the old dream of the secret of life. (*AN* 123)

Both master-building and modern alchemist, engineer and magician, the novelist must follow the rules of this master or surely he will fail. So too must the editor and publisher of fiction. Deeply concerned about illustration and any other form of supplementation of the author's work by someone or some agency other than the author, James sternly warns us that,

> Anything that relieves responsible prose of the duty of being, while placed before us, good enough, interesting enough and, if the question be of picture, pictorial enough, above all *in itself*, does it the worst of services, and may well inspire in the lover of literature certain lively questions as to the future of that institution. (*AN* 332)

If mastery is a matter of control, James is certainly on the right track. While James confesses that he is frequently at a loss to explain how and where his stories first developed, he claims utter responsibility for his 'relation with the reader ... as to which I felt no one to be trusted but myself' (*AN* 55).

The image of self as master is constructed in the prefaces through passages such as these, and James's critics for many generations have quoted such passages to prove the validity of their readings. James was a tremendous success at building a monument to his mastery, but he knew the fate of Ozymandias and other great masters before and since: 'Nothing beside remains. Round the decay / Of that colossal wreck, boundless and bare / The lone and level sands stretch far away.'[3] James was no less committed to a different sort of relation to his reader, one more personal if uncomfortable. He presents himself in the prefaces as the awe-struck young writer, as we have seen, but this is only one moment in the unfolding history of his authorial consciousness. This is the autobiographic narrative in the prefaces, the double figuration of James as speaking subject and as the subject spoken about.

Eve Sedgwick notes the autobiographic form of the prefaces without naming it: 'James's most usual gesture in the prefaces is to figure his relation to the past as the intensely charged relationship between the author of the prefaces and the often much younger man who wrote the novels and stories to which the prefaces are appended – or between either of these men and a yet younger figure who represents the fiction itself' (214). Sedgwick argues that 'The speaking self of the prefaces does not attempt to merge with the potentially shaming or shamed figurations of its younger self, younger fictions, younger heroes; its attempt is to love them' (216). Yet within the prefaces, both separation of younger and older selves and any potential merger are illusion: the younger self and the 'speaking subject' in the prefaces are already unified. The apparent separation of authorial identity into past and present selves is a rhetorical device that enables James to create a Self that is both historicised and abundantly mature. When James writes in the first preface 'These notes represent, over a considerable course, the continuity of an artist's endeavour, the growth of his whole operative consciousness' (*AN* 4), he suggests that the prefaces will offer a complete history of authorial consciousness, and therefore a complete image of the authorial self. Yet James almost immediately admits there is no such thing as plenitude in art: 'Really, universally, relations stop nowhere, and the exquisite problem of the artist is eternally but to draw, by a geometry of his own, the circle within which they shall happily *appear* to do so' (*AN* 5; emphasis James's). The distinction of younger and older selves is an appearance, an illusion of the historicised plot in the prefaces, which draws the circle, leaving the union somewhere outside its circumference.

The illusion is a trick of metaphor. The young author of *Roderick Hudson*, the earliest novel in the Edition, is characterised as a novice explorer with a new command. 'I recall again the quite uplifted sense with which my idea, such as it was, permitted me at last to put quite out to sea. I had but hugged the shore on sundry previous small occasions; bumping about, to acquire skill, in the shallow waters and sandy coves of the "short story" and master as yet of no vessel constructed to carry a sale.' The metaphor allows historical continuity and development. The young writer learns his craft in shallow, safe waters gaining experience as he awaits some external event – a merchant command or an idea suited to the longer novel – that will test his skill. There is both physical and temporal continuity between this young sailor and the captain who soon marvelled at how 'the blue southern sea seemed to spread immediately before me and the breath of the spice-islands to be already in the breeze' (*AN* 4). Certainly this metaphor lends an aura of mastery, as James propels himself on a career that builds in rank and distance until such time as he circles the globe and returns with the goods and these tales about how he acquired them. Yet the older, wiser, mature artist separates himself from this hopeful wanderer because, looking back, James knows that hopes, like ships, are often dashed. James suggests as much in the second preface, to *The American*. He remembers that the *Atlantic* had begun serial publication before he was finished writing the novel, and detecting a problem in the plot, he found himself stymied:

> I ask myself indeed if, possibly, recognizing after I was launched the danger of an inordinate leak – since the ship has truly a hole in its side more than sufficient to have sunk it – I may not have managed, as a counsel of mere despair, to stop my ears against the noise of waters and *pretend* to myself I was afloat; being indubitably, in any case, at sea, with no harbour of refuge till the end of my serial voyage. (*AN* 21)

When the hopes and ambitions of the young writer confront the realities of his profession, the metaphor sinks. While James is often engaged with watery metaphors in the prefaces, and in one instance he compares himself finding the idea for 'The Aspern Papers' to Columbus coming upon San Salvador, he will not place himself on a shoreless sea again. The metaphor of youthful explorer is not entirely lost to time; it evolves.

Whereas in the first preface James figures himself as the young captain about to set sail for blue southern seas, in the third preface, to *The Portrait of a Lady*, he has more modest geographical ambitions. Both *Roderick Hudson* and *The Portrait of a Lady* were begun in Italy, James contends, but he fashions himself writing the latter novel not as a global explorer, but as a stationary people watcher:

> the waterside life, the wondrous lagoon spread before me, and the ceaseless human chatter of Venice came in at my windows, to which I seem to myself to have been constantly driven, in the fruit-less fidget of composition, as if to see whether, out in the blue channel, the ship of some right suggestion, of some better phrase, of the next happy twist of my subject, the next true touch for my canvas, might n't come into sight. (*AN* 40)

He has separated himself from the ship, fashioning himself as the recipient of the ship's goods rather than the captain who would bring those goods to port. In this sense he is, like Hawthorne before him, at some Custom House, some border between the world of suggestion and the world of composition. While in the fourth preface James becomes mobile once again, he is no less local than in the preface to *Portrait*: 'the prime idea' for *The Princess Casamassima*, 'was unmistakeably the ripe round fruit of perambulation' (*AN* 59). James becomes an explorer of his own immediate world, and the familiar streets of London become 'the great grey Babylon' and then 'a garden bristling with immense illustrative flora' (*AN* 59). By the writing of *The Wings of the Dove*, James declares in the sixteenth preface, he becomes 'the wary adventurer' walking 'round and round' his subject. The discovered world was no longer a beautiful garden but some unidentifiable place 'with secrets and compartments, with possible treacheries and traps; it might have a great deal to give, but would probably ask for equal services in return, and would collect this debt to the last shilling' (*AN* 289). James remains the explorer, but he narrows his scope and grows more cautious with age.

The metaphor extends from James as novelist to James as author of the New York Edition itself. While James may never imagine himself in 1907 setting sail to discover islands and extend his geometry around the globe, in his role as master-builder of the monument and model reader, he becomes a guide. He is constantly 'remount[ing] the stream of time' to find the all-but-forgotten origins of his stories (*AN* 183). Unable to recall the precise origin of *The Portrait of a Lady*, James says that he is 'quite unable to track the footsteps' of the characters who became Isabel Archer, Ralph Touchett, Madame Merle and Gilbert Osmond (*AN* 53). Perhaps most tellingly of the differences between youth and age, and also of the continuity that joins them, James transforms the uncharted expanses into walled gardens. The 'blue southern sea' that lay before James as he wrote *Roderick Hudson* becomes 'some sweet old overtangled walled garden' in which James, as he revises the novel and writes the preface to it, can find 'a safe paradise of self-criticism' (*AN* 10). The garden for James is an image of 'a palpable imaginable *visitable* past' (*AN* 164); whereas the spice islands and uncharted seas of his youth are finally unimaginable and unreachable. James abandons the metaphor of vast exploration for this reason. It represents a future that exists only as a hope in the distant past. It is a road not taken (a subject that intrigued James in 'The Jolly Corner' and other stories). As guide, however, James is able to lead his reader where he will. Offering himself as the exemplary reader, James explains that into an author's 'very footsteps the responsive, the imaginative steps of the docile reader that I consentingly become for him all comfortably sink; his vision, superimposed on my own as an image in cut paper is applied to a sharp shadow on a wall, matches, at every point, without excess of deficiency' (*AN* 336). Here James offers the reader an armchair exploration of the world, taming the metaphor and transforming it into one of vicarious but precisely controlled experience. He is, then, no less the master for fashioning himself as docile, consenting and comfortable.

James uses a second system of metaphor to provide continuity between the younger self as writer and the older self as reader and reviser. Throughout the prefaces, James figures himself as a painter. When he refers to the work of revising, for instance, he becomes 'the anxious artist' who places his old canvas on the easel. He 'has to wipe it over, in the first place, to see; he has to "clean it up," say, or to varnish it anew, or at the least to place it in a light' (*AN* 10). This metaphor, however, extends backward to the time of first writing. While at work on *The Spoils of Poynton*, for instance, James 'as a painter' wanted from his subjects their 'passions, the faculty, the forces of their beauty' (*AN* 127). Such elements 'gave out the vague pictorial glow which forms the first appeal of a living "subject" to the painter's consciousness,' James explains in the preface to *What Maisie Knew* (*AN* 141). The metaphor of writer as painter is also used to characterise those in the literary canon: 'many an expert painter, as for instance Dickens and Walter Scott, as for instance even, in the main, so subtle a hand as that of R.L. Stevenson, has preferred to leave the task' of writing about a young woman 'unattempted' (*AN* 49). By the final preface, as James incorporates the work of the New York Edition into the historical narrative that includes work on the Edition itself, he considers the metaphor outright: as a writer, James is like a painter because both are 'inclined to the idea of the particular attaching case *plus* some near individual view of it' – that is, James understands fiction as both subject and perception of the subject – 'that nearness quite having thus to become an imagined observer's, a projected, charmed painter's or poet's ... close and sensitive contact with it' (*AN* 328). Here, the writer-as-painter becomes the writer-as-painter-*or-poet*, for both have an individual and subjective vision to articulate in images. For James, 'all art is *expression*, and is thereby vividness' (*AN* 324): the painter and poet (and novelist) express both subject and subjectivity, and this is how and why James remains an 'active, responsible agent', as McWhirter explains, in and around his text, for the subjectivity of fiction is the expression of authorial consciousness.

We can understand the trajectory traced by these metaphors as the self constructed in and as James's authorial consciousness as he writes the prefaces. 'Tell me what the artist is, and I will tell you of what he has *been* conscious' (*AN* 46): while the novels and tales of the Edition tell us what the artist is, the prefaces show us the facets of the Self of which James is conscious. Or more accurately, he shows us facets of which he wants his readers to be conscious. As Armstrong and Sedgwick point out, James's identity appears dual – past self and present self, failed dramatist and masterful novelist. That which appears dual, however, is really a multiplication of metaphor that leads to differences among them, but differences that are not so great as to lose the trajectory traced here. The trains of both metaphor systems – the adventurer and the painter – retain coherent meaning. The prefaces portray contingent selves, separated by time and task, that gradually accumulate and form one highly crafted Self. This structure resembles a genre of autobiography that James Olney calls duplex autobiographical form. In this form, the autobiographical subject, often beginning from birth, gradually develops into the narrating autobiographer. Throughout this form, the autobiographer is an apparent subject, unlike the ostensibly objective autobiographical voice in Olney's simplex form, which is the voice of a distant historian writing as if transparent and unrelated to the autobiographical subject. In duplex form, the present creates itself as it recreates the past, working towards a union of subject and narrator. Gradually, the younger self becomes the autobiographer, and the story of the past becomes the story of writing about the past. This is precisely what appears to happen in the prefaces, as the younger Henry James, whom we see struggling with the creation of Rowland Mallet in *Roderick Hudson* and Isabel Archer in *The Portrait of a Lady*, becomes the elder author-as-painter returning to his early work 'with due care and with a bottle of varnish and a brush' to bring the older work back to life (*AN* 11). The permutations of metaphor creates what James Olney calls the *daimon*, the 'dominant faculty or function or tendency that formed [only] a part of his whole self' (39). One would assume that the *daimon* of the New York Edition would be the literary Master, for that is often the voice with which James speaks; it is that, and it is something much more personable, born of the sense of responsibility, that James, writing the prefaces, feels for his art, for his relation to it, and through it for the often elusive reader.

Whereas James Olney describes the formal characteristics of the form that James employs in the prefaces, Judith Butler provides a theoretical framework for understanding the repetition of metaphors that accumulate in James's construction of self. The very repetition of the metaphors of writer as painter, for instance, suggests that 'identity is not self-identical' (315); James's identity in the prefaces is not uniform, perpetual, evident, unique. And it should not be, for James is constructing an identity that will serve the public, attracting readers (consumers) to his works, just as Clare Vawdrey spawns a public persona-turned-person to do the same. James's self in the prefaces is a literary performance, and as such it has no prior subject. As Butler explains in 'Imitation and Gender Insubordination', 'the performance constitutes the appearance of a "subject" as its effect' (315). The subject is produced through the expression; it is not the producer of expression. James as explorer and revisionary painter, as young writer and as master, are products of the present moment of the prefaces. The metaphors of self constitute a self that is an effect of James's performance in the prefaces.

In this sense, James's story 'The Birthplace' may offer a better literary correlative than 'The Private Life' for the work of the prefaces. Morris Gedge and his wife Isabel are hired to live in the birthplace of a great writer, to keep up the property and guide guests through the rooms of the estate. They nearly lose their livelihood, however, because Mr Gedge seeks to know the now deceased author intimately and factually before he will act as duomo. He wanders the house looking for signs and knowledge that will lead him to some sense of certainty about the celebrated writer. Until he feels this certainty, he cannot properly instruct paying visitors. Eventually, Gedge learns to perform his role rather than to recite facts. Of facts, James writes this: 'nine tenths of the artist's interest in them is that of what he shall add to them and how he shall turn them' (*AN* 163). Gedge makes the birthplace a noteworthy stop on any literary tour of England, for he conjures an image of the author that is vital and compelling to his visitors. The prefaces, like the birthplace, offer a performance of authorial identity and not the author himself – and indeed the notion of 'the author himself' is at best debatable in any poststructuralist context. As Butler indicates, performance of the Self constitutes the Self. It is the origin even as it represents itself as a repetition of some displaced and unplaceable original.

In the final preface, published a full two years after the first volume appeared, James looks back on his great work and on his wilful construction of Self. He fashioned himself a master, controlling every detail of composition and literary architecture, while he remained almost helpless in his quest for ideas, for germs of stories, that he would find in the air and stumble over in his evening perambulations about London and Venice. As he prepares himself for the last word, he revises his initial statement that these notes – these prefaces – represent the unfolding of his entire consciousness, his crafted self. Now, he thinks, his consciousness must become part of the reading process. 'The rate at which new readings, new conductors of sense interposed, to make my total sense at all right, became, to this wonderful tune, the very record and mirror of the general adventure of one's intelligence.' Reading his own works, selected and collected to present a fairly controlled image of himself as author, James is pleased. He sounds a note of concern almost immediately, however, as he considers the dangers of reading. 'What I have been most aware of asking myself, however, is how writers, on such occasions of "revision," arrive at that successful resistance to the confident assault of the new reading which appears in the great majority of examples to have marked their course' (*AN* 342). No matter how carefully he controls his self-image, no matter how deep he makes the trail for others to follow him through his texts, James experiences the reader's will as an assault for he knows that he cannot control reading, interpretation, evaluation, or even the Self he has constructed and now must leave to its own devices. James soothes himself by recalling that his work and the complex self he fashions in the prefaces will remain, and his relation to them 'is essentially traceable, and in that fact abides', he writes in the final paragraph, 'the incomparable luxury of the artist' (*AN* 348), for as long as that self remains traceable as a spirit 'brooding' over the text, Henry James survives (*AN* 339).

Notes

1   On the architecture of the New York Edition, see especially Michael Anesko's chapter 'The Eclectic Architecture of Henry James's New York Edition' in *'Friction with the Market': Henry James and the Profession of Authorship*, chapter 8; and Stuart Culver 39–57.

2   For ease of reference, all references to the New York Edition prefaces are to *The Art of the Novel*, ed. R.P. Blackmur (Boston: Northeastern University Press, 1984), and will be noted in the text as *AN*.

3   Percy Bysshe Shelley, 'Ozymandias' ll. 12–14. See Culver 39–57.

Works cited

Anesko, Michael, *'Friction with the Market': Henry James and the Profession of Authorship*. New York: Oxford University Press, 1986.

Armstrong, Paul B., 'Reading James's Prefaces and Reading James'. *Henry James's New York Edition: The Construction of Authorship*. Ed. David McWhirter. Stanford: Stanford University Press, 1995, pp. 125–37.

Butler, Judith, 'Imitation and Gender Insubordination'. *Inside/Out: Lesbian Theories,Gay Theories*. Ed. Diana Fuss. New York: Routledge, 1991. Rpt. In *The Lesbian and Gay Studies Reader*. Ed. Henry Abelove, Michele Aina Barale, and David M. Halperin. New York: Routledge, 1993, pp. 307–20.

Culver, Stuart, 'Ozymandias and the Mastery of Ruins: The Design of the New York Edition. *Henry James's New York Edition: The Construction of Authorship*. Ed. David McWhirter. Stanford: Stanford University Press, 1995, pp. 39–57.

Edel, Leon, *Henry James: The Master; 1901–1916*. Philadelphia: Lippincott, 1972.

Habegger, Alfred, 'New York Monumentalism and Hidden Family Corpses'. *Henry James's New York Edition: The Construction of Authorship*. Ed. David McWhirter. Stanford: Stanford University Press, 1995, pp. 185–205.

Holly, Carol, 'The Emotional Aftermath of the New York Edition.' *Henry James's New York Edition: The Construction of Authorship*. Ed. David McWhirter. Stanford: Stanford University Press, 1995, pp. 167–84.

Jacobson, Marcia, *Henry James and the Mass Market*. Alabama: University of Alabama Press, 1983.

James, Henry, *The Art of the Novel*. Ed. R.P. Blackmur. Boston: Northeastern University Press, 1984.

—— 'The Birthplace'. *The Selected Novels and Tales of Henry James*. Vol. 17. New York: Charles Scribner's Sons, 1907.

—— 'The Private Life'. *The Selected Novels and Tales of Henry James*. Vol. 17. New York: Charles Scribner's Sons, 1907.

McWhirter, David, 'Introduction: "The Whole Chain of Relation and Responsibility": Henry James and the New York Edition'. *Henry James's New York Edition: The Construction of Authorship*. Ed. David McWhirter. Stanford: Stanford University Press, 1995, pp. 1–19.

Olney, James, *Metaphors of Self: the Meaning of Autobiography*. Princeton: Princeton University Press, 1972.

Pearson, John H., *The Prefaces of Henry James: Framing the Modern Reader*. University Park, PA: Pennsylvania State University Press, 1997.

Posnock, Ross, 'Breaking the Aura of Henry James'. *Henry James's New York Edition: The Construction of Authorship*. Ed. David McWhirter. Stanford: Stanford University Press, 1995, pp. 23–38.

Rowe, John Carlos, *The Other Henry James*. Durham, NC: Duke University Press, 1998.

Salmon, Richard, *Henry James and the Culture of Publicity*. Cambridge: Cambridge University Press, 1997.

Sedgwick, Eve Kosofsky, 'Shame and Performativity: Henry James's New York Edition Prefaces'. *Henry James's New York Edition: The Construction of Authorship*. Ed. David McWhirter. Stanford: Stanford University Press, 1995, pp. 206–39.

Shelley, Percy Bysshe, 'Ozymandias'. *The Norton Anthology of Poetry*. Ed. Alexander W. Allison. New York: Norton & Co., 1970, p. 667.

3
'Who is "We"?' The 'Daily Paper' Projects and the Journalism Manifestos of W.T. Stead

Laurel Brake

This is an essay about W.T. Stead's transformation from editor and journalist into an entrepreneurial publisher and theoriser of journalism in the modern period. Stead's writing between 1886 and 1904 was a constant process of self-fashioning through theory and practice of a developing profession and his place within it. How was he to combine commercial journalism with responsible journalism? The 'we' of his question interrogates at once the public editorial 'we', the personal journalist or editor, and the imagined community of readers – the Democracy whom, in Stead's view, newspapers represent. What I want to explore is the play between Stead's trope of 'Americanization', by which he meant entrepreneurial, commercial, cutting-edge journalism, and a competing ideology in which his spiritual and political agendas join to defeat it in its irresponsible guise. Stead's commitment to 'Americanization'[1] stretches from 1871, the date of his first job at the Darlington daily *The Northern Echo*, through to 1902 when he published 'The Americanization of the World or The Trend of the Twentieth Century' as a *Review of Reviews* Extra. I examine this commerce–ethics tension through two versions of a 'Daily Paper' in 1893 and 1904, devised by Stead as his re-entry into daily journalism from the margins of editing a monthly review. In the first instance, the title never progressed beyond a grand scheme and an indicative 'sample' issue, and in 1904 the paper folded after a month.

In his effort to reconcile commerce with ethics, Stead rethinks the contemporary economy of the newspaper industry. His 'Daily Paper' projects seek to avoid an economic structure in which power and control rest with the proprietor, a structure that hampers responsible journalism. This was the economy that had resulted in Stead's enforced departure from the *Pall Mall Gazette*. In the 'Daily Papers' Stead opts to remain 'outside' the capital arrangements of mainstream journalism by fashioning an economy in which the editor retains control: in 1893 he issues shares for would-be subscribers to purchase in advance, and in 1904 he requires prepaid subscriptions. He offers *readers* the opportunity of becoming proprietors, readers whose primary power is their initial choice to subscribe or not. He doesn't obscure where the power lies: 'I have a clear majority of the ordinary shares .... I can always override all opposition, and the company becomes but another term for myself' (*RR* November 1893: 463). But as we shall see, in Stead's vision of responsible journalism the reader is positioned as a participant in dialogue with the editor, through local distribution 'depots' which function as community clubs; through a network of editor's scouts whose business is to inform the editor of readers' views; and through the facilitation of direct communication between reader and editor, by correspondence collected from readers and deposited at the depot by newsboys and girls.

Stead's company plan typifies the 'personal' journalism defiantly developed by him and by other new journalists. Stead's justification of the issue of shares under the conditions outlined above includes both a profit scheme for shareholders that envisages civic groups pooling their dividends for charitable expenditure in the 'Civic Community' (*RR* October 1893: 349), and the dissemination of the 'responsible' contents of the journal which, from 1893, is seen as 'not so much as a dividend-earning, salary-paying machine, as a *nexus* between a great body of men and women who are actuated by a common faith and a common resolve which they are prepared to demonstrate by united action' (*RR* October 1893: 347). This notion is developed in the December number, where one future outcome of such a paper is envisaged in a Christmas story, as a 'Fellowship'. The social function of the 1904 scheme is evident in Stead's notion of a 'Civic Church' of which the newspaper is a hub. However, in retrospect, the mismatch between the 'mass', lower-middle-class/artisan readership of Stead's imagined niche market and the requirement to put down a relatively large sum of money was a glaring and ideological failure of Stead's commercial judgement. So was the mismatch between that popular readership and the paper's contents. Although the first was religious and the second secular, both excluded all reports of vice-ridden aspects of modern urban culture: the racing tips as well as the stock market reports. They may usefully be compared with other innovative models of the press at the time – British socialist and American investigative/muckraking, for example.

Tributes to Stead in 1912 when he died on board the *Titanic* are a direct result of Stead's transformation of journalism from 'old' to 'new':

> He struck the personal note. He acclimatised the 'interview.' He developed the 'crossheads.' He extended the scope of the special article and the signed contribution. He introduced pictorial illustration. All these were the outward signs of the current of fresh vigour and greater vividness of presentment which were an expression of his personality. (Anon. 18 April 1912: 12c)

At a time when journalism was of decidedly low status, his willing *self*-identification as, above all, a 'journalist' was self-conscious and anomalous, as were his commitment to the development of the fourth estate and his insistent attention throughout his career to its visibility as a growing, dignified and powerful profession.

Editing a monthly from 1890 did not pay the bills, and from 1890 Stead set up his own publishing house from which base he not only issued the monthly *Review of Reviews* but also other journals (a penny monthly called *Help. A Journal of Social Service* (1891–2) and *Borderland* (1894–97) a quarterly review of psychic research) whose topics were not served by the format of the *RR*, and also a stream of books, pamphlets, extras, annuals and reprints, many of which he wrote himself. It is in these, as well as in the *Review*, that the steady, annual pronouncements on the nature and theory of journalism appear. It is a rich archive.

Stead's self-fashioning is a pervasive part of current critical comment on this maverick figure. Hypocrisy is alleged or implied by commentators such as Judith Walkowitz and Lucy Bland in analyses of his sexual prurience in his 'investigative' journalism. Moreover, serial 'womanising' and the resultant personal anguish of himself, his wife and his family are clear from correspondence, including Stead's letters to himself.[2] The public voice, then, is also echoed by a reflexive personal battle, which underlies the dramatic shift in his journalism practice from the 1880s to the 1890s and after: the fissures in the discourse lead to his ultimate (enforced) abandonment of commercial journalism, but also his attempt to reconcile it with other, evangelical discourses that had been clamouring for his full attention throughout his life. The 'imperfect' Stead that Walkowitz and Bland 'see' is also and nevertheless a reformer and activist. His prurience does not cancel his advanced views on the education and employment of women, and his sensationalism may also be read as a bid to new readers and part of best practice in the journalism of his day. It is an aspect of his contribution over three decades to the transformation of English journalism.

The arena of W.T. Stead's productivity was wide, its rate prodigious and its variety notable, determined only by what was most topical, newsworthy and, in his view, best commanding his attention. Thus international conflict in Russia and in Southern Africa, the age of consent, homosexuality, and the state of the Navy at home, women's rights, international peace, spiritualism, and psychic research all at various times (and often simultaneously) were objects of his interest, campaigns and publications. I contend, however, that amidst this cacophony of discourse the dominant terms remain journalist and journalism. Stead's self-fashioning involved the adoption of two basic rules associated specifically with the new journalism: remaining open to the contemporary and new – as the lifeblood of the enterprising newsman, and of *making* news through a proactive, investigative role that emphasises the agency of the journalist. In the last analysis, Stead's representation of the ideal journalist amounts to a journalist/leader of a 'Civic Church', comprising the assets and power of two types of minister, the minister of religion and the prime minister of party and government.

Stead's biography is germane to the particular profile of his career as a late nineteenth-century Anglophone journalist, notably his northern roots, his family's evangelical dissenting Christianity, his amateur entry into the profession, his apprenticeship in provincial journalism, and the philanthropic adult pursuits of his siblings who were London missionaries and settlement workers. They help anchor Stead's practice and project *outside* mainstream English journalism, in so far as that was essentially commercial; even while he drifted into the centre and appeared to define the present and future of journalism in the 1880s, he remained attentive to the values and community of his origins. For example, in *Help* (1891–2), dedicated to 'Social Service', Stead opens the first number with the statement: 'its chief object will be to help the helpless and those who need to be helped ...by preaching the Gospel of the Citizen Christ' (2–3). In 'Government by Newspapers', in the 1998 *Annual*, Stead endorses W.R. Hearst's dedication in the *New York Journal* to 'action': 'Action ...is the distinguishing mark of the new journalism' (Stead RR *Annual for 1898* 184). This axiom is directly linked to a technique of the new journalism – investigation: 'The new journal of to-day prints the news too, but it does more. It does not wait for things to turn up. It turns them up' (Stead *Annual for 1898* 184). Additionally, the framework in which this chapter on the *New York*

Journal is lodged is evangelical, as part of an investigation that comprises the whole of the shilling *Annual,* entitled 'Satan's Invisible World Displayed. Or Despairing Democracy. A Study of Greater New York'. It is in turn a 'companion' to Stead's earlier best-seller, *If Christ Came to Chicago* (1892).

Stead's departure from the *PMG* at the sensitive age of 40 also became, in the event, a premature departure from the world of daily journalism, and from the high status and power attaching to one of its organ's editors. If at 22 Stead had been a youthful editor, his journalism career also peaked at an early age. By 41 he was out to grass editing a monthly, whose relation to news was distant, and whose relation to power was crippled by the lapse of time between numbers and by its inability to respond to important events as they happened. It is not surprising that Stead made serious efforts to return to daily journalism from the platform of the monthly *Review of Reviews* and his publishing imprint at Mowbray House.

It is to Stead's self-fashioning in his journalism manifestos, which combine discourses of commercial journalism and evangelical transformation, that I now turn. More than any of his contemporaries, Stead wrote about his profession as well as practising it. In a discourse that characteristically in the profession remains chary of theory, Stead is anomalous: he repeatedly attempts to pin down the significance of current practice through critical reflection on his own and others' journalism, to fly alternatives in theory and practice, and to situate journalism in culture generally and with respect to government in particular.

Once Stead left the North of England and the exigencies of editing a morning daily, his opportunities for combining his spiritual and social mission with commercial journalism were enhanced. The role of the *Pall Mall Gazette* as an *evening* paper – to epitomise the morning's news and to cover in depth selected items – left far more space for 'feature' stories and time for investigative journalism. It gave Stead more opportunity to pursue his vision of a spiritually and socially responsible press. Moreover, Stead's evangelical background and character *chimed* with the developing journalism of the 1880s and 1890s. Evangelical diction and sermonising harmonised with the personalising and sensation of the 'new journalism', and Nonconformity's identification with ordinary men and women fuelled the commercial drive to increase sales and readers to include the populous, through reduction of the cover price and other devices such as competitions. It is perhaps *because* of Stead's identification between the two, and *because* of the overlaps between them, that, unlike so many of his generation, Stead is wholeheartedly willing to identify as a journalist and to campaign to develop and improve the profession.

The juggling that Stead had maintained for fifteen years between his evangelicism and his journalism began to fail in the late 1880s.[3] The dissension that developed between the editor of the *PMG* and his Quaker proprietor Yates Thompson in the aftermath of 'The Maiden Tribute' campaign was not caused by Stead's imprisonment *per se*, but by the tainting of the journal's reputation with 'coarseness' which resulted in a loss of sales.[4] It represented the clash of Stead's evangelical programme and the commercial realities of mainstream higher journalism.

However, Whyte notes Stead's immediate impatience with the limited power base of the monthly he then established, 'how dissatisfied he was to become with the *Review of Reviews* – how inadequate and altogether futile he was to find it as a political organ' (Whyte 2: 55). By March 1890, only three issues into the *Review*, Stead penned a thoughtful and extensive critique of *The Times* in a 'Character Sketch' of that benchmark daily. Stead's attempt to return to daily journalism did not take long: within four years of having begun to edit the *Review* the first *Daily Paper* is bound into its pages, and a decade later the *Paper* is launched as an independent broadsheet. Although the two projects are quite different in format and content, their title significantly remains the same, *The Daily Paper*. The baldness of the name discloses their similarity and core value for Stead: the return to daily journalism. His disappointment on the failure of the first 'magazine paper ... a pocket paper which a man can double up in one fold and put into his pocket' (quoted in Whyte 2: 331) is palpable. Stead was shaken, but it is indicative of how deeply he wished to return to mainstream journalism that he nursed his ambitions for a decade. The two projects may be viewed as *fresh* attempts by Stead to fashion a daily that will join responsible journalism with popular. But as well as Stead himself changing in the decade that separates the projects, the markets that the papers are geared to enter are quite different. The former pre-dates the mass readership of the *Daily Mail*; the latter includes the cheap and bright *Mail* as a formidable rival for the niche Stead might have once hoped to occupy with *his* 'Daily Paper'.

From his earliest years at the Darlington *Northern Echo* Stead saw journalism as part of his Christian life and mission. By 1886, in the two articles on journalism provoked by his experience of editing a London daily in which his evangelicism and mainstream journalism clashed, Stead had evolved a complex vision of the role of responsible journalism in culture and society. Both these articles appeared in a journal associated with religion.[5] But Stead shifts the model from 'class journalism' to the burgeoning daily mainstream newspaper press. Unlike contemporaries, the all-important context and measure of daily journalism for Stead is the health of society and politics, not the success of the business. The new role of mainstream journalism is theorised by Stead as a religious and civic duty, authorised as a legacy from the past, and represented as a continuity rather than a revolution. Stead's formulation in these articles is the origin of many of the models that follow.

In 'The Future of Journalism', responsible journalists and their newspapers are to be part of a national social and political matrix, of which they are the hub. An infrastructure of Major Generals and Journalistic Travellers is proposed; the first who represent the alter-ego of the editor are planted in each district, to identify local associates who would receive free copies of the newspaper and from whom public opinion would be canvassed; they seem to be a version of resident reporters. The Travellers represent the 'perambulating alter ego ... of the editor at the centre', who would make periodic visits and take 'full and accurate knowledge from the associates' (Stead November 1886: 672). This structure, Stead points out, provides a potential network for the organisation of public meetings on important issues. For Stead, the aim of the structure is to bear out his claim in 'Government by Journalism' that the press, rather than government, is the structure of direct democracy. To this end the press both canvasses public opinion and enters into dialogue with it, through its newspapers and the Major Generals and Travellers. As Stead sums up in 'The Future of Journalism',

> Such a newspaper would indeed be a great secular or Civic Church and democratic university ... the very soul of our national unity; and its great central idea would be the self-sacrifice of the individual for the salvation of the community, the practical realization of the religious idea in national politics and social reform. (Stead November 1886: 678)

This notion of the Civic Church is to be developed elaborately in 1894 in Stead's analysis of Chicago, and in the *Review of Review Annuals* that followed in 1898, 1900, 1902 and 1903, on the problems of urban America and on the global implications of American culture. In all these narratives journalism and particular editors as well as the Civic Centre or Civic Church are central.

The penny *Daily* that Stead envisaged and published in 1893 was *not* a new *Times*. It aimed lower down the market; it was not a broadsheet but more like a magazine; and although with 40 pages it appeared much longer than the usual daily, it cost only a penny. In many respects it was a daily analogue of the *Review of Reviews*, whose format it resembled:

> The *Daily Paper* is almost exactly the shape of the *Review of Reviews* and consists of a neatly folded, pasted and trimmed pamphlet of forty pages ... a cross between the *Pall Mall Gazette* and *Tit Bits* ... it avowedly aims at throwing a bridge over the abyss which separates the millions who read weekly miscellanies from the comparative few who read the daily papers. (*RR* November 1893: 464)

The majority of the copy of the 1893 *Daily Paper* was political; but the second largest category was religious. Its legend is 'For the Union of all who Love, in the Service of all who Suffer', and the rationale for the date of the sample issue is that 4 October was the Saint's Day of St Francis of Assisi. In adding religion prominently to the usual dominance of political discourse of the daily press, Stead is bidding for women as well as men readers, well in advance of the *Daily Mail*. Journalism itself was a topic, with articles on political reporting and advertising. An illustrated piece – 'The Reading Public and the Press' – actually treats the distribution activities of W.H. Smith's and reads suspiciously like an advertisement posing as an article. The choice of Smith's for this treatment underlines Stead's commercial strategy and how far his projected journalism practice in the *DP* had altered from the sensationalism of the 'Maiden Tribute' in 1885, which Smith's banned from its sales points. The *Daily Paper* of 1893 also had practical features: a 'Business and Pleasure Diary' of the day; and 'News of the Day, with Maps', in short, accessible, 'digest' paragraphs, reminiscent of the *Review of Reviews*.

The Civic Church makes only a shadowy appearance in Stead's editorial afterwards, 'Of Things Undone and to be Done'. It is almost a throwaway in a discussion of the inclusion of correspondence in future issues, which echoes its fictional location in 'the future' in the December *RR* number, in which reference to the 'Civic Church' occurs in the 'future' section of the story 'Two and Two Make Four' (*RR* December 1893: 555), but there is none of the detail outlined in the

1886 vision of an elaborate infrastructure. However, there is an *advert* for "The Daily Paper' Publications' that gestures towards the notion of the newspaper at the centre of secular and religious life and a programme of reading. Included are 52 titles of a projected Popular Library at threepence a week, which begin with The Bible; a penny Saturday weekly paper containing the best of the *DP*; a halfpenny weekly and threepenny monthly fiction paper collecting the *Daily Paper*'s serial; a penny Sunday paper; a halfpenny *Daily Paper Tracts*; and a threepenny *Daily Paper Extras*. This plan of catering to the spectrum of the market, or the market niches, is pursued in subsequent manifestos such as the *RR Annual* of 1900 and in 1904.

Stead, like other publishers, places adverts for other parts of his list in the new Advertising Supplement, so there is an advert for the *Review of Reviews* with a religious slant appropriate to the *Daily Paper*. As Stead acknowledges in 'Advertising as a Fine Art', advertising is an income stream increasingly important at the time to the finances of the press. Mooting a policy of 'edited' adverts admissible to the pages of a journal only if, like other copy, they are 'good', Stead creates adverts in this sample number to illustrate his ideas. However, these strictures on the morality of adverts did not preclude him from including 'matrimonial adverts' in his advertising manifesto, a type of copy that at the time was deemed sensationalist. Clearly a populist genre that might attract a huge number of readers and media attention, it does not materialise in the sample issue, ensuring that issue's primary 'note' is that of respectability.

Including religious copy, articles on art and cookery, and a fictional serial, the sample issue of 1893 includes specific features designated for women readers alongside similarly targeted articles for men. The fiction, for example, is spiked with educational matter, reflecting Stead's particular regret that women remained uninformed about current affairs,[6] as well as the common perception that fiction was 'light' and morally dangerous. Stead's idea of a particular kind of *journalistic* fiction is interesting, and it is one that he takes up again in the *Review of Reviews* in 1903. In 1893, it is called 'The Romance of the World'. Possessing 'all the fascination of a romance', it is to be 'constructed out of the living facts of contemporary life in such a way that no one who reads the story can fail to be *au courant* with the events of the world in which he lives' (*DP* 1893: 32). Claiming that in England in 1893 'no first-class newspaper demeans its columns by the publication of a novel in instalments', Stead introduces his plan to recruit women as well as male readers to his new daily as revolutionary;[7] and he is critically eloquent and suggestive about this genre, whose factual fiction he relates to the fictional facticity of news itself:

> There are millions of human beings, especially among the young and among women, who will never read anything unless it is served up to them in the form of fiction. As a newspaper only deals with fiction of another sort and religiously abstains from publishing fiction that is honestly labelled such, it fails to secure as readers those whose only literary diet is romance. (Stead November 1893, quoted in Whyte 2: 332)

Perhaps the aspect of the sample of the new daily of 1893 most likely to attract women readers and to alienate men is the psychic research and spiritualism that pervade the issue. There are several interviews, as one might expect of an editor who pioneered the new genre in the 1880s. That with Lady Brooke is explained by Stead as 'A Telepathic Automatic Interview'. A 'Note' states:

> The application of automatic telepathy to journalism is no longer a dream ... telepathic communication exact and instantaneous has been established between Dunrobin Castle and Dover railway station, a distance of over 600 miles. The documents and evidence in proof of this apparently incredible statement are at our office for the inspection of the Psychical Research Society. (*DP* 1893: 8)

There is also a Spiritualist element in an interview with the actress Miss Robins, on 'The National Theatre of the Press'. Responding to her plea to include theatre reviews in his journalism, Stead, who had never been to the theatre in Britain, provides a solution that will meet his suspicion that true, serious theatre has been displaced by 'the buffoon and the ballet dancer'. The new National Theatre will exist in the paper 'on the astral plane': 'you and your community will start – on the astral plane of course – the National Theatre, which would be really existing in London if the serious people had not abandoned the stage .... Every week we will publish the list of pieces that would have been played if the National Theatre had existed' (*DP* 1893: 15). The idea of theatre coverage, *without* the spiritualist dimension, is resurrected in 1903 in the prospectus for the new venture and, when that fails, materialises in the *Review of Reviews* later in 1904.[8]

Just as the 1893 *Daily Paper* was failing, Stead, who was in Chicago, was clarifying his ideas about the infrastructure of the Civic Church, which in 1886 he had conceived in terms of *newspaper* government. The refined Chicago model of the Civic Church was to be translated into his plans for the 1904 daily. The dates of the Chicago visits in 1893 and 1894 and the publication of *If Christ Came to Chicago* in 1894 are crucial, sandwiching as they do the experiment and failure of the 1893 paper. The common gestation period for the 1893 newspaper and the flourishing of the Civic Church idea, in which HQ is now lodged not in a newspaper but in municipal government, re-enforces what we already know of the connection in Stead's mind between journalism, government and the church, and retrospectively makes the similar connection in the 1903 experiment more foreseeable.

In 1904, having learned from his 1893 experiment, Stead re-imagined the daily in important respects – price, size, distribution and, perhaps most significantly, secularity. However, in excluding 'everything that ought not to be read in the family' he again refused to accept the culture of his potential readership. 'Racing, betting in all forms, including that great gambling arena the Stock Exchange, will not be reported, neither shall I publish any adverts which minister to the vices of the day' (Stead 4 January 1904 Supplement: 2a). These exclusions are all aspects of male culture, and shibboleths of working- and middle-class masculinity. By identifying the 'family' as his moral barometer Stead was appropriating the categories of women and children to authorise his evangelical programme. At the same time, Stead's 1903–4 venture may also be read as a fascinating attempt to embrace progressive formulations of gender, with women constituting a serious element of the new public sphere and readership. Like Thackeray in *Cornhill,* Stead was set on family readers but, more audaciously than the *Cornhill,* for a *newspaper* audience. Stead's primary distribution system,[9] for example, involved home delivery by 1 pm, while men were out to work, and the 'politics' of the new venture were to be the politics of the fireside and home:

> to endeavour in all political matters to supersede the atmosphere of the Stock Exchange, and of the pulpit, of the tap-room and of the House of Commons .... For all these other institutions are exclusively male, and ... have the vices, the prejudices, and false perspective that would be found in any institutions as exclusively monopolised by the other sex. The home is neither male nor female. In that microcosm of the better world that is to be both man and woman play an equal part and there is fulfilled the prayer that a little child shall lead them. (Stead 4 January 1904: 6b)

By excluding 'betting' and 'vice' of all types, Stead was flying in the face of new journalism's adjustment, from the *Star* of 1888 onwards, to definitions of 'news' that met demands of the new readers. In other respects, Stead is more accommodating to his target mass audience in 1904, being prepared to 'bait our hook with as many attractive lures as experience can suggest or imagination can invent' (Stead 4 January 1904, Supplement: 2a). So, there are prizes, puzzles and illustrations; there is also serial fiction and 'tales of sensational adventures' as 'it is necessary to put the foot of your ladder very low down if you have to get the people who are at the bottom to begin to climb' (ibid.).

In 1904, then, Stead aims to get lower down the social scale than his *RR* readers who are primarily being offered digests of the higher journalism. As this formulation actually appears in the first issue, and not merely in the *RR* publicity for the *Daily News*, its tone may well have been found insulting to new subscribers, men and women alike. But, in imposing his exclusions on the potential male purchaser, the person who both identifies most with the genre of the daily and has the purchasing power to subscribe, Stead seems unlikely to succeed with a class of readers already extravagantly being wooed in the market by popular dailies that had no such scruples.

In the interim between 1893 and 1904, Stead updated many of the ideas for the new daily through sustained attention to W.R. Hearst's *New York Journal*. Crucially, it was *not* the contents of Hearst's paper so much as his fund of stylistic ideas about popular journalism – how to respond to public opinion – that Stead mapped on to his own evangelical notion of a Civic Church with a newspaper at its hub.

In common with other young journalists in the 1860s and 1870s, Stead's interest in the press of the United States was keen from the beginning of his career,[10] and while he was later to criticise and interrogate American journalism, he also *inter alia* admired and customised it for British journalism. His responsiveness to urban America and to its press *despite his disapproval* may be gauged by his celebration of the unreformed, carnivalesque New York *Journal* under Hearst's earliest days as editor: 'The *Journal* was like Broadway in print. Broadway at high noon, with cars swinging backwards and forwards along the tracks, and the myriad multitudes streaming this way and that – life everywhere, but one common governing purpose or direction nowhere .... this feverish chaos of sensationalism' (Stead *Annual for 1898* 183). Stead addresses Hearst's American journalism and other examples repeatedly between 1898 and 1903 and, in that six-year period, half of the *RR Annuals* are dedicated to American or Anglo-American topics:

'Satan's Invisible World, or Despairing Democracy' (1898), which is 'A Study of Greater New York'; 'Mr. Carnegie's Conundrum' (1900), which consists of a detailed comparison of the US and the UK; and 'The Americanization of the World' (1902). Two of them, 1898 and 1902, discuss the Hearst press by name.

The fourth chapter of the 1898 *Annual* is entitled 'Government by Newspaper'. In it Stead parallels a long quotation from his own 1886 'Government by Journalism' with an equally lengthy piece from a *New York Journal* leader, and thus the link is made between Stead's British-based notion and the example of an American newspaper in which 'Action ... is the distinguishing mark' (Stead 'Satan' 184). Although the *Journal* and Hearst appear to fall short of Stead's ideal 'to redeem New York' (Stead 186), Stead is careful to trace Hearst's economic process of building the *Journal*, by undercutting the cover price of his rivals and luring their staff by paying them over the odds. He also observes the multiplicity of editions among the two New York popularist papers, daily morning and evening, and Sunday editions, all 'profusely illustrated' (Stead 183).

It is later in the *Annual* that Stead makes the link between the newspaper and the Civic Church. In this 1898 model, the Civic Church remains lodged in City Hall, but the function of the daily populist newspaper is enhanced and becomes the policing arm of the state. Here Stead's fantasy of the union of evangelicism and journalism is at its most authoritarian: journalism

> might perhaps be recognised as a power in the State, to whose initiative might be left by statute the task of appointing the Inquisitor and of bringing cases before the Inquisition .... But if the Journalism that Acts is to do its share in the cleansing of the Augean stable of municipal corruption, it could hardly find a more legitimate field for development than in providing a ... tribunal for the purpose of dragging out of the darkness and secrecy in which they flourish those evils which can never be dealt with until they are accurately located, and brought within the range of public opinion by the searchlight of the Inquisition. (Stead 194)

Stead thus authorises the most proactive investigative journalism as delivering up to the state culprits it identifies and turns in.

If the 1898 *Annual* reveals an extreme form of Stead's preoccupation with national control (rather than governance) through the press, it also yields one of his most interesting analyses of contemporary social space at a local level. That it involves the press is indicative not only of Stead's personal involvement in journalism, but also the high tide of this media form at the turn of the century. Stead's idea is of a 'Newspaper Area'; defined in terms of social geography as well as the logistics of distribution, it is 'the most real and living area of all those into which the social organism is divided', one which 'is rigidly limited by the distance from the printing office in which a newspaper can be delivered before breakfast' (Stead 24–5). Embedded in Stead's plan for distribution of the 1904 *Daily Paper*, it is to be the mechanism of creating communities of subscribers around local 'depots' that house reading rooms and community resources. But there is an important proviso: Stead's 1904 newspaper is *an afternoon* paper.

In the light of these local and national models, Stead's projection of an international, Imperial model in 1900, in 'Mr Carnegie's Conundrum', is perhaps not unexpected. Stead the pacifist is here reacting against an unwelcome form of British Imperialism, 'the unregenerate Jingo demon' that he associates with 'yellow journalism', not in Hearst's *Journal*, but in the London *Times*. Stead's scheme involves a 'Look-Out Man' in each country, who would identify sympathetic 'leading journalists' with whom he 'would enter into a more or less informal alliance'.

Stead's last plan for expenditure of Carnegie's fortune is a detailed model for a nest of papers. This has developed significantly from that first projection of related publications in the sample advert in 1893. In 'The Endowed Newspaper' in the 1900 *Annual* there is a three-tier model: 1) a *Twopenny Times* whose losses would be paid for by 2) a more popular, halfpenny newspaper, the *Daily Paper*, which is modelled on the *Daily Mail* in Britain and the New York *Journal* in the US; this halfpenny derivative would have the run of all the copy of its 'twopenny contemporary, but would be independently edited with a view to circulation'; 3) a news-sheet, the *Daily Visitor*, would be distributed free of charge and 'depend for its profits upon the advertisements' (Stead 153). '[H]aving affiliated journals in every town in the land', the imprint could 'organise a news service of its own, which it would share with [likeminded] newspapers in all parts of the world.' There is a considerable element of self-conscious fantasy in Stead's limning of this grandiose, if visionary, blueprint for an alternative press baron, late in a life of modest wealth and of poor financial management. Most of these did not materialise when the *Daily Paper* was launched in 1904. Yet the prescience of this 1900 plan is undeniable at the beginning of a century that was to see the consolidation of press ownership.

By 1902 in the *Review of Review Annual* Stead positively defends 'yellow journalism' and the newspapers which carry it as quintessentially American: 'it is in the newspaper offices that the drive, bustle and intense strain of American life is pre-eminently centred, and so-called "yellow" journals are those where the national characteristics find the freest scope and widest range' (Stead 'Americanization' 295). Stead endorses Hearst's *New York Journal* and other 'loud' newspapers like it: the 'metaphoric roar of the *Journal*' is necessary for 'the cosmopolitan, polyglot, very busy millions of people' to whom it appeals, over 'the well-bred whisper of diplomacy' (Stead 'Americanization' 297). For Stead, these aids to easier access to news and education, to communication with the populous, and to dissemination of investigative journalism serve as model prototypes as he approaches his final attempt at a daily paper.

Many of the ideas mooted in the *Annuals* appear in the Prospectus for the 12-page penny broadsheet. Stead incorporates the notion of the Newspaper Area, for example, in his distribution structure, which allows for local depots or clubs, local intercourse between the paper and its readers, and a plan for eventual 'local' editions, with customised editorial content and adverts. The *identity* rather than the anonymity of the editor featured in the advance publicity and in the paper itself, the first issue of which included a signed address to his readers on the front page. Like the American objects of Stead's admiration, both copious illustration and a daily front-page caricature were important, populist ingredients of the new paper. Its first number makes every effort to be as wide-ranging and spectacularly broad-based as the American *Journal* and *World*, featuring an interview with the Pope, a main news story about a royal visit, a Bairns' page, an article about the Girl Messenger Brigade, and fiscal and political news. Its proactive, investigative story in keeping with its social mission is a statistical report on the incidence of Sunday visitors to public houses in Paddington, which would remind readers of Chicago. The first number also draws on other earlier work. The issue of coloured reproductions echoes his subscription drive for the *Review of Reviews* in 1901. The inclusion of a daily epitome of the morning papers follows his practice in the *PMG*, while in the Prospectus it is titled 'A 'Review of Reviews' of the Morning Papers'. Its 'serial story' has been given a trial run in the *Review of Reviews*, from which it transfers, but with a title from the previous 'Daily Paper' of 1893, 'Romance of the World's Life'.

The materialisation of these collected notions in the publication of a daily broadsheet represents a significantly more serious attempt to

1. The launching of the *Daily Paper, Review of Reviews.* January 1904

re-enter the mainstream of journalism on Stead's part than the single sample of 1893. By its last issue in February 1904, however, advertising had seeped away, and only now does Stead release news of his illness as the explanation of its failure. But this is doubtful. Its failure is probably a result of three factors: 1) an altered market, now including the unstoppable *Daily Mail*, which already claimed many of Stead's potential readers; 2) his limited financial backing which necessitated pre-paid subscriptions; and 3) his exclusion of aspects of popular culture that threatened the otherwise commercial character of the paper, which did draw on the best of new journalism practice. Late in his career, Stead's attempts to reinvent daily journalism and himself as an editor are eloquent illustrations of the ideological, social and historical contingencies of the trope of individual 'self-fashioning'. But his path to the daily papers, which function for him and us as a sign of his preoccupation with journalism, is strewn with a series of manifestos on journalism second to none in the period. The *Review of Reviews* gave Stead a publishing platform, which he exploited prodigiously. It allowed him freedom to fashion his life and journalism according to his admittedly eclectic and contradictory 'self', and to explore alternatives to the commercial model of the mass market daily that developed so preternaturally in the US and the UK during these years.

Notes

1   I have taken the term from the title of Stead's *Review of Reviews Annual* for 1902, 'The Americanization of the World, or The Trend of the Twentieth Century'.
2   Lloyd notes that every year on his birthday, Stead wrote a letter to himself (42).
3   During a visit to Paris in April 1888, Stead told Emily Crawford that 'his "boss" wanted to "chuck" him, and [that] he wanted to make an independent journalistic situation for himself' (Whyte 1: 256).
4   Kingsmill notes that at the time W.H. Smith's banned the *PMG* from its bookstalls, and that the press was united in its condemnation, with the exception of Frank Harris who was then editing the London *Evening News*, itself a popularist, sensationalist but Tory paper (18). However, the general public supported Stead.
5   On the religious character of the *CR*, see Brake 51–62.
6   See the first volume of the *Review of Reviews* (1890) in which Stead sets up a competition for women readers that requires them to read his monthly column 'The Progress of the World' for six months, and to sit an examination on its contents.
7   The radical evening paper the *Star* included serial fiction from its inception in 1888, as did the dummy run (only) of the *Daily Mail* (on the front page) in 1896. For serial fiction in newspapers see Law 2000.
8   Stead trails his forthcoming (virgin) tour of the London theatres in the prospectus for 'The Daily Paper' in the December 1903 issue of *RR* (580), and 'First Impressions of the Theatre' is serialised from July 1904.

9 The paper could be bought from newsboys and newsagents in town, but at twice the price of subscription by advanced payment, which Stead deemed 'indispensable' in the prospectus.

10 As an unpaid contributor to the *Northern Echo* in August 1870, Stead writes to its editor (who was soon to leave for experience in America), 'I wish we had more American news in our paper. Gold at so much and cotton at so much – that is about all we get from our Press. Could you not do something in the way of producing union among our scattered English family?' (Whyte 1: 24).

Works cited

Anon., 'Books and Bookmen'. *The Star* 20 April 1912.

Anon., 'W.T. Stead'. *Daily Chronicle* 19 April 1912, 6c

Anon., 'The Sinking of the *Titanic*. Some Notable Victims. Mr W.T. Stead's Career'. *The Times* 18 April 1912, 12a–c.

Anon., 'William Thomas Stead'. *Modern Men from the Scots Observer*. London 1890, 62–8.

Anon., ed., *Interview* [3 January 1891] *with Mr. Stead on 'The Church of the Future' Together with Criticisms, Press Opinions and Unpublished Correspondence Relating Thereto*. London, 1891.

Arnold, Matthew, 'Up to Easter'. *Nineteenth Century* May 1887, 629–43.

Bagehot, Walter, 'The First Edinburgh Reviewers'. *National Review* October 1855, 253–84.

Baylen, J.O., 'The 'New Journalism' in Late Victorian Britain'. *Australian Journal of Politics and History*. 18 (December 1972), 367–85.

Bland, Lucy, *Banishing the Beast*. Harmondsworth: Penguin, 1995.

'Blowitz', 'Journalism as a Profession'. *Contemporary Review*. 63 (January 1983), 36–46.

Brake, Laurel, 'Theories of Formation: the *Nineteenth Century*, 1877'. *Subjugated Knowledges*. Basingstoke and London: Macmillan, 1994, pp. 51–62.

Crawford, Emily, 'Journalism as a Profession for Women'. *Contemporary Review*, September 1893, 363–71.

Fairbaums, W.N., compiler, Scrapbook of Cuttings. Enfield, 1913.

Finot, Jean, with a Preface by W.T. Stead, *The Death Agony of the 'Science' of Race*. London, 1911.

Greg, W.R., 'The Newspaper Press'. *Edinburgh Review*. October 1855, 470–98.

Jones, Victor Pierce, *Saint or Sensationalist? The Story of W.T. Stead 1849–1912*. East Wittering, West Sussex, 1988.

Kingsmill, Hugh, *After Puritanism, 1850–1900*. London, 1929.

Law, Graham, *Serialising Fiction in the Victorian Press*. Basingstoke: Macmillan, 2000.

Lloyd, Chris, *Attacking the Devil. 130 Years of the 'Northern Echo'*. Darlington, 1999.

Luckhurst, Roger, *The Invention of Telepathy*. Oxford, 2002.

Merle, Gibbons, 'Newspaper Press'. *Westminster Review* January 1829, 216–27.

—— 'Weekly Newspapers'. *Westminster Review* April 1829, 466–80.

—— 'Provincial Newspaper Press'. *Westminster Review* January 1830, 69–103.

—— 'Journalism'. *Westminster Review* January 1833,195–208.

'S' [Stout, W.E.?] 'W.T. Stead'. *Westminster Gazette*, 17 April 1912, 1–2.

Stead, Estelle, *Personal and Spiritual Reminiscences*. London, 1913.

Stead, W.T., 'Character Sketch: March. The *Times*'. *Review of Reviews*, March 1890, 185–91.

—— *The Revival of 1905*. London, 1905.

—— ed., *The Daily Paper* 4 January-9 February 1904.

—— 'Supplement'. [Prospectus] *The Daily Paper*. 4 January 1904, 1–4.

—— 'The Daily Paper. By its Founder, Editor and Proprietor'. *Review of Reviews*. December 1903, 571–83.

—— 'The Coming of the New Paper'. Chapter 39 'To be Continued in our Next', *Review of Reviews* November 1903, 524–8.

—— *The Despised Sex*. London: Grant Richards (reprint of most of 'In Our Midst'), 1903.

—— 'The Twisters of the Tail of the Jumping Cat', in 'In Our Midst'. *Review of Review Annual for 1903*. London, 1903, 63–6.

—— 'The Americanisation of the World'. *Review of Reviews Annual for 1902*. London, 1902.

—— 'The British-American United States' and 'The United States of Europe' in 'Mr. Carnegie's Conundrum'. *Review of Reviews Annual for 1900*. London, 1900, 107–16, 126–8.

—— 'Satan's Invisible World Displayed or Despairing Democracy. A Study of Greater New York', *Review of Reviews Annual for 1898*. London, 1898.

—— ed., *Borderland. A Quarterly Review and Index*. London, 1894–7.

—— *If Christ Came to Chicago*. London, 1894.

—— 'A New Year's Greeting. Exit the *Daily Paper*. To the Readers of *The Review of Reviews*'. *Review of Reviews*. January 1894, [3].

—— *A Journalist on Journalism*, ed. Edwin H. Stout. London, 1892.

—— 'The London Morning Dailies that Are and Are to Be'. Sell's *Press Guide*. London, 1892.

—— ed., *Help. A Journal of Social Service*. London, 1891–2.

—— ed., *Portraits and Autographs. An Album for the People*. London, 1890.

—— 'The Future of Journalism'. *Contemporary Review* November 1886, 663–79.

—— 'Government by Journalism'. *Contemporary Review* May 1886, 653–74.

Scott, J.W. Robertson, *The Story of the Pall Mall Gazette*. London, 1950.

Stephenson, John, 'W.T. Stead'. Darlington, 1987. 8pp.

Walkowitz, Judith, *Prostitution and Victorian Society*. Cambridge, 1980.

—— *City of Dreadful Delight*. London, 1992.

Watson, Aaron, *A Newspaper Man's Memories*. London, 1928.

Whyte, Frederic, *The Life of W.T. Stead*. 2 vols. London, 1925.

Wiener, Joel, ed., *Papers for the Millions*. Westport, Conn., 1988.

4
A Novelist of Character: Becoming Lucas Malet

Talia Shaffer

> The Baron can highly recommend *The Wages of Sin*, by LUCAS
> MALET. 'I am informed,' says the [Baron], 'that this is the nom
> de plume of an Authoress. This MALET should be Femalet.'
>
> *Punch*

Once among the most famous, controversial and successful novelists of
the turn of the century, 'Lucas Malet' (Mary St Leger Kingsley Harrison)
is virtually forgotten today, and the decline of her reputation is partly
due to the same reason she became famous in the first place: her name.
'Lucas Malet' is deliberately indeterminate. Male or female? English or
French? Its ambiguity was, in fact, its point. The name's unplaceability
lifted her out of all the ordinary categories by which Victorians constructed identity. In this case, the construction of a pseudonym facilitated the invention of an entirely new kind of persona. The name
'Lucas Malet' not only replaced her existing filial and marital names,
but also, crucially, came to signify certain genealogies, desires, gender
identifications and personal traits. But equally importantly, becoming
'Lucas Malet' allowed her to escape the legacy of her famous father,
Charles Kingsley. Understanding the complexities of this relationship
can help elucidate the career of an exemplary late Victorian woman
writer and show how difficult it was to achieve an independent identity. In the public mind Malet was regarded as a kind of inferior repetition of that original man. Malet's paternal ambivalence and familial
rewriting simply could not be understood in the crude terms of the
turn-of-the-century literary marketplace. In other words, what we see
here is a clash between the marketplace's demand for the reassuring
reiteration of known quantities, the saleability of sequels and an

author's need to establish herself as an autonomous identity. Malet was 'sold' as the daughter of Charles Kingsley in spite of the fact that she spent a lifetime spent trying to mystify that connection. In this chapter I will discuss what it meant to become 'Lucas Malet' – not only to escape a crushingly strong paternal influence, but also to invent a different model of female authorship.

Malet's writing career began in 1882, when she had to find a name under which to publish her first novel, *Mrs. Lorimer: A Study in Black and White*. Interestingly, she never seemed to consider using her husband's last name (perhaps because her writing career began just as her marriage was disintegrating). Another obvious choice for a pseudonym would have been her mother's maiden name, Grenfell, and Malet's avoidance of this option may indicate a reluctance to identify herself with her mother's lineage.[1] Nor did she want to affiliate herself with the powerful Kingsley clan. Instead, she renamed herself after her grandmother Mary Lucas Kingsley and her father's great-aunt Malet. She chose this pseudonym 'in order that my work might be judged on its merits – quite apart from and independent of my father's reputation' (Dolman 149). Indeed, in several interviews Malet stressed that 'Miss Malet ... was a very clever woman, it seems, and it was from her that we inherited whatever brains we happen to have' (Whitelock 785). Malet reconstructed her lineage around these female ancestors not only through naming, but also through fetishised objects. 'I always like to have this writing-table for my use,' she told an interviewer. 'It belonged to my father's mother, who was a most remarkable woman, from whom my father and uncles undoubtedly derived much of their talent. So I fancy her table has some special virtue in it which may communicate itself to me' (Smith). In these pronouncements, Malet was working to re-centre the family on its originary matriarch. Mary Lucas became the great trunk from which all the Kingsley branches grew, making Charles, Henry, George and Mary all equally inferior boughs.

Although the new name commemorated Malet's participation in a specifically female history, it also sounded unmistakably male. The masculinity of 'Lucas Malet' alluded to Malet's belief that she had a man's mind. As interviewer Mary Angela Dickens wrote:

> To begin at the very beginning, however, Lucas Malet has one grave and fundamental quarrel with Fate. It turned her out a woman, and not a man! She herself is of opinion that Nature jumbled things up altogether in the construction of her whole family and distributed male and female characteristics at random! (522)

Indeed, Malet's masculine self-identification functioned on several levels. For one thing, it was a shorthand way of explaining a shift in the Kingsley family. In the mid-nineteenth century, the famous Kingsley writers were the three brothers, Charles, George and Henry. But in the next generation, it was only their daughters who became successful writers. Malet was a leading novelist; her sister Rose was a respected authority on art, travel and gardening; and her cousin Mary was the African traveller. The Kingsley sons were notoriously less successful, although they had had a far more expensive education. Malet explained this situation by assuming that literary ambition and skill were 'male ... characteristics' and that such characteristics could float independently of the recipient's actual gender. In other words, she read her own writerly talent as a masculine trait, and therefore read herself as internally male.

Malet also behaved in stereotypically masculine ways. She liked her friends to call her Lucas, and she had a large, commanding presence (Srebrnik 'Re-Subjection' 194). As an interviewer commented, 'one gets the impression of talking with a clever man rather than to a woman. There is the masculine repose of both thought and expression, a man's well-digested point of view upon most subjects ...' (*New-York Daily Tribune* 18). Her bold and idiosyncratic lifestyle and her risqué novels foregrounded sexual honesty. Harry Furniss described her as 'the first of the modern school of lady novelists to throw a literary bomb into the centre of squeamish people loaded with what she called "the great and cruel riddle of sex"' (Furniss 19–20). 'Courage, courage, courage!' was her motto, in conversation as in life. She had, recalled Violet Hunt, 'the effect of being rather terrible when roused. She put everything rather strikingly – and her friends round the tea table would murmur restrainingly, "Mary, Mary!"' By believing that she was internally male, Malet could justify and naturalise behaviour that she might otherwise have had to regulate. Instead of reading her assertiveness as a failure to adhere to feminine norms, she could claim it as fidelity to her inner truth, thereby licensing herself to continue writing and speaking in ways she might otherwise have been forced to muffle.

'Masculinity' was frequently adduced as a problem with Malet's fiction. 'I do not mean to include Lucas Malet's novels amongst "feminine fiction,"' wrote Janet E. Hogarth anxiously. 'They are altogether too virile, and yet there is a touch of exaggeration, which does not suggest masculine authorship' (Hogarth 538). Thirty years later, the same reviewer summed up Malet's career: 'It was in no sense "woman's work"' (Courtney 230–1). In this case Janet Hogarth Courtney seems to mean it as praise; similarly, her husband, the influential critic W.L. Courtney, consistently described Malet's writing as 'masculine' in *The Feminine Note in Fiction*, using it to indicate Malet's cleverness, daring and strength. Similarly, *The Times* noted the 'masculine audacity' of Malet's most famous novel, *The History of Sir Richard Calmady* ('Recent Novels'). In *Harper's Weekly*, James Macarthur publicly struggled with the problem of how to read a book that showed all the hallmarks of male authorship. At first he admitted grudgingly, '*Sir Richard Calmady* is amazingly, one might say diabolically, clever. It would almost cheat the elect into believing that it was a great book. Also it is astonishingly virile, and in parts voluptuous, coming from a woman' (Macarthur 'Notes' 1160). Macarthur clearly resents a novel that poses such a challenge to his literary taxonomy. A few months later, however, Macarthur reconsidered. Whereas Hardy or Tolstoy produce powerful realism, Macarthur argued, their female counterpart offers a grotesquely degenerate 'taste for the abnormal', an 'almost brutal realism' that lacks spiritual grace (Macarthur 'Animadversions' 474). Malet's masculine realism was appalling because it did not come from a man.

Malet did not reject the accusations of masculinity, but instead inhabited and embraced them. By writing under a man's name, thinking of herself as having a man's mind, she evaded the critics' urgent directives to curb herself.[2] Malet frequently wrote from the point of view of a male main character, and often used a male narrator, as in *Colonel Enderby's Wife* (1885), *The Carissima* (1893), *The Gateless Barrier* (1900), *The History of Sir Richard Calmady* (1901), *The Far Horizon* (1907) and *Adrian Savage* (1911). The masculine identification helped excuse the novels' focus on controversial matters. The prevalence of male points of view also indicates that Malet was comfortable inhabiting a male subjectivity. When warned that her interest in physical disabilities, morbid eroticism and psychologically aberrant behaviour did not befit a woman writer, Malet was able to counteract this social pressure by believing herself truly, inwardly, male.

But perhaps the most important reason that Malet wanted to assert her masculinity was that it provided a readily understood code for her own desires. During Malet's time, contemporary sexological theory connected gender identification with 'inverted' sexuality, so Malet may have deliberately tried to look masculine as a way of signalling her sexual affiliations. While it is, of course, problematic to try to assign modern nomenclature to nineteenth-century erotic attractions, there is no doubt that the most profound emotional bonds Malet formed were those with other women. As an adult, Malet adopted a teenaged cousin, Gabrielle Vallings. This incidentally deflected potential public critiques by demonstrating that she had the requisite maternal instinct even if she had not borne children herself. Malet and Vallings were inseparable, wrote prefaces for each other's novels, and Malet bequeathed Vallings all the Kingsley papers. A character in one of Malet's novels is named Gabrielle St. Leger, combining Vallings' first name and Malet's middle name, as if she were the product of their union. This novel was dedicated to Vallings as 'a love-token'. Vallings' nieces, Angela Covey-Crump and Brenda Hudson-Perramon, both 'believe that Malet found heterosexual relationships to be distasteful. Miss Hudson-Perramon believes that Malet persuaded Vallings to remain single' (Srebrnik 'Re-subjection' 211). This intriguing comment is supported by an anecdote privately recorded by Violet Hunt:

> She once took me down to her dining room in her new house in Egerton Crescent to shew me the portrait of her father Charles Kingsley and I informed her that when I was six at Sidney Sussex College, Cambridge he had stooped and given me a kiss. 'Then I will too,' she said, and did so. It was a curious sensation.' (Hunt notes)

That Malet may have felt predominantly same-sex desire is borne out by the fact that several of her novels have overtly lesbian love plots, including *The History of Sir Richard Calmady* (1901) and *The Survivors* (1923). In *The History of Sir Richard Calmady*, a young woman explicitly announces her passion for an older woman, and the narrative works to facilitate their union as a couple. Malet's characteristic male perspective may also have facilitated her writing coded lesbian desires; under the heterosexual cover of male characters like Adrian Savage, Dominic Iglesias, Sir Richard Calmady, Laurence Rivers, Anthony Hammond or Colonel Enderby, she can describe erotic longing for unavailable, forbidden, female bodies.

Along with the considerable evidence of Malet's persistent personal and literary interest in same-sex female relationships, there is also evidence of an almost equally persistent fascination with celibacy. Starting as early as her 1885 article, 'The Youngest of the Saints', and moving through all her major novels (*Colonel Enderby's Wife* (1885), *A Counsel of Perfection* (1888), *The Wages of Sin* (1890), *The Gateless Barrier* (1900), *The History of Sir Richard Calmady* (1901)), Malet proclaims the spiritual glory of sexual self-renunciation. Lovers steel themselves into a disembodied adoration of the beloved, experiencing their self-sacrifice as salutary discipline and/or deserved punishment for the unruly body. Again, the thematics of Malet's fiction correlate to events in her life. In new biographical work on Malet, Patricia Lorimer Lundberg has argued that one reason Malet's marriage fell apart was her fear of pregnancy and consequent reluctance to sleep with her husband. The nieces' comment that Malet urged Vallings to remain single, too, could indicate not just that Malet wanted an exclusive relationship with Vallings, but also that Malet urged Vallings to maintain the celibacy Malet herself prized.

It seems that inversion theory helped Malet form a coherent sense of self, but that her final answer to the problem of illicit desires was either to discipline herself into celibacy – or, as we shall see, to recode those desires into socially acceptable venues. Becoming 'Lucas Malet' meant deliberately abandoning the names that marked her married/ unmarried status: Kingsley, Harrison. It meant, instead, to assume a persona that was marked by gender fluidity and sexual possibility. It placed her in an all-female lineage while simultaneously confirming her self-identification as an invert.

'Lucas Malet' is just as indeterminate in nationality as it is in gender terms. Although the name derives from English families, it looks French (just as the name comes from women but sounds masculine). Frenchness, like maleness, was part of Malet's voluntary affiliations. 'I am much more given,' she told interviewer Frederick Dolman, 'to reading French than English fiction, and any little knowledge I may have of style and method I have so learnt.' She went on to critique George Sand and Victor Hugo, preferring Balzac, Gautier, Flaubert, de Maupassant, Bourget, Zola, Daudet and Loti (Dolman 149). Her choices reveal a predilection for the more shocking contemporary French writers; her public preference for Zola and Gautier is especially startling. Janet E. Courtney recalled 'she was very fond of French life and French literature. Balzac and Maupassant had much to say in her work; perhaps also Huysmans and the Symbolists' (238). Malet spent a good deal of time in France and Switzerland. She and Vallings finally moved to Montreux, in Switzerland, permanently in 1924 (Srebrnik 'Lucas Malet' 184). French and Swiss scenes figure prominently in her fiction, and in *Adrian Savage*, the dominant perspective is that of a Frenchman hopelessly in love with the beautiful Gabrielle St. Leger. Identifying herself with French literature gave Malet a model for her writing. To be French meant to be experimental in style, sexually explicit in content, psychologically deft in characterisation, unconventional in lifestyle. The French represented an artistic tradition completely distinct from the morally uplifting homilies expected from British matrons, or the strenuously improving literature associated with her father. As Stephen Gwynn pointed out, 'the Kingsleys ... were known as almost fanatically English' (481). Charles Kingsley was descended from an ancient English family, chaplain to Queen Victoria, adviser to the Prince of Wales, and Canon of Westminster Abbey where a marble bust of him was placed after his death.[3] Against her father's place at the centre of approved British thought, Malet wrote from the experimental Francophile edge. That Francophone pseudonym asserted her membership in an alternative national heritage, conferring the dignity of a tradition on her idiosyncratic work.

But if the name 'Lucas Malet' was psychologically empowering, it was financially problematic, as it inhibited her sales, according to James L. Ford, who complained:

that she was not long ago made known to the entire reading public of this country is due to various causes, not the least important of which is the circumstance that she has chosen to write under the name of 'Lucas Malet,' a pseudonym which reveals nothing as to her identity or sex, and which it is very easy to spell wrong. For this reason the shallow-pated ones who do so much of the reading in this country do not, as a general thing, talk about her, even if they happen to have read some of her books, because they cannot remember whether they should say 'him' or 'her.' In short, Mrs. Mary St Leger Harrison's unfortunate choice of a nom de plume has cost her a vast amount of ... conversational advertising. (Ford 232)

It is interesting that James L. Ford himself emphatically corrects this unfortunate choice of pseudonym by giving her full personal name, stressing her marriage twice over ('Mrs' and 'Harrison'). Reviewers often abandoned use of the Malet pseudonym in order to assert Malet's participation in the Kingsley or Harrison lineage. Malet, however, liked to be called Lucas and signed even personal letters with her pseudonym, sometimes adding her full string of names, or her full set of initials, MSLKH, in a subsidiary and explanatory position at the bottom of the page.

One reason reviewers insisted on calling her Mrs Harrison may have been the influence of her rival, the woman who published under the name Mrs Humphry Ward. Ward was also related to a famous literary family, being the niece of Matthew Arnold. Whether Mary Ward deliberately chose to become Mrs Humphry or was pushed into it by publishers – a point over which Ward scholars debate today – the fact remains that affiliating herself with her husband was a canny marketing strategy. Malet was bitterly jealous of Ward's royalties (Cartwright 172). In 1932, Jane E. Courtney reminisced that at the turn of the century, Malet, Ward and May Sinclair led English fiction, and comparisons between Malet and Ward were critical commonplaces (231). Ward was also writing innovative fiction that asked profound questions about religious faith, women's roles and social work at the turn of the century. But her cognomen, her three-volume realist novel format and her later anti-suffrage work all colluded to fix an image of Ward as unalterably conservative. Ward, in other words, represented a path not taken for Malet. Ward's pseudonym connoted respectability, marital obedience and financial success, some of which might well have accrued to Malet had she chosen to publish as a wife, under the name of Mrs William Harrison.

Yet the public overwhelmingly preferred to identify Malet as a daughter. 'The daughter of Charles Kingsley', as Malet was inevitably known, was a title that dogged her, inspired her, annoyed her and fundamentally shaped her life. It meant that a mature female novelist was perpetually positioned in the filial role to a Victorian sage. Critics judged her against his standards, read her as his successor. Reviewers ritually mentioned her parentage in the first or second paragraphs of the reviews. Twenty-five years after Kingsley's death, a reviewer who had never seen him insisted on making this connection: 'Mrs. Harrison is tall and large, distinctly English in appearance, and reminiscent, I should imagine, of her father, Charles Kingsley,' wrote William Wallace Whitelock in the *New York Times*, stressing her official married name and her daughtership at once (785). Reviewers often claimed that her eyes, her height, her mouth, recalled Charles Kingsley, selectively reading her body parts to prove that she was her father over again. By 1898 reviewers could mention her filial status as common knowledge that none the less needed repetition: 'Lucas Malet, who is, it will be remembered, the daughter of the late Charles Kingsley ...' ('Lucas Malet' *New-York Daily Tribune* 18). The sympathetic reviewer and biographer Stephen Gwynn read Malet's entire personality as a Kingsley inheritance:

> Charles Kingsley's daughter preaches through the same art the same
> ideal as Charles Kingsley preached, sees life and the world through
> the same eyes – an ideal modified by many contributing influences,
> yet still essentially the same ideal of strength and courage – eyes

which look on life from the standpoint of another sex and of a younger generation, but eyes trained with the same training and desiring the same beauty. (Gwynn 480–1)

Kingsley was also assumed to be her audience. One reviewer excoriated her for having written a novel that would have disappointed her father, by then long dead ('Deformed' 342). If the 'anxiety of influence' against one's literary fathers is powerful enough as it is, how much more powerful would it be when one's entire culture is speaking the voice of that father. As Patricia Srebrnik writes, 'How much more severe the anxiety must be for the woman author whose actual biological father is widely acclaimed as one of the primary architects of the ideological and literary structures which confine her' ('Re-Subjection' 195).

Some association between Malet and Kingsley was inevitable. As those reviewers noted, she did in fact resemble her father. Malet married Kingsley's worshipful curate, William Harrison, shortly after her father died, and the couple moved to Clovelly, which had been her father's parish. Harrison admired Kingsley greatly, thought about publishing a biography of him, and may indeed have been attracted to Malet in so far as she represented an accessible extension of his hero. Meanwhile, Malet chose to marry a man thirteen years her senior who could not have been more closely professionally identified with her father, just after her father's death. It is hard not to read this as an attempt to marry a father-substitute.

In terms of personality and talents, Malet was perhaps the closest to Kingsley of any of his four children. She inherited his writerly facility, his artistic ability and his intensity of belief. Like Kingsley, Malet pursued professional artistic training before turning to fiction. Like Kingsley, Malet passionately preached political and religious ideas in her fiction. Like Kingsley, Malet enjoyed writing occasional children's stories. Of the four Kingsley children, she was the only fiction writer and she finished his last novel posthumously, managing to ventriloquise his voice so flawlessly no reviewer could tell where her additions came in. Her favourite novel was her children's book, *Little Peter*, because she felt it was the closest to her father's style (Smith). Indeed, she told interviewer Mary Angela Dickens that 'she finds herself grow nearer to her father with every year she lives' (524). More prosaically, Malet also quite directly inherited his books and papers and the royalties on that estate. Malet inherited, too, what we now know, thanks to Susan Chitty, to be Kingsley's morbid interest in masochistic sexuality.

In all these respects, it was easy for the public to read Malet as simply another Kingsley, the next item in the series.

The series had, in fact, become one of the primary ways Victorian readers understood literary production. In the latter half of the nineteenth century, Victorians were accustomed to literary work that occurred in instalments, either from month to month (serial publication) or every few years (series fiction with recurring characters was published amongst others by Anthony Trollope, Charlotte Yonge and Margaret Oliphant). They were accustomed to a fictional record that defied closure, a record that was continually modified and diversified and extended, interrupted at regular intervals, responsive to readers' concerns, a tale that had the complex ebb and flow of actual life and might well play out in something approximating real time. In their magisterial *The Victorian Serial*, Linda K. Hughes and Michael Lund argue that 'the serial form was more than an economic strategy. It was also a literary form attuned to fundamental tendencies in the age at large' (8). The serial, they argue, participated in the Victorian rethinking of time, in everything from investment strategies geology to biology and embryology, where time was beginning to be understood as a series of events over a long duration rather than a few catastrophic events (4–7). Laurie Langbauer picks up on this idea in her *Novels of Everyday Life: The Series in English Fiction, 1850–1930*, suggesting that series fiction fits into commodity capitalism inasmuch as 'the same story is not so much efficiently recycled as it is repackaged and marketed anew as the next installment' (51). Hughes and Lund and Langbauer together offer a powerfully persuasive analysis of the way late Victorian readers were trained to expect and enjoy a tale that occurred in occasional instalments over a long duration. Thus the Kingsley family could be seen as comprising multiple local expressions of the same intrinsic spirit over generations. The Kingsleys, in short, were a series, a serial publication, of one persona. This model lies behind Stephen Gwynn's assertion:

> The family to which Lucas Malet belongs has thrown up in two generations an astonishing number of notable persons, varying extremely in temperament and achievement, yet essentially akin by nature. A passion for adventure, intellectual or physical, a supreme sense of the glory of life, a love of freedom amounting to absolute disregard of convention, were as characteristic of Henry and George Kingsley, Lucas Malet's uncles, as they were of her father, and ... her cousin Miss Mary Kingsley, the explorer. And those same character-

istics are written large and bold over Lucas Malet's whole work. (Gwynn 480)

Malet and her cousin Mary Kingsley were the latest instalment in the Kingsley story. This provided a reassuringly predictable narrative for the public, but of course it leached all individuality out of Malet's (or Mary Kingsley's) work.

As the daughter of Charles Kingsley, too, Malet was sheltered from the desperately competitive world of the 1880s and 1890s literary marketplace. Malet sent her first novel, *Mrs. Lorimer: A Study in Black and White* (1882) to the Kingsley family's publishers, Macmillan. The reader disliked the manuscript, although the terms of the review demonstrate how much pressure s/he was under to find a way to accept a Kingsley novel. 'On the whole [I] must confess that I see only moderate merits in it,' wrote Macmillan's reader. Complaining about its dreary style, trivial incidents and vapid characters, the reader concluded: 'The fact I fear it must be stamped with the fatal brand of "mediocrity." I have tried to persuade myself into a more approving frame of mind, but to no purpose.' Given another chance, the reader confessed continuing inability to find merit in the text: 'I've read very carefully the second half of Mrs Lorimer and with the best will in the world I cannot see anything striking or remarkable in it in any way .... The thing is a romance of the type of wh. one we return a couple of dozen or more per annum.' The reader added, and then crossed out, 'I wish that I could' ('Macmillan'). The reluctance to give a bad review is evident in the tone ('I must confess', 'I fear', 'I have tried to persuade myself', 'with the best will in the world', 'I wish that I could'). Macmillan could lose its very lucrative hold over the Kingsley estate if it alienated the family. Furthermore, although they may not have known this, Malet was the next heir to that estate. The review makes it clear that if Malet had been an ordinary writer, *Mrs. Lorimer* would never have been published. Yet the novel was accepted in June 1882, in spite of the reader's report. It received sparse but fairly respectful reviews, again, probably better treatment than it would have received had its author been someone less well connected.

However, if Malet's Kingsley heritage favoured her entry into the literary marketplace, it must be said that she did what she could to frustrate such favouritism. Publishing under a pseudonym was one such trick, although, interestingly, Macmillan's reader did not bother with it, confidently recording her as 'Mrs. Harrison' and clarifying in the next line, 'Mrs. Kingsley Harrison, I mean.' Within Macmillan, then, there was no pretence about who had written the novel. The pseudonym was swiftly uncovered; by 1885, reviewers were confidently assuming readers were aware of her real identity and gender, although there were still pockets of ignorance as late as 1896, when a reviewer for the *New York Times* called her 'Mr. Malet'.

Although the pseudonym worked only spottily, Malet had another trick to evade her family's influence. She left Macmillan immediately after *Mrs. Lorimer* and began publishing with several other houses, including Methuen, Kegan Paul, Hutchinson, and Dodd, Mead. Anxious to get good terms, she used a literary agent, then a new innovation, to help her place her work with different publishers (Gillies). This unpredictability made it difficult for her to get decent terms for her novels. Whereas her father had built a mutually beneficial relationship with a single firm over decades, Malet played the market, ending up with wildly divergent contracts, with publishers unwilling to wait for her to compose, with agents who unconsciously misrepresented her work, and with publishers who ignored her explicit directives (Gillies, Lundberg). In other words, after 1882 Malet distanced herself from the Kingsley name so swiftly and completely it actually damaged her career, rendering it impossible for her to get the kind of special consideration Macmillan had given her first novel. As in the case of her pseudonym, her relations with publishers demonstrates anew that her urgency to escape the family identification was great enough to make her willing to sacrifice financial stability.

Malet evaded the Kingsley name partly because, for all her fidelity to her father's memory, she was fiercely antagonistic to her father's precepts. In interviews, she generally tried to delineate her difference from her famous parent. In that very same interview with Mary Angela Dickens where she had enthused that 'she finds herself grow nearer to her father', Malet asserted that she had led a miserably isolated childhood, speaking of it with 'vehement horror' (523). She particularly resented her father's dictum that she could not read novels until after she turned 20, when she was finally allowed to start reading Charlotte Yonge. She was angry enough about this policy to describe it to several of her interviewers (Dickens 523; Smith; Tooley 187). Her marriage to Kingsley's acolyte worsened in the 1880s and led to separation by the 1890s. During this stressful period, Malet began to express increasing distaste for the ideas her father and her husband both held dear. She complained about her husband's notions in the preface to a volume of his sermons (Malet 'Preface').

She expressed bitterness about the difficulties of life in her father's beloved Clovelly parish (Dolman 146). Publicising her pro-Catholic sympathies as early as her article 'The Youngest of the Saints' in 1885, Malet's long journey away from her father's Anglican loyalties climaxed in 1902, when she took the almost unimaginable step of converting to Catholicism. Kingsley, of course, had been the most famous anti-Catholic debater in England, whose accusations spurred Newman to write his *Apologia Pro Vita Sua*.

Interestingly, the serial paradigm of Victorian thought managed to accommodate even Malet's Catholicism. Janet E. Hogarth suggested that

> Kingsley's daughter, quite apart from her own idiosyncrasies of temperament, must almost have been born an adherent of the flesh-and-blood school of robust religious thinking. She ought also to have been born a Protestant, but perhaps muscular Christianity, when it takes feminine shape ... is apt to seek satisfaction in a religion which makes other appeals to the senses. (535)

Hogarth here manages to explain Malet's spectacularly rebellious Catholic conversion as an inherited muscular Christianity gone bad. The habit of reading serially encouraged Victorian critics to try to prove that each instalment was, somehow, a progressive, logical extension of the same story. Malet's actually vexed relations with her father could not be read in the serial paradigm. After all, a later chapter does not usually attack an earlier component, or declare independence and march off to be its own story.

But Malet's writing did just that; she fought against her father's legacy in interviews, prefaces and fiction. Although she literally lived on the proceeds of Kingsley's literary estate, she could not resist condemning it. In that posthumously published and co-authored novel of Kingsley's, *The Tutor's Story*, Malet added a highly ambivalent preface. She begins by claiming that although she had inherited her father's literary remains upon her mother's death in 1892, it was not until 1915 that she examined them; whether true or not, the assertion demonstrates her anxiety to show she was a reluctant and belated reader of his writing. The Preface opens up an implied space for her career by suggesting that, between 1892 and 1915, she had no time to worry about her father's work, being otherwise occupied in writing her own books. Indeed, finishing the father's unfinished book is at least as much an act of aggressive competitiveness as it is an act of homage. Her ambivalence is perhaps most visible in this passage:

> I have tried to preserve peculiarities of style, and maintain a moral and emotional unity throughout – to maintain, further, a certain freshness and complicity of outlook which has the rather pathetic charm of a 'day that is dead.' I, personally, hold no brief for that day either in its literary, social, or political methods. Yet I find the charm a very real one. (Malet 'Prefatory Note' vii)

In this passage she tacitly defines the 'charm' of her father's style as deriving from both inexperience ('freshness') and conventionality ('complicity'). By contrast, Malet tacitly constructs herself as an experienced, mature, independent thinker who patronises the fresh young thoughts of a beginner, thus reversing the usual parent–child assumptions.

Indeed, Malet violently reacted against the mid-Victorian values promulgated by her father. Not surprisingly, as she told an interviewer in 1897, 'there were points upon which, even young as she was, she ventured to differ from him. To-day, she acknowledges that she has diverged greatly from many of the views which he held' (Tooley 188–9). Perhaps the point in which she most differed from Kingsley concerned his treatment of women. Here is a telling exchange with interviewer Frederick Dolman: '"Did you write any books during Mr. Kingsley's lifetime?" "No, I never wrote until some time after his death. And I am not altogether sure he would have cared about my working. He held the old-fashioned and chivalrous notion that women should be treated *en princesse,* should be provided for, worked for, not permitted to struggle with the world at first hand"' (Dolman 147). The passage is reminiscent of the famous diary entry in which Virginia Woolf imagines how her father's life would have forestalled her own writing: 'Father's birthday. He would have been 96, yes, today; & could have been 96, like other people one has known; but mercifully was not. His life would have entirely ended mine. What would have happened? No writing, no books; – inconceivable' (Woolf 208). Like Woolf, Malet also required her father's death to write. She had to see herself as displacing or replacing him, while her culture viewed her as his continuation.

Not surprisingly, this resentment of her father was worked out in her novels, particularly two produced as her career was taking off. *A Counsel of Perfection* (1888) is a close examination of the problems of daughterly fidelity. Lydia Casteen reluctantly has to give up the prospect of marriage in order to continue to minister to her selfish father, a strict scholar who remains sublimely unconscious of her suffering or her sacrifice. Indeed, Lydia has to find comfort in the selflessness of a martyrdom nobody else will appreciate. It is probably not coincidental that Malet produced this novel just after emerging as a published novelist while living in Clovelly, the town associated with her father's boyhood, and just as all the reviewers were starting to unmask her identity and compare her to her father. *A Counsel of Perfection* clearly works through the feelings of reluctantly serving an all-powerful paternal intellectual.

The main character in her next major novel, *The Wages of Sin* (1890), is closely based on Kingsley. James Colthurst has Kingsley's stammer, Kingsley's artistic hands, Kingsley's controversial socialist realism and Kingsley's sexual self-hatred. Colthurst is positioned as an erring but heroic figure in an English culture that persistently misunderstands and belittles his magnificent moral attributes. Yet the Kingsleyan figure in *The Wages of Sin* has an arc that bears no relation to Kingsley's own life. Kingsley himself was blissfully happily married, a devoted father, a beloved and respectable Victorian sage, professor at Cambridge, highly successful author, religious mentor to the royal family and guide to many young 'muscular Christians'. But in James Colthurst, Malet writes an alternative Kingsley, one who is systematically denied any kind of success. Refused the wife he loves, given an illegitimate family he despises and neglects, thwarted of professional achievements, feared by respectable society, James Colthurst ultimately dies in what may well be suicide. Interestingly, the woman with whom Colthurst is in love is clearly an autobiographical figure, a young woman named Mary Crookenden (echoing Malet's real name, Mary Kingsley), who, like Malet, attends the Slade School but drops out to pursue a relationship with an older man. Although Mary and Colthurst love each other, Colthurst's depression and self-hatred wreck their relationship, leaving Mary a cool, lofty, untouchable ideal in Colthurst's mind. And when Colthurst dies, Mary begins travelling all over the world in an absolute freedom that is no less welcome because it has been forced upon her by tragedy.

It is tempting, but perhaps dangerously reductive, to assert that in Colthurst Malet was getting her revenge against her more famous father, cutting him down to size and placing herself as the unattainable object of desire. Obviously, the construction of a fictional character is motivated by many interacting needs, not all of them rooted in the author's psychology, and not all of them deducible by readers. But it is probably safe to say that Colthurst is a case study of a less fortunate, and therefore less threatening, Kingsley, while Mary is a case study of what Malet herself might have wanted to be, an inaccessible beloved, and the fact that such an alternative emerged in the pages of this novel denotes what is certainly a more complex daughterly relation than that of the faithful inheritor. That Mary Crookenden experiences the death of Colthurst as a kind of liberation as well as a catastrophe does seem to encode some of Malet's own ambivalence.

What it meant to be the 'daughter of Charles Kingsley', then, was to be a reluctant heir, a rebel and a rewriter, rather than an imitator. Malet swerved from the faithful reiteration her Victorian audience demanded. She refused to be a sequel. Instead, Malet wrote her own family lineage and perpetuated it herself. We have already seen how the name 'Lucas Malet' places Malet as the heir of her great-aunt and grandmother rather than of the Kingsley men. Such alternative ancestry was only the beginning of a new kind of family structure. Far from looking for literary foremothers, Malet rejected direct parental relations. Instead she charted, in life and in fiction, fruitful relationships that moved laterally through the family. As Eve Kosofsky Sedgwick enjoins, 'Forget the Name of the Father. Think about your uncles and your aunts' (59).

We have already seen that Malet renamed herself after her great-aunt and adopted her young relative Gabrielle Vallings. Malet also had a very close relationship with her nephew Ranulph Kingsley (Lundberg). She also lived with her sister Rose for much of her life, even during her marriage. In short, although Malet had an unhappy marriage and a vexed relationship with her father, the permanent, nurturing, vital relationships in her life were with laterally related family members.

The pairing of nurturing aunt and the adoring niece or nephew are central in much of Malet's mature fiction. In *The Wages of Sin* (1890), Mary Crookenden is brought up by an aunt and uncle. After her ill-fated relationship with Colthurst, she permits her adoring cousin Lance to tag along behind her in her travels, and the narrative hints that eventually she will reward his fidelity. In *The Gateless Barrier* (1900), a young man is haunted by a charming ghost who turns out to be the spirit of his great-aunt. The ardent young man and the shy maiden fall in love. Their affair cannot be consummated, for just as the ghostly great-aunt is about to eat the bread and sip the wine that will re-embody her, she disappears, returning to the world of death. The hero, however, has a passionate private cult for her memory, which governs the rest of his life. *Adrian Savage* (1911) offers a love triangle involving cousins. These avuncular relationships are sometimes played out in marriage, in which a young woman marries a much older man who nurtures her paternally. In *Colonel Enderby's Wife,* for instance the ageing and ailing Colonel Enderby suffers heart problems alone as his lovely young wife dances the night through.

The quantity of avuncular and lateral relationships in Malet's fiction may be most easily seen if we trace the familial relations of one character, Katherine Calmady, in her most famous novel, *The History of Sir Richard Calmady.* Katherine is brought up by a charming, courtly great-aunt and her female companion. She marries Sir Richard Calmady but he dies shortly, and during her long widowhood, Katherine contracts an ardent relationship with a young cousin, Honoria St Quentin. Honoria declares her love for Katherine quite openly:

> 'You see – I know it sounds as if I was rather a beast – perhaps I am – but I never cared for anyone – really to care, I mean – till I cared for you.' 'My dear!' – Katherine said again, wondering, shrinking somewhat, at once touched and almost repulsed. The younger woman's attitude was so far removed from her own experience. 'Does it displease you? Does it seem to you unnatural?' Honoria asked quickly. 'A little,' Lady Calmady answered, smiling, yet very tenderly. (415–16)

In spite of Katherine's orthodox rejection of Honoria's adoration, Katherine keeps Honoria near her and eventually the two women manage to move in together. Their passion is depicted as a purified, sexless affection, but it is marked by physical caresses and small endearments neither woman uses for anyone else. The Katherine–Honoria nexus is clearly the most emotionally fulfilling relationship in the novel.

Celibate cousinly relationships flourish in Katherine's vicinity. Katherine's cousin by marriage, the ascetic clergyman Julius March, develops a profound, private passion for her. Katherine's son, the younger Richard Calmady, falls in love with two cousins in turn. First, he has relations with the carnal and voluptuous Helen. Sex with Helen has catastrophic consequences, devastating him both physically and emotionally. He recovers by falling in love with, and marrying, the chaste Honoria. But, as I have argued elsewhere, the Richard–Honoria relationship appears to be a celibate marriage (Schaffer). In fact, its main purpose appears to be to facilitate Honoria's cohabitation with

Katherine. At the end of the novel, Richard and Honoria adopt a nephew, Dickie. In short, Katherine is brought up by an aunt; chooses a niece as her loving companion; that niece in turn appropriates a nephew. Families replicate not through direct parent–child perpetuation but laterally, through avuncular relationships.

Although Victorian novels are notorious for having cousins fall in love, Malet outdoes herself in *Sir Richard Calmady*. The final chapter of the novel shows a whole network of erotically charged cousinships, as Honoria and her cousin Katherine stroll blissfully together arm in arm, Honoria and her cousin Richard have contracted a celibate marriage, Honoria caresses her handsome nephew Dickie, and Julius continues to worship his cousin Katherine. None of these four familial attractions has been, or apparently will be, consummated, but the tension of controlled desire suspends the characters in place. The characters' sexual refusals are not read as tragic failure, fear or sterility. They are, rather, seen as triumphs.

Thus in her own life and in her fiction, Malet systematically imagined lateral avuncular, cousinly or sororal relationships, or adoptive/marital patronage relationships, as the ideal. These relationships often verge perilously close to erotic consummation, only to be diverted into safe celibacy at the last moment in order to produce a holy, purified adoration.

What I am trying to suggest is that the adoptive avuncular relationship became Malet's way of escaping the complex of competing emotions provoked by perpetual comparison with her father and her own inchoate feelings for Vallings. Although she worked through her complex relationship with Kingsley in many texts, she was primarily interested in imagining an alternative sort of family rather than being trapped within the binary opposition of obedience or rebellion. She revised her public persona of helpless daughterly subservience by making herself into a powerful mentoring aunt. She made herself the great-niece of Mrs Lucas instead of the daughter of Charles Kingsley. She also disciplined her perhaps socially unacceptable desires for other women by rechannelling them into familial relations and resolutely de-eroticising them. Changing a passion for women into a celibate, avuncular/sororal mentorship, Malet could safely have contact with her beloved. Indeed, she could feel that her suffering was salutary, her self-discipline a spiritual achievement.

Eve Kosofsky Sedgwick has demonstrated that uncles and aunts play a central role in another turn-of-the-century text, *The Importance of Being Earnest*. In her view, the 'avunculate' acts as an alternative form of family that provides relief from traditional forms of patriarchy and the stiflingly Oedipal and biological bonds of the nuclear family. Part of the comedy of *Earnest*, in fact, is the multitude of unruly and shifting familial possibilities gleefully generated by its characters before the Name of the Father comes down heavy-handedly in the last scene, placing Jack and Algy permanently in a hierarchical relation to each other and to the other characters (Sedgwick 52–72). What Wilde did on stage is what Malet wrote in her own life, as she emphasised her cousinly, avuncular, adoptive and sisterly affiliations to evade identification with the Name of the Father.

But Malet's avuncular alternative can also be seen as part of a generational shift away from the heavy emphasis on patriarchal lineage and marital propagation in the nineteenth century. Edward Said has suggested that modernism tends to depict childbearing as either impossible or unpleasant, instead developing a set of substitute bonds to compensate for the lack of biological reproduction.

> What I am describing is the transition from a failed idea or possibility of filiation to a kind of compensatory order that, whether it is a party, an institution, a culture, a set of beliefs, or even a world-vision, provides men and women with a new form of relationship, which I have been calling affiliation but which is also a new system. (Said 19)

In other words, in high modernism people turn away from traditional filiation towards affiliation: a voluntary formation of loose social ties ruled by collegiality and consensus. To put it in the terms we have been using here, by the early twentieth century readers might be loosening their serial paradigm in order to read in a more associative, impressionist, relativist way. No longer expecting Victorian series, they were now reading modernist texts. Malet, composing a lateral family at the turn of the century, appears to be making something like the affiliative move Said describes. In this respect, she may have begun in a densely repetitive serial familial situation, but she ends up in a loose adoptive network linked by indirect associations. If her life story started as a Trollope series, it was ending as a Woolf novel.

Unfortunately, Malet's avuncular alternative was not particularly marketable. In the nineteenth century, her relation to Kingsley sold books. Her relation to Kingsley also sold a way of understanding Malet's challenging work. Malet's controversial subjects and direct honesty and jarring ideas could be put into a reassuring context if she was seen as a member of a colourful Kingsley clan, simply expressing inherited traits, and if those qualities could be reconfigured as repetitions of her father's beloved eccentricities. Stephen Gwynn's analysis of Malet as 'Charles Kingsley's daughter preach[ing] through the same art the same ideal as Charles Kingsley preached', was just the sort of reassuring gloss the Victorian market wanted.

After the turn of the century, however, reaction began to set in against the Victorian sages. The tutor of the Prince of Wales, the avatar of cleanliness and muscles and English decency, could hardly achieve respect in the modernist mindset. In the twentieth century, Malet's affiliation with Kingsley damaged her deeply. Ironically, just as Malet was constructing non-traditional family structures and writing experimental modernist texts and non-realistic psychological narratives about subjects that included disease, delirium, lesbianism, masochism and erotic obsessions, she began to be read as the most hidebound of Victorian survivals. Her later novels got fewer and fewer reviews. Janet E. Courtney simply dismisses her last nine novels as unworthy to stand with her turn-of-the-century masterpieces (240). In her only major obituary, in 1931, *The Times* wrote: 'In the literary history of the last quarter of the nineteenth and the first quarter of the twentieth century Lucas Malet can hardly be denied a secure place. She was a very slow writer, and there were often long intervals during which she published nothing.' She is remembered here, perversely, for what and when she did not write. The obituary writer grudgingly admits that Malet 'can hardly be denied' a place in literary history, as if s/he would like to deny it, and, of course, it did not take long until even these residual threads of reputation had dissolved.

Being Lucas Malet, then, helped her establish a particular sort of writerly persona that had more psychological than financial value, more personal than political applicability. Being Lucas Malet meant constructing oneself as the heir of a great-aunt and setting in motion a sequence of avuncular relationships that replaced the nuclear family with a much more lateral, voluntary and capacious notion of family. It meant replacing the patriarchal Kingsleys with a more feminist lineage. Being Lucas Malet meant affirming the masculine and Francophilic traits that Malet felt determined her social behaviour, her writing style and perhaps her 'inverted' desires; it meant confirming and even publicising this unconventional self. Being Lucas Malet meant not being Mary Harrison, the wife of a conventional clergyman. It most certainly meant not being Mary Kingsley, the daughter of Charles Kingsley. From 1892 to 1915 – from the time she inherited her father's papers until the time she read them – a major career could form. Slipping into the space outside her father's name, working through her father's silence, this woman writer could claim her own identity. The unmarketable, unplaceable name gave her the space to forge a different self, and for a few decades at the turn of the century, it worked. But it worked at the cost of the financial stability she would have derived from her recognised participation in a solid brand, the Kingsley product.

The last official public word on Malet was that obituary in *The Times,* and it sums up the contradictions of her career. The writer alternates between biographical material about 'Mrs Harrison' and literary evaluation of 'Lucas Malet'. The oscillations between the two subjects of this review – the dutiful wife/daughter, the ambitious novelist – immortalise the indeterminacy of her public identity. The first line announces her real name to be 'Mrs Mary St. Leger Harrison', and the second sentence establishes her relation to Charles Kingsley and lists his achievements. It seems as if the obituary intends to reduce Malet to her properly filial role permanently. But the headline tells a different story. In large type it reads: '"Lucas Malet": A Novelist of Character'. Thus her pseudonym visually triumphs over the biographical small print. With the name 'Lucas Malet' quite literally above all, the conventionalising project of the obituary is called into question; we read the Kingsley history in the context of a name that is defiantly, deliberately, non-Kingsley. Interestingly, however, 'Lucas Malet' is in quotation marks, as if to remind us that it is a fiction, a construct. The obituary writer must quote Malet's own composition in order to name her. By 'A Novelist of Character', the writer probably meant that she was a psychological novelist, studying the vagaries of human characters. But Malet was also a 'novelist of character' in a second sense, for composing a pseudonym gave herself a new character, a particular sort of persona with her own genealogy, nationality, gender and affiliative community. In fact, she was not only a literary character herself, but a being composed of characters, a self ratified and articulated by the letters that formed her adopted name. Finally, Malet was a 'novelist of character' in a third respect: she had the strength to surrender the financial resources available to the Kingsleys in order to claim her own truth. She had the character to delineate her own character as a novelist. Throughout her long life, the 'daughter of Charles Kingsley' had the character to write 'Lucas Malet'.

Notes

1   I do not discuss Malet's relationship with her mother here, partly because of space constraints and partly because in this article I am focusing on Malet's participation in a literary lineage that was construed as exclusively paternal. Malet's reviews overwhelmingly stressed her famous father and excluded her mother completely. However, Malet's relationship with Frances Grenfell Kingsley was clearly stormy. In various interviews, Malet tacitly critiqued her mother's neediness, sickness and absence from her daughter's life, and Patricia Lorimer Lundberg argues that Malet avoided taking care of her mother as she aged.
2   For instance, a reviewer in 1900 mourned, 'her slight sketches of American society betray a lightness of touch and a dexterity of manipulation which she might profitably seek to cultivate. Instead of which, she wastes her abilities on the vain effort to be awe-inspiring and gruesome' ('A Budget').
3   The Kingsley family traced its lineage back to the twelfth-century knight Ranulph de Kingsley (Chitty 23).

Works cited

'Baron de Book-Worms', 'Our Booking-Office', *Punch* 21 March 1891, 141.

'A Budget of New Books', *Blackwood's Edinburgh Magazine* 168 (November 1900), 732.

Cartwright, Julia, *A Bright Remembrance: The Diaries of Julia Cartwright 1851–1924*, ed. Angela Emanuel. London: Weidenfeld and Nicolson, 1989.

Chitty, Susan, *The Beast and the Monk: A Life of Charles Kingsley*. London: Hodder and Stoughton, 1974.

Courtney, Janet E., 'A Novelist of the 'Nineties', *Fortnightly Review* 137 (1932), 230–41.

Courtney, W.L., *The Feminine Note in Fiction*. London: Chapman and Hall, 1904.

'The Deformed Reformed', *Outlook*. 12 October 1901, 342.

Dickens, Mary Angela, 'A Talk with "Lucas Malet"', *Windsor Magazine* X (1899), 522–4.

Dolman, Frederick, '"Lucas Malet" at Home: A Chat with the Daughter of Charles Kingsley', *The Young Woman: A Monthly Journal and Review* 4 (1896), 145–9.

Ford, James L., 'The Author of "Sir Richard Calmady"', *Bookman* 14 (1901), 232–4.

Furniss, Harry, *Some Victorian Women: Good, Bad, and Indifferent*. London: John Lane, 1923.

Gillies, Mary Ann, *The Professional Literary Agent in Britain: 1880–1920*. Unpublished.

Gwynn, Stephen, 'Sir Richard Calmady', *New Liberal Review* 2 (1901–2), 480–8.

Hogarth, Janet E., 'Lucas Malet's Novels', *Fortnightly Review* 77 (1902), 532–40.

Hughes, Linda K. and Lund, Michael, *The Victorian Serial*. Charlottesville: University Press of Virginia, 1991.

Hunt, Violet, Unpublished autobiographical notes in the Ford Madox Ford Collection at Cornell University, Box 63.006.

Langbauer, Laurie, *Novels of Everyday Life: The Series in English Fiction, 1850–1930*. Ithaca: Cornell University Press, 1999.

'Lucas Malet: An American Visitor's Portrait of the Novelist', *New-York Daily Tribune* 27 February 1898 (Sunday Supplement), 18.

'"Lucas Malet": A Novelist of Character', *The Times* 29 October 1931, 14.

Lundberg, Patricia Lorimer, '"An Inward Necessity": The Writer's Life of Lucas Malet'. Unpublished biography, 2001.

Macarthur, James, 'Notes of a Bookman', *Harper's Weekly* 45 (16 November 1901): 1160.

—— 'Some Animadversions on the Abnormal in Art', *Harper's Weekly* 46 (12 April 1901): 424.

Malet, Lucas, *The History of Sir Richard Calmady*. London: Methuen, 1901.

—— 'Preface'. William Harrison, *Clovelly Sermons*. London: Methuen, 1898, pp. vii–xi.

—— 'The Youngest of the Saints', *Fortnightly Review* new series 38 (September 1885), 395–412.

—— 'Prefatory Note'. Charles Kingsley and Lucas Malet, *The Tutor's Story*. New York: Dodd, Mead, and Company, 1916, p. vii.

New York Times, 12 December 12 1896 (Saturday Supplement), 2.

Reader's Report, Mrs. Lorimer. 'The Archives of Macmillan & Co., 1854–1924'. Cambridge: Chadwyck-Healey, 1982. Vol. 1, Part 1, Reel 1: 128.

'Recent Novels', *The Times* 16 September 1901, 12.

Said, Edward W., *The World, the Text, and the Critic*. Cambridge, Mass.: Harvard University Press, 1983.

Schaffer, Talia, 'Introduction'. Lucas Malet, *The History of Sir Richard Calmady*. University Press of Birmingham, forthcoming.

Sedgwick, Eve Kosofsky, 'Tales of the Avunculate: Queer Tutelage in *The Importance of Being Earnest*', *Tendencies*. Durham, NC: Duke University Press, 1993, pp. 52–72.

Smith, Laura Alex, 'Western Women of Note'. *Western Weekly News* 29 January 1898.

Srebrnik, Patricia Thomas, 'Lucas Malet (Mary St. Leger Kingsley Harrison)', *Dictionary of Literary Biography* vol. 153, ed. George M. Johnson. Detroit: Gale Research, 1995, pp. 177–85.

—— 'The Re-subjection of "Lucas Malet": Charles Kingsley's Daughter and the Response to Muscular Christianity', *Muscular Christianity: Embodying The Victorian Age*. Ed. Donald E. Hall. Cambridge: Cambridge University Press, 1995, pp. 194–214.

Tooley, Sarah, 'Lucas Malet (Mrs. Harrison)', *Woman at Home* December 1897, 187–9.

Whitelock, William Wallace, 'Lucas Malet: A Visit to the Home of Charles Kingsley's Daughter and a Talk With Her', *New York Times* 26 October 1901, 785.

Woolf, Virginia, *The Diary of Virginia Woolf, vol. 3 1925–1930*. Ed. Anne Olivier Bell with Andrew McNeillie. New York and London: Harcourt Brace Jovanovich, 1980.

5
Irony, Ethics and Self-Fashioning in George Moore's *Confessions of a Young Man*

Annette Federico

The vogue for self-fashioning in England at the turn of the century has been well documented in recent scholarship and, as the essays in this book prove, the self-mythologies and authorial identities that proliferated in the literary market were extraordinarily diverse, by turns playful, arrogant, self-protective, subversive. In this essay, I want to think about the ethical implications of self-fashioning, and in particular the uses of irony in artistic self-invention and as a potentially activist stance against the apparent finality of middle-class assumptions about the ends of life – happiness, utility, respectability and material success. For even in the book market, self-fashioning involves more than adopting a pseudonym, toying with gender roles, manipulating photographs or managing one's celebrity. Self-fashioning also gestures towards a new ethical sensibility, for it deliberately undermines cherished Victorian beliefs in character, truth, reality and fidelity to fact – Oscar Wilde's 'The Decay of Lying' (1889) and Max Beerbohm's 'A Defence of Cosmetics' (1894) are both in effect ironic polemics for artifice and subjectivism against these mid-Victorian values. Ironic self-fashioning is an ethical position; and if, as the philosopher Alasdair MacIntyre argues, ethical beliefs presuppose a sociology (19), then various late century practices of self-fashioning – by advertisers and public relations people, artists and writers, politicians, and even ordinary consumers who wear rouge or sport velveteen – indicate a change in people's attitudes to individual agency and social responsibility, a new way of thinking about the self and one's choices in life. Jil Larson explains this shift simply and persuasively in *Ethics and Narrative in the English Novel, 1880–1914*:

> the ethos of the late-century ... is marked not by a deontological escape from self or a paradoxically strong-willed refusal of choice

but instead by anxious yet flexibly ethical searching, an openness to the surprising and unusual, and an ambivalence poised between regard for Victorian morality and attention to the ethical relevance of that which lies beyond moral authority.

... Self-fashioning is an ethical concept radically divergent from mid-Victorian understandings of the self as determined by family, social convention, and deontological morality. The focus on the inner life is also new, a departure from the Victorian ethos of looking outward to others and defining oneself through vigorous agency with the world. (32–3)

According to Larson, the late century writer's new attitude of 'introspection, rebellion, and self-fashioning' is characteristic of a generation's self-consciousness in an age of transition; hesitation, ambivalence and individualism mark many late Victorian texts because of contradictory needs to assert a normative vision, on the one hand, and to stake out one's subjective impressions, on the other (38–41).

Larson's discussion of agency, emotion, gender and aesthetics in certain late century writers (Hardy, Wilde, James and Conrad) is illuminating in the context of authorial self-invention. I would like to build on her work by asking how the deliberate construction of an authorial identity participates more generally in a generation's acute awareness of its own subjectivities, and the consequences of this new ethic for late Victorian society, which, by 1900, had fashioned itself as a very modern, fully industrialised, increasingly democratic state. I shall be using the American philosopher Richard Rorty, who has had much to say about the ambiguous value of ironic self-revision in liberal societies.[1] Rorty advocates what he has called 'redescription', the life-long activity of placing vocabularies and metaphors beside one another in an ongoing effort at self-creation, rather than accepting a 'final vocabulary' that has been given to one by others (*CIS* 39). For Rorty, the opposite of irony is common sense, 'For that is the watchword of those who unselfconsciously describe everything important in terms of the final vocabulary to which they and those around them are habituated' (*CIS* 74). Rorty prefers the attitude of the 'liberal ironist' who accepts the contingency of her beliefs and recognises that instead of finding out the truth, her task should be to play vocabularies off one another. In poets, artists and intellectuals this activity may quite literally involve inventing new metaphors. Rorty refers to Nietzsche's idea of self-knowledge as self-creation:

> The process of coming to know oneself, confronting one's contingency, tracking one's causes home, is identical with the process of inventing a new language – that is, thinking up some new metaphors. ... To fail as a poet – and thus, for Nietzsche, to fail as a human being – is to accept somebody else's description of oneself, to execute a previously prepared program, to write, at most, elegant variations on previously written poems. So the only way to trace home the causes of one's being as one is would be *to tell a story about one's causes in a new language*. (*CIS* 27–8; my emphasis)

Although Larson does not focus on Rorty in her study, like me she finds his work helpful in understanding a certain ethical position in a particular historical context, what she calls 'late Victorian liberal ironists' (Larson 11). That such an attitude is even possible is a matter of historical contingency. For example, as different as were Freud, Nietzsche and Proust, argues Rorty, each was able to add new metaphors and new vocabularies to Western culture because 'it somehow became possible, toward the end of the nineteenth century, to take the activity of redescription more lightly than it had ever been taken before' (*CIS* 39). But, he notes, we would be wrong to look at this phenomenon in metaphysical terms – as 'the march of the World Spirit toward clearer self-consciousness, or as the length of man's mind gradually coming to match that of the universe' (*CIS* 39). Such an interpretation would betray the spirit of playfulness and irony which links Nietzsche, Proust and other figures, something that is 'the product of their shared ability to appreciate the power of redescribing, the power of language to make new and different things possible and important' (*CIS* 39).

George Moore's *Confessions of a Young Man* (1888) is an especially promising text for testing out this 'power of redescribing' in turn-of-the-century British culture and society. *Confessions* is a clever and paradoxical book, and for many critics an important one in the development of literary modernism.[2] The pressures of redescription, of imposing new metaphors on the world and of ironic self-creation are felt by both the reader (reactions to the book ranged from bewildered admiration to revulsion)[3] and the narrator, Edward Dayne, whose utter self-involvement, as well as his curious explorations into literature and art, make him an intriguing example of a late Victorian liberal ironist. Of course, George Moore the autobiographical author is also implicated in this pose, adding a peculiar angle to the notion of self-fashioning, for *Confessions* represents the first stage in his authorial self-construction. As Elizabeth Grubgeld has shown in her study of the author's 'autogenous self', throughout his career Moore engaged in projects of self-invention in his autobiographies, memoirs and essays (Grubgeld ix–xiii). For Moore this autogenous process was almost always tied to art criticism and public intellectualism – Oscar Wilde was right when he quipped that 'George Moore has conducted his whole education in public' (Harris 278). Moore was in fact very serious about his autodidacticism. All his autobiographical works are largely about his education in letters which, for Moore, always incriminates 'life'. Yet his tone is often playfully aloof; he is intellectually promiscuous or, in Adrian Frazier's words, 'a Don Juan of the mind' (161). His eclecticism was certainly part of his public identity, but it was not just a pose, as Wilde must have recognised; it was a frank commitment to a life-long process that involved acquiring many points of view and, especially, seeking specific kinds of knowledge (circumscribed by the world and personal history) by way of art and literature – that is, he redescribes himself at this period of his life through his experiences with many different French and English texts. *Confessions* is Moore's first experiment with self-creation through literature as the narrator traces his early affection for Shelley, Gautier, Balzac, Baudelaire and Pater, with notable references to the symbolists and other 'minor awakenings' (Moore 165), including Zola, Flaubert and the Goncourts. Chapter 10 is entirely an account of the narrator's readings of English authors; it is all literary criticism. This enterprise is close to Wilde's in 'The Decay of Lying' and 'The Critic as Artist' (1891), and both writers take their jabs at Victorian prudery, too. Yet there is an important difference between Moore and Wilde. Max Beerbohm said that Moore presented 'in the midst of an artificial civilisation the spectacle of one absolutely natural man', whereas Wilde was 'a conscious and deliberate piece of work', a man of masks and poses (quoted in Grubgeld 37). Holbrook Jackson, in 1913, understood Moore's situation well:

> the real influences of his life were Flaubert and the naturalists on the one side, and their corollaries in the graphic arts, Manet and the impressionists, on the other. For the rest he insisted upon England accepting the impressionists; abandoned realism; introduced into [England] the work of Verlaine and Rimbaud, and the autobiography of indiscretion; flirted with the Irish Literary Movement, and its vague mysticism – and remained George Moore. (63–4)

Thus Moore's form of self-fashioning involved a steady dedication to the creation of an inner life that would be true to an ideal of outward self-presentation, an ideal 'George Moore'. This person would honour all the various tastes, propensities and idiosyncrasies – what he calls in *Confessions* 'the instinctiveness of my likes and dislikes' (Moore 81) – which were to propel him in so many different literary directions. People like Moore and Wilde are ironists partly because they read a variety of literature and literary criticism so they will not get trapped in the vocabulary of one single book (Rorty *CIS* 81).

Moore's story is about 'the artistic development of me, Edward Dayne' (Moore 165), it is a record of a person's 'mental digestions' (180). It dramatises *the process* of self-fashioning in a way no other book of the period did, at least not with the same irony and insouciance. And it is a self-reflexive performance, as Moore's later Prefaces, additions and revisions show. According to Grubgeld, the language of the novel 'reflects commercial needs and is rhetorical in origin rather than romantically self-expressive. At no point in the text's history is a sincere authorial voice accessible' (Grubgeld 51). Moore was worried that people would misread the authorial voice and therefore the whole tone of the book, and he was at pains to explain to his first translator that 'My book is a *satire*' (quoted in Dick 11). *Confessions* therefore has the subversive edge that is part of the rhetoric of satire;[4] despite the narrator's pose of snobbery and detachment, it is, like most satires, radically moral. *Confessions* is partly directed against the prudery and platitudes of Victorian society, where a young girl cannot read an 'immoral' novel but may spend her mornings poring over the Colin Campbell divorce case in the newspapers. 'Who shall come forward and make you answer?' is the rhetorical question the book asks its readers. 'Oh, vile, filthy, hypocritical century, I at least scorn you,' says the accusing narrator (Moore 165). *Confessions* is also a brisk, witty confrontation with the 'hypocritical reader' who accepts the identity respectable society has imposed upon her, rather than excavating her past for that ideal self, playing with the possibilities of selfhood. Frazier justly calls *Confessions* 'a *Sartor Resartus* for the end of the century' (165).

Confessions not only displays a new ethical position for modern people; it also offers alternative ideas about the self. Moore throughout suggests that there is a contingency of selfhood: 'What I have ... chance bestowed, and still bestows, upon me. ... Nor am I exaggerating when I say I might equally have been a Pharaoh, an ostler, a pimp, an archbishop' (Moore 49). At the same time, he asserts the existence of what he called, after Schopenhauer, 'instinct' or 'brain instinct'

(Moore 63) – which is to say, certain tendencies to which we should lend an ear, tendencies that are strange, idiosyncratic and unclaimed by anyone else's criteria. Scholars have recognised the influence of Schopenhauer in Moore's attraction to 'instinct' as an irrational and determining factor in our lives, and the pessimism such a deterministic view implies. But as I see it, for Moore 'instinct' represents our deepest, most unexplainable motivations, and not at all necessarily a capitulation to the universe and blind will. According to Rorty, 'Finding out about our unconscious motives is not just an intriguing exercise, but more like a moral obligation' ('Freud' 145). Unlike an earlier genera- tion, Moore and many of his decadent, and later modernist, contemporaries embraced this obligation – indeed, they exulted in it. Chance and instinct are not necessarily antithetical:

> Chance! What a field for psychical investigations is at once opened up; how we may tear to shreds our past lives in search of – what? Of the Chance that made us. ... Chance, or the conditions of life under which we live, sent, of course thousands of creatures across my way who were powerless to benefit me; but then an instinct of which I knew nothing, of which I was not even conscious, withdrew me from them, and I was attracted to others. (Moore 62)

Dayne uses both people and books as food for his self-creation – 'Books are like individuals,' he says (Moore 76), and after they have been 'digested' (Moore 62), he moves on to other sources of nourishment. 'To read freely, extensively, has always been my ambition,' says Dayne (Moore 101), but he also recognises that books cannot supply every need or satisfy every instinct: 'Contact with the world is in me the generating force; without it what invention I have is thin and sterile' (Moore 101). Rorty's ironists (who are also sometimes literary critics) likewise

> spend their time placing books in the context of other books, figures in the context of other figures. This placing is done in the same way as we place a new friend or enemy in the context of old friends and enemies. In the course of doing so, we revise our opinions of both the old and the new. We revise our own moral identity by revising our own final vocabulary. (*CIS* 80)

But importantly the moral influences of certain friends and certain books remain with us: 'the chance reading of a book' creates a far-reaching chain of consequences for Moore's narrator. 'Never shall I open these books again, but were I to live for a thousand years, their power in my soul would remain unshaken,' he says. '*I am what they made me*' (Moore 80; my emphasis).

Moore's stylistic experiments, his 'decadent' philosophy and his evolving self-presentations from young bohemian to man of letters to the sage of Ebury Street testify to an ongoing commitment to reinventing both himself and the genre that has come to be called 'life-writing' as Moore uses voices and styles from literary and art criticism, philosophy, the family saga, drama and the novel.[5] Yet if his entire career was a self-conscious ritual of aesthetic and intellectual sampling, it was not because he was a dilettante, nor simply because he was interested in wearing masks or adopting alternative identities. His autobiographical personae involve an ironic attitude towards his own life,[6] and in *Confessions*, especially, he asserts a Nietzschean commitment to the quest for self-creation through books, art and experience. At the same time, as I have suggested, *Confessions* accepts the role chance plays in our lives. This, too, is a peculiarly modern feeling: 'we are all too ready to forget that in fact everything to do with our life is chance,' according to Freud (quoted in Rorty *CIS* 31). Grubgeld argues persuasively that the narrator of *Confessions* must reject 'the concept of individual moral choice central to the ethics (and aesthetics) of Evangelical Protestantism. But he uses deterministic language in a way that supports the primacy of individual will' (Grubgeld 42). The novel begins, famously, with the presentation of a mutable and plastic self: 'I came into the world apparently with a nature like a smooth sheet of wax, bearing no impress, but capable of receiving any' (Moore 49). His 'self-will and an impetuous temperament' never lead the narrator astray, yet he admits he is capable of being 'moulded into all shapes' by the chances of life (Moore 49). For Grubgeld and Frazier, this contradictory position, basically a dialectic between determinism and freedom (Frazier 166), is close to Moore's own psychology. As I have noted, he liked Schopenhauer's idea of a person's being ruled by 'instinct', and acknowledged Schopenhauer's influence in the 1889 Preface.[7] Yet he also felt that whatever happened in his life had to be right, and he believed that one should never be ashamed of the way one's life turns out. To me, this does not necessarily suggest a deterministic view. If a person imposes symbolic significance on life's accidents, or sees a pattern or narrative in the contingencies of life, it may be self-deceiving, it may even justify cruelty or wantonness, but it also may be liberating, an important tool in constructing oneself and articulating one's values.[8] Freud has taught us that by

> seeing every human being as consciously or unconsciously acting out an idiosyncratic fantasy, we can see the distinctively human, as opposed to animal, portion of each human life as the use for symbolic purposes of every particular person, object, situation, event, and word encountered in later life. This process amounts to redescribing them, thereby saying of them all, 'Thus I willed it'. (Rorty *CIS* 36–7)

If Moore's *Confessions* moves between self-assertion and capitulation to fate it may be due less directly to Schopenhauer than to a writer's difficult experiments, in the 1880s and 1890s, in setting a Schopenhauerian vocabulary of instinct beside a Nietzschean vocabulary of will. Moore claimed in the 1904 Preface that although he wrote his novel before he read Nietzsche, the doctrine of Zarathustra 'though hardly formulated, is in the "Confessions," as Darwin is in Wallace' (Moore 41).[9] *Confessions* also anticipates the yet-to-be articulated Freudian vocabulary of the ego or the unconscious, as in Dayne's dialogue with Conscience (added to the 1889 French edition): 'Have I not drawn the intense ego out of the clouds of semi-consciousness, and realized it? And surely, the rescue and the individualization of the ego is the first step' (Moore 219). My point is that the whole method of *Confessions* reveals a person who accepts and enjoys the peculiarly modern task of comparing vocabularies and rescuing the ego. Moore links this task with Aestheticism because that movement represents a challenge to the ugliness, conformity and commercialism of Victorian society. Several critics have noted the connection between *Confessions of a Young Man* and Moore's campaign against the straitjacket imposed on writers by the conventions of Victorian publishers and the circulating libraries. For these reasons they see him as a subversive or political writer: David Weir says Moore's 'activism and aestheticism' encouraged literary modernism (102), Susan Dick claims that 'the reformer's social criticism goes hand in hand with the aesthete's claim to detachment' (11), and Douglas A. Hughes calls him 'a revolutionary writer' (v). It is certainly true that to Moore and many of his contemporaries Aestheticism represented social hope, the *refashioning of the world* into something better. To the unimaginative person, it seems 'monstrous' to 'expect to fashion the whole world into conformity with your aestheticisms ... a vain dream, and if realised it would result in an impossible world. A wife and children are the basis of existence, and it is folly to cry out because an appeal to such interests as these meets with response ... it will be so till the end of time' (Moore 111). Thus the imagined reply from the characterless bourgeois who is content with an existing vocabulary, with other people's plans for his life: 'it will be so till the end of time.' The truly radical nature of self-fashioning as an *ethical* position is that it can lead to world-fashioning, to utopian politics and the revision of social platitudes such as 'a wife and children are the basis of existence'. By the 1890s, people were beginning to appreciate the full implications of the movement (some might say this is among the reasons Wilde was destroyed); they were beginning to see that the aesthetes' turn towards literature and art had as much to do with radical ethical, social and political ideas as it did with hothouse flowers, wallpaper designs and erotic pictures. Holbrook Jackson wrote that by the 1890s people were convinced that they were 'passing not only from one social system to another, but from one morality to another, from one culture to another, and from one religion to a dozen or more' (31). I agree with Weir and Dick that *Confessions of a Young Man* is a potentially activist book, but it is one not only because of Moore's war on Mudie's. It is also an important text in its emphasis on playful self-construction as a legitimate ethical and even political position. The character Edward Dayne (or the author George Moore) is, to return to Rorty, a role model for ordinary people bent on their own private acts of self-creation in a liberal society. Writers make up new metaphors, tropes and redescriptions, so they remake the world anew, they keep demanding that people see the world, and their own lives, melioristically, involvedly, romantically. Louis Menand sums up this view: 'the activity of redescription in which the poet is engaged might be a paradigm of self-realization in a liberal regime in which private activities are pursued in the interest of one kind of fulfillment and public activities are pursued in interests of a different kind of fulfillment' (Menand 364). Thus Rorty, very much like George Moore and the aesthetes, wants a 'poeticized' culture (*CIS* 53). By this he means that liberal societies should shift attention away from Enlightenment values of reason and scientific rationalism toward areas that '*are* at the forefront of culture, those which excite the imagination of the young, namely, art and utopian politics' (*CIS* 52). There is anti-democratic language in *Confessions*, to be sure – ironic remarks opposing universal education (Moore 140), for example, and the recalcitrance of his Irish tenants (Moore 123, 181). But anything that aids in freeing the ideal self and assists the project of autonomy is championed; open and liberal institutions are preferred to the dull proprieties of the respectable villa or the cramped morality of the philanthropist. Thus the tavern is better than the club because it is more liberal: 'everyone can go to the tavern, and no place in England where everyone can go is considered respectable' (Moore 139). The music hall is hailed as 'the one thing in England that is free, that is spontaneous' (Moore 145) for 'the music hall is a protest against the villa, the circulating library, the club, and for this the 'all is inexpressibly dear to me' (Moore 147). Art in general is an 'outcry' against middle-class respectability and 'the life of the artist should be a practical protest against the so-called decencies of life' (Moore 139).

If vocabularies for ironists are 'tools rather than mirrors' (Rorty 'Freud' 158), the title that Moore chose for his book may have been meant to suggest a religious vocabulary, a disclosure of deviance, doubt, or sinfulness. 'St. Augustine,' wrote Moore in the 1889 Preface, 'wrote the story of a God-tortured soul; would it not be interesting to write the story of an art-tortured soul?' (Moore 35). The book indeed confesses a conversion through poetry from Christianity to paganism, from the world of 'lacerated saints and a crucified Redeemer' to 'a love of life and beauty' (Moore 78). The book is gleefully and irreverently secular, but it cannot be classed as a lubricious confession intended merely to shock and titillate – these are not the confessions of a sensualist, and indeed, Moore rejected the idea of using a picture of a young woman on the book's cover because it would be misleading: 'My confessions are purely literary,' he wrote (quoted. in Dick 1). Also, the narrator's egotism – his flaunting unorthodoxies and frank self-justifications – seem to undermine the self-disciplining impulse of confessional writing. The book is not humble, but accusatory:

> You sighed, O hypocritical friend, and you threw the magazine on the wicker table, where such things lie, and you murmured something about leaving the world a little better than you found it, and you went down to dinner and lost consciousness of the world in the animal enjoyment of your stomach. I hold out my hand to you, I embrace you, you are my brother, and I say, undeceive yourself, you will leave the world no better than you found it. The pig that is being slaughtered as I write this line will leave the world better than it found it, but you will leave only a putrid carcase fit for nothing but the grave. (Moore 179)

Moore's irony makes this passage tilt towards the comic, but it is still every bit as harsh as parts of *Sartor Resartus*! For Moore's narrator is boldly, deliberately free of shame. 'I am ashamed of nothing – I am a writer; 'tis my profession to be ashamed of nothing but to be ashamed,' he says to his Conscience (Moore 218). Unlike Wilde's remorseful self-searching in *De Profundis* (1905) or Edmund Gosse's poignant appraisal of his childhood and self-becoming in *Father and Son* (1907), Moore's confession is slanted for the reader by an ironic pose of shameless indecency, a pose he felt was necessary for anyone who takes a serious interest in literature – or in himself. In fact, Moore criticised Gosse's sensitive autobiography because he could not overcome 'that sense of decency, *which as a writer you should not have*' (quoted in Frazier 371). 'Decency' only inhibits the exuberant curiosity and individualisation necessary to a writer of the modern age. Moore consistently foregrounds an ethic of self-fashioning against a Kantian morality of categorical imperatives: individualisation is against duty, self-enlargement is against obedience, irony is against common sense, passion is against pity and philanthropy. For some sophisticated readers, and not just the librarians at Mudie's, this revisionist sensibility was more difficult to understand than Moore's formal inventiveness. Upon finishing *Confessions*, Walter Pater wrote to 'dear, audacious Moore' that he did not question the book's style or the author's literary faculty, but he did question his morality.[10]

Although Moore seems to embody the ironist's attitude of experimentation and self-invention, he sees the possibility of self-invention as itself contingent – a matter of accident or chance. His father's death, for example, when Moore is eighteen, is an event that frees him to begin the process of self-creation: 'no further need of being a soldier, of being anything but myself,' he says (Moore 53). 'His death gave me the power to create myself – that is to say, to create a complete and absolute self out of the partial self which was all that the restraints of home had permitted; this future self, this ideal George Moore, beckoned me, lured me like a ghost' (Moore 196). Moore seriously wonders who he would be if his father had not died – as he should. Pursuing an ideal self is not a plan of life available to everyone and, as Rorty claims, it cannot be guaranteed by or embodied in social institutions, even in liberal societies. 'Autonomy is not something that all human beings have within them and which society can release by ceasing to repress them. It is something which certain particular human beings hope to attain by self-creation, and which a few actually do' (Rorty *CIS* 65). *Confessions of a Young Man* dramatises this belief for certain particular modern people. The maid-of-all-work, Emma, may represent Moore's understanding of the contingencies of autonomous self-fashioning.

Life to Emma means being born in a slum, working seventeen hours a day, knowing nothing of London, being unable to read, eventually being thrown out of doors and taking to drink. 'There is no hope for you,' Moore writes (135) because a person like Emma, ignorant and poor, is simply unable to take an interest in herself. Moore's narrative imagination allows him to follow the trajectory of her depressing career (later more completely and more hopefully, perhaps, in *Esther Waters*), but Emma is not interested in where she comes from and how she will turn out – and taking an interest in oneself is what self-fashioning means, ethically and psychologically. That is why Moore taunts the 'hypocritical reader' whose moral superiority and cherished 'respectability' makes it impossible for her to recognise the urgent message of the book. 'This is a magical *tête-a-tête*,' he says, 'such a one as will never happen in your life again' (Moore 179). His hope rests in the young men who will read his book, young men with similar temperaments and yearnings: 'I yield my place, do you eat and drink as I have; do you be young as I was. I have written it!' (Moore 191). The future of a meaningfully free and liberal society rests not on a Kantian notion of moral imperatives, but on the self-creating abilities of the next generation.

If *Confessions of a Young Man* is a deliberate ethical performance, one that announces a new and important attitude towards the self as something malleable, shifting and rebellious, it is also a literary performance. The book initiates a new style, in *both* the literary and ethical senses; in fact, it is all style.[11] In *Decadence and the Making of Modernism*, David Weir argues that *Confessions* belongs to the new century rather than to the old precisely for formal reasons: 'The relative absence of conventionality; the lack of a clear generic identity; a varied and inventive style; a shifting, contradictory thematic focus; and a certain simple but invaluable documentary quality make Moore's *Confessions* an extremely malleable text – incomplete in itself, but a mine of possibility' (102). This generic and stylistic inventiveness unquestionably signals Moore's radical departure from the customs and proprieties of mid-Victorian fiction; but the text's malleability and incompleteness also perfectly parallel the narrator's idea of the self as an unfinished potentiality, a personality in the making. When working on *Confessions* Moore was 'living extravagantly through ceaseless self-invention, discovering and indulging all that made him himself. Moore was coming into a purely elective form of identity. He was not to be defined by where he was born, by schooling, by religious training, or even by the customs of his family' (Frazier 161). Yet in seeking this elective and ideal self, Moore, unlike other writers of the period, did not create an alternative self, he did not adopt a pseudonym, he did not merely construct an 'author function'.[12] He even mocks that pose in the description in *Confessions* of the 'enormous young man' who becomes a literary success and takes to speaking of the British public as 'B.P.' and of the magazine as 'the mag' (Moore 183). Instead, Moore asserted a contradictory, unruly, quasi-instinctive self, one both ironic and sincere, cynical and sentimental, fictional and autobiographical. Thus, as both Frazier and Grubgeld rightly point out, the enormous significance of Moore's instructions to remove the name 'Edward Dayne' from the title-page of *Confessions* and substitute 'George Moore' (Frazier 165–6; Grubgeld 52–63). 'With this stroke,' argues Frazier, 'autobiographical fiction became a fictionalised autobiography' (165). Moore's project thereby takes on more interest, in my view, for both the ethical and aesthetic entrepreneurs of late Victorian society, for he accepts as his own the perversity and foolishness of the character Edward Dayne while at the same time inventing a character who can be used as a model by readers seeking new vocabularies, new attitudes towards modern life.[13]

Confessions presents a challenge to the average person's concept of ethical conduct and of morality. There is certainly the deliberately transgressive rhetoric of sin, as in Dayne's delight in 'this long narrative of a sinful life' (Moore 179). And the narrator's exaggerated grief at the ascendancy of pity and justice in the modern world in Chapter 8, a satire of a certain pagan strain of the decadence, is a kind of 'echo-augury' (Moore 49) of Nietzsche's ambition to revalue all values. 'We are weary of pity, we are weary of being good,' he cries. 'We are weary of tears and effusions, and our refuge – the British Museum – is the wide sea shore and the wind of the ocean. There, there is real joy in the flesh; our statues are naked, but we are ashamed, and our nakedness is indecency' (Moore 126). In passages like this, Moore both mocks the decadent pose and affirms its commitment to be unashamed, to experiment with life.

But the book is also morally challenging and enlarging because it represents an historically important assertion of creative autonomy against 'the so-called decencies of modern life' (Moore 139), the habits of common sense and duty. Rorty argues that the 'metaphysical' view of morality 'is woven into the public rhetoric of modern liberal societies' (*CIS* 82). The rhetoric of these societies – and surely Victorian England was one – takes for granted that there are real essences, laws, or truths in the world which it is our duty to discover. Thus there is a firm distinction 'between the moral and the 'merely' aesthetic – a distinction which is often used to relegate 'literature' to a subordinate position within culture and to suggest that novels and poems are irrelevant to moral reflection' (*CIS* 82). Throughout *Confessions* the narrator has been seeking moral guidance through his instinctive likes and dislikes for certain novels and poems; he has been 'eager for some adequate philosophy of life' (Moore 54) and has gone to Shelley at first, then Gautier, Baudelaire, Pater and, most of all, Balzac for moral guidance and reflection (Moore 101). But these moral advisers provided him with no final set of guidelines. He falls in love with the symbolists, the naturalists, the realists, and each time he forgives himself for his infatuations. 'I do not regret my errors, my follies; it is not well to know at once the limitations of life and things. I should be less than nothing had it not been for my enthusiasms; they were the saving clause in my life' (Moore 97). Even when he feels he is a failure, in a marvellous piece of interior monologue – 'I can do nothing, nothing; my novel I know is worthless; my life is a weak leaf, it will flutter out of sight presently' (Moore 168) – he also says that he does not repent, he regrets nothing (Moore 180). And Moore, like Edward Dayne, lets stand his youthful missteps and reconsiderations because 'to withdraw them would be unmanly, unintellectual, and no one may re-write his confessions' (Moore 40).[14]

So it is fitting that at the end of *Confessions*, as he bids future readers to cultivate curiosity about their past, to find out who they want to be, the narrator sits at his table in the shabby London lodging-house, 'haggard and overworn' from his rigorous adventures, and recommences the writing of his novel (Moore 192). Having accepted that there is no one truth to the exclusion of other truths, no one book or literary movement to the exclusion of other books and literary movements, he commits himself to the task of creation in the ongoing effort to remake the world. And the young man remains as a model of individualisation: 'But can I do aught for this youth, does he need my supervision?' wrote Moore retrospectively in 1904. 'He was himself, that was his genius; and I sit and gaze' (Moore 37).

At one point, in a rather Freudian reflection, Moore comments, 'That I should have forgotten so much in ten years seems incredible, and it will be deemed impossible by many, but that is because few are aware of how little they know of the details of life, even of their own, and are incapable of appreciating the influence of their past upon their present. The visible world is visible only to a few, the moral world is a closed book to nearly all' (Moore 150). The narrator of *Confessions* accepts the opacity of reality and the inscrutability of the moral world; his task instead is to understand the influence of his past upon his present, and thereby fashion an ideal self out of 'the labyrinth of [his] desires' (Moore 49). This may be the ethos which, for better or worse, informs our understanding of literary modernism – and after.

Notes

1   Rorty, a pragmatist, has been a controversial philosopher among philosophers chiefly because of his rejection of such time-honoured philosophical pursuits as truth, reality and objectivity. Robert Brandom's 'Introduction' in *Rorty and His Critics* lays out the principal grounds of dispute (ix–xx). He has been better received among literature professors because of his view that literary criticism is more useful than philosophy, with its chain-dragging heritage of truth-seeking and absolutism. The promising thing about literary critics is that they can always change their interpretation of a text when they read another interpretation of the same text, or place the text beside other texts. Thus Rorty advocates 'ironists': people who play vocabularies against one another, who are good at redescribing situations, who are not interested in seeking a picture of reality or truth or goodness. Literary critics are better at redescription than philosophers, whose training has historically been on the scientific model of direct inquiry. I feel it is important to note that Rorty sees ironic self-fashioning as a private matter, unconnected with one's public or political responsibilities in liberal societies.
2   See, for example, Weir 102, 113–18; and Frazier 156–8. Graham Hough: 'I think it is likely that neither the title nor the contents of Joyce's *Portrait of the Artist as a Young Man* would have been quite the same in 1916 if it had not been for the prior existence of Moore's *Confessions of a Young Man* in 1886. And there are other resemblances [between Joyce and Moore] more strongly marked' (Hough 138).
3   For reviews and reactions to the book, see Frazier 163–5.
4   In *Irony's Edge: The Theory and Politics of Irony*, Linda Hutcheon explains the contradictions and nuances of irony and the different uses to which it is put (see especially pp. 1–57). Satire tends to use irony as a form of ridicule, but she points out that 'there is a wide tonal range possible' even when satire is meant as a corrective, 'from the playfully teasing to the scornful and disdainful' (53). Nevertheless, Hutcheon concludes that there is always an emotive aspect to ironic discourse. Moore was very sensitive to this affective dimension and worried about how the book would be understood in translation. 'If my translator is a young man you may tell him that the irony of the English disappears somewhat in the French. I achieve I think a lighter and more spirited phrase, and there is always the touch of exaggeration which the French fails to convey. In English I have my tongue in my cheek, in French I am deadly serious' (quoted in Dick 11).
5   Grubgeld deals with Moore's developing attitudes to autobiographical writing in great detail. According to Frazier, by 1905, 'he came to believe that what he did best was write autobiographically. ... his autobiographies

are fundamentally not falsifications of experience, but bold and writerly uses of it' (Frazier xv–xvi).

6 Grubgeld writes that Moore viewed 'his own life as an ironic action of a specifically parodic nature' (ix). Grubgeld's book is a scrupulous treatment of Moore's autobiographies and their relation to his construction of the autobiographical speaker.

7 Schopenhauer was the fashionable philosopher of the decadence, and he was an influence on Moore in the 1880s. In the 1889 Preface, he wrote, 'I owe much of my mind to Schopenhauer' (Moore 36).

8 Another philosopher, Alasdair MacIntyre, has argued for the importance of narrative in social formation, in identity and in ethics. In *After Virtue* MacIntyre explains that in classical mythology, in tragedy and in medieval quest tales human life was rendered intelligible when it was cast in 'the unity of a narrative which links birth to death' (206); MacIntyre offers the hypothesis that 'generally to adopt a stance on the virtues will be to adopt a stance on the narrative character of human life' (144). Some twentieth-century philosophers have challenged this paradigm; existentialism, for instance, sees the individual life as a series of random, unconnected episodes.

9 David Weir points out, however, that although Moore and James Joyce were temporarily infatuated with Nietzsche, his writings had no real consequences for their works (Weir 133–9). I am more interested in looking at how Nietzsche's emphasis on self-creation and youthful exuberance is displayed in the ethical development of Edward Dayne than I am in determining any direct influence Nietzsche's works may have had on Moore.

10 Pater wrote to Moore: 'Of course there are many things in the book I don't agree with. But then, in the case of so satiric a book, I suppose one is hardly expected to agree or disagree. – What I cannot doubt of is the literary faculty displayed. '"Thou com'st in such a questionable shape!" – I feel inclined to say, on finishing your book: "shape" – morally, I mean; not in reference to style' (quoted in Donoghue 75). Moore was so pleased with this letter he cited it in full in the 1904 Preface to the English edition of *Confessions*.

11 I am thinking of Nietzsche's use of 'style' as a self-conscious way of living one's life, so that the literary style of *Confessions* is one aspect of its ethical claim to self-fashioning, especially through cultivating an aesthetic temperament. Nietzsche wrote: 'To "give style" to one's character – a great and rare art! It is practised by those who survey all the strengths and weaknesses of their nature and then fit them in an artistic plan until every one of them appears as art and reason and even weaknesses delight the eye. Here a large mass of second nature has been added; there a piece of original nature has been removed – both times through long practice and daily work at it. ... For one thing is needful: that a human being should *attain* satisfaction with himself, whether it be by means of this or that poetry and art; only then is a human being at all tolerable to behold' (Nietzsche 232).

12 Frazier has a different view, explaining that Moore 'studiously elaborated a complex and developing identity for public consumption' (166). In his biography Frazier distinguishes between 'GM', the man who is the subject of the biography, and 'George Moore' the author.

13   This is why I think it is significant that Edward Dayne presents himself as an aesthete, an aspiring artist and writer, *and* a literary critic. Rorty: 'Ironists read literary critics and take them for moral advisors, simply because such critics have an exceptionally large range of acquaintance. They are moral advisors not because they have special access to moral truth but because they have been around. They have read more books ...' (*CIS* 80–1).

14   I read this as another of Moore's links with Nietzsche, and a more optimistic view of human life than that offered by Schopenhauer. See, for example, *The Gay Science*, pp. 273–4. In the introduction to his translation of that book, Walter Kaufmann writes: 'A modern poet has asked: "What still has weight?"' In his parable of the madman (section 125 [pp. 181–2]) Nietzsche suggests that during the Victorian era this question was not yet asked widely, but that before long the sense that whatever we do is of hardly any consequence will spread like a disease. This terrifying sense of weightlessness might be called *nihilism* ... Now it occurs to Nietzsche that the belief that whatever I do now I shall do again and again, eternally, may cure this weightlessness by becoming 'the greatest weight" (17–18). Moore's insistence that he is unashamed, without regrets, and will let stand what he has written in his confessions is something like Nietzsche's greatest weight, or 'Thus I willed it.'

Works cited

Brandom, Robert B., 'Introduction.' *Rorty and His Critics*. Ed. Robert B. Brandom. Oxford: Blackwell, 2000, pp. vii–xx.

Dick, Susan, 'Introduction'. *Confessions of a Young Man*. Ed. Susan Dick. Montreal: McGill-Queen's University Press, 1972, pp. 1–22.

Donoghue, Denis, *Walter Pater: Lover of Strange Souls*. New York: Knopf, 1995.

Frazier, Adrian. *George Moore 1852–1933*. New Haven: Yale University Press, 2000.

Grubgeld, Elizabeth, *George Moore and the Autogenous Self: The Autobiography and Fiction*. Syracuse: Syracuse University Press, 1994.

Harris, Frank, *Oscar Wilde*. 1916. East Lansing: Michigan State University Press, 1959.

Hughes, Douglas A., 'Introduction'. *The Man of Wax: Critical Essays on George Moore*. Ed. Douglas A. Hughes. New York: New York University Press, 1971, pp. v–xxvi.

Hutcheon, Linda, *Irony's Edge: The Theory and Politics of Irony*. London: Routledge, 1995.

Jackson, Holbrook, *The Eighteen Nineties*. 1913. New York: Capricorn Books, 1966.

Larson, Jil, *Ethics and Narrative in the English Novel, 1880–1914*. Cambridge: Cambridge University Press, 2001.

MacIntyre, Alasdair, *After Virtue*. Notre Dame: University of Notre Dame Press, 1984.

Menand, Louis, 'Pragmatism and Poets: A Response to Richard Poirier'. *The Revival of Pragmatism*. Ed. Morris Dickstein. Durham, NC: Duke University Press, 1999, pp. 362–9.

Moore, George, *Confessions of a Young Man*. Ed. Susan Dick. Montreal: McGill-Queen's University Press, 1972.

Nietzsche, Friedrich, *The Gay Science*. Trans. Walter Kaufmann. New York: Vintage, 1974.

Rorty, Richard, *Contingency, Irony, and Solidarity*. Cambridge: Cambridge University Press, 1989.

—— 'Freud and Moral Reflection'. *Essays on Heidegger and Others*. Cambridge: Cambridge University Press, 1997, pp. 143–63.

Weir, David, *Decadence and the Making of Modernism*. Amherst: University of Massachusetts Press, 1995.

6
Interstitial Identities: Vernon Lee and the Spaces In-Between

Hilary Fraser

> Beginnings and endings may be the sustaining myths of the
> middle years; but in the *fin de siècle*, we find ourselves in the
> moment of transit where space and time cross to produce
> complex figures of difference and identity, past and present,
> inside and outside, inclusion and exclusion.
>
> (Bhabha 1)

It is in the borderland of the century, that 'moment of transit' when
boundaries are at once so momentous and so permeable, that Homi
Bhabha, writing in 1994, locates those '"in-between" spaces' which
'provide the terrain for elaborating strategies of selfhood ... that initiate new signs of identity' (1). His definition at the end of the twentieth
century of the crucial historical conditions for the post-colonial intellectual project suggests interesting ways of framing a discussion of
subject formation at the turn of the previous century. Bhabha's insistence on the complex constellation of subject positions, 'of race,
gender, generation, institutional location, geopolitical locale, sexual
orientation', that inhabit any individual's claim to identity in the
modern world, and his exhortation to think 'beyond narratives of originary and initial subjectivities', rather than to focus 'on those moments
or processes that are produced in the articulation of cultural differences' (1), seem particularly pertinent to the case of one *fin-de-siècle*
figure, the art historian, essayist, aesthetician and fiction-writer Vernon
Lee (1856–1935). The paradigmatic 'in-between' identity for post-
colonialism is the diasporic subject. Stuart Hall writes of diasporic
peoples 'who have succeeded in remaking themselves and fashioning
new kinds of cultural identity by, consciously or unconsciously,

drawing on more than one cultural *repertoire'* (206) in ways that have both a literal and a metaphorical resonance for Vernon Lee, an Englishwoman born in France, who spent most of her life in Italy and wrote principally on Italian and British cultural history:

> They are people who belong to more than one world, speak more than one language ... inhabit more than one identity, have more than one home; who have learned to negotiate and translate between cultures, and who, because they are irrecoverably the product of several interlocking histories and cultures, have learned to live with, and indeed to speak from, *difference.* They speak from the 'in-between' of different cultures, always unsettling the assumptions of one culture from the perspective of another, and thus finding ways of being both *the same as* and at the same time *different from* the others amongst which they live. (Hall 206)

Whilst the privileged Vernon Lee, one of the colonising class of English in nineteenth-century Italy, can hardly be said to occupy the same ethnic and social position as those 'translated men (and women)' that Salman Rushdie describes in his essay in *Imaginary Homelands* (17), dispersed by diaspora and unable to return to their homelands, she does, like them, speak as an exile 'from the in-between of different cultures', speak 'from difference'. Moreover, her borderline condition, as a subject formed in the in-between *fin-de-siècle* moment of history as well as in the liminal spaces of geography, may be said to inform her displacement and re-inscription of other domains of difference. In the introductory chapter, 'Borderlines', of her book *Sexual Anarchy: Gender and Culture at the Fin de Siècle* (1990), Elaine Showalter focuses on sexual difference as 'one of the threatened borders of the *fin de siècle'* (4) in ways that are clearly relevant to Vernon Lee, whose adoption of a masculine style of dress (tailored black dresses with high Gladstone collars being her preferred mode), passionate friendships with women, literary explorations of androgyny and same-sex desire, and fashioning of a 'third sex' authorial identity disrupted the conventional sexual binary. In terms of her sexuality and her gendered self-construction also, then, Lee inhabited an identity that was fundamentally transgressive and relational, built across categories rather than bound by them.

This essay tracks Lee's mapping of the spaces in-between. It considers the ways in which those borderline negotiations that Bhabha sees as the defining characteristic of the *fin-de-siècle* moment may be said to produce and authorise a hybrid subjectivity 'in-between the designations of identity' (Bhabha 3) and to inform and define her intellectual work – in particular, her performative engagements, both independently and relatively, with history, visuality and modernity.

I

'Finally we arrive at Il Palmerino. We saw a *sibyl*, in a tailor-made black dress, vine-dresser's hat and apron, sowing seeds. It advanced – it was Vernon' (Field, 264). Thus begins the account in Michael Field's journal of the visit by Katherine Bradley and Edith Cooper in 1901 to the Italian home of Vernon Lee, where she lived with her 'bosom-friend' Clementine (Kit) Anstruther-Thompson in a house described as having 'like its mistress ... no central unity of purpose' (264). Throughout the passage, the visiting female poets – who were themselves by no means conventional as regards either their sexuality or their choice of authorial identity (being a lesbian couple, aunt and niece, who published collaboratively under the signature 'Michael Field') – describe their hosts in such a way as to suggest connections between their cross-cultural and transsexual positionality. The fact that these 'immense tailor-made women' (264) fit no more comfortably into this rural Italian scene than they do into conventional female dress, whether middle-class English or Italian peasant, is suggested by the fact that their huge sheep dog gets into a fight with the dog of a neighbour, identified as 'Vernon's great enemy' (264). The 'dominant long back of Anstruther', herself characterised as 'a splendid example of the thorough-bred English woman', is described as looming over the combatants 'like the leaning tower of Pisa' (264), while after the dog fight Vernon calls the cowering poets into the house for dinner in 'a voice, cool as a man's' (265).

I offer this vignette of Vernon Lee in Italy as a way of entering a discussion of how her transgressive authorial and sexual identity might be seen to articulate with her cross-cultural identity. Lee was born Violet Paget on 14 October 1856, at Château Saint Léonard near Boulogne, the only child of her mother's second marriage. Her father, Henry Fergusen Paget, was the son of a French émigré nobleman and an English woman, and was brought up in Warsaw and Petersburg; her mother, who had been raised and educated in England but went to live in France as an adult, was the daughter of a wealthy businessman born in Kingston, Jamaica of an old-established colonial family. In a letter to Kit Anstruther-Thompson, Vernon Lee ironically describes her mixed ancestry, refusing – indeed mocking – a romantic narrative of origins for herself: 'Oh no, I am not descended from the "Kings of England till Edward III, the Counts of Flanders and Hainault, and *many* Kings of France" – I fear – only from a few inhuman and often rather drunken Jamaican planters, who have left me this bad constitution' (quoted in Gunn 15).

If Violet Paget's family background and complicated national and cultural inheritance formed the basis of an unusually multicultural identity, this was compounded by her continental upbringing. The young Violet led a nomadic existence with her family, who shifted constantly from one European location to another throughout her childhood, until they finally settled on Florence, moving in 1889 to the Villa Il Palmerino at nearby Maiano, where she was to live until her death in 1935. As the English girl moved between Nice, Paris, Thun, Rome, and numerous other European centres, and was, as she later wrote, brought up as a German child on Teutonic romance and sentiment by a series of governesses she describes as a 'dim procession of Germania's daughters' (quoted in Gunn 29), it became harder than ever to fix her national identity. She was later to write in her volume *The Sentimental Traveller*, 'We shifted our quarters invariably every six months, and, by dint of shifting, crossed Europe's length and breadth in several directions', with the result that 'my friends, even the nearest and dearest, imagine me to have been born and brought up in a gypsy-cart, at any rate metaphorically' (quoted in Gunn 27, 25).

It is hardly surprising, then, that she was, in terms of her social, national and cultural identity, hard to place. Although Bernard Shaw described her as 'English of the English' (quoted in Gunn 2), her biographer, Peter Gunn, notes that 'Among the English society in which she moved the difference in her upbringing was marked not only by the slightly foreign precision of her vocabulary and intonation but also by the frequent use of gesture, particularly Italian in its graceful appropriateness or in its vehemence, when reinforcing a point' (90). For Maurice Baring, 'She opened and stimulated the mind more than any English person or than any person, however cultivated, who has always lived in England could have done' (Baring 87). He wrote admiringly of her cosmopolitan sensibility and linguistic mastery: 'She has always understood the finer shades of Italian feeling, and German and French feelings as well. She speaks French like a Frenchwoman of the seventeenth century, so a Frenchman said to me one day, and it is always a great pleasure to me to listen to her unhesitating, forcible, direct Italian. Indeed her Italian is just as nervous as, and sometimes less complicated than, her English' (89). In short, Vernon Lee was like her own mother, of whom her close friend Mme Duclaux declared, 'one could never think of her as wholly French or wholly English – "she came from Cosmopolis"'(quoted in Gunn 18–19).

To what extent did being hard to place lead to a sense of displacement, a consciousness of alienation and exile, of the 'unhomely' (which, for Bhabha, though 'a paradigmatic colonial and postcolonial condition', has broader historical and cultural resonances [Bhabha 9])? Gunn notes that 'In England Vernon Lee never found herself completely at home' and felt that her 'sympathies were too international to be acceptable even to the least insular among her English friends', quoting from a letter written in 1900 in which she describes how 'with Mabel Price I am actually treated as an alien and barely an acquaintance by her people ... I fancy all expatriated people, and perhaps all really independent ones are apt to pay this price'. And from another written from Europe to Kit in which she explains, 'It's funny, though I feel so much more English than anything else (in fact only English) I cannot feel well in body or mind save on this sufficiently big and sufficiently aired and warmed continent' (Gunn 167–8). She writes about 'the English' not as one of them, but as an observer. Of Oscar Wilde, for example, whom she met in 1881, she writes to her mother, 'I think the creature is clever, and that a good half of his absurdities are mere laughing at people', adding, 'The English don't see that' (quoted in Gunn 78). Elsewhere she opines, 'These English have no more imagination than pint pots' (quoted in Gunn 123). And yet she was similarly out of place on the Continent. The Marchesa Medici, who knew her in her youth, recalls Miss Paget as 'a very distinct and peculiarly outstanding figure of the Florence of our young days' (quoted in Gunn 172). And when we read her descriptions of her bicycling expeditions in the countryside around Rome in the 1890s, of hurtling down steep hills in 'an annihilation of both space and time' (Lee *Spirit of Rome* 47), a rather extraordinary manifestation of the New Woman in rural Italy, it is clear that she must have cut a striking figure.

II

What I would like to suggest is that the consciousness of her cultural hybridity, of 'being in-between', is fundamental to Vernon Lee's self-construction and becomes a defining feature of her writing on art, place, cultural history and aesthetics. It is not insignificant that she wrote a volume with the title *Limbo*, for it is a condition and a trope to which she regularly alludes. 'I am usually in two places at a time,' she confesses in *Limbo* (60), and the urgency of her need to delineate her complex and bipartisan relationship to place may suggest that it stands in for other, perhaps unspeakable subject positions. Some 'in-between' identities were easier to articulate for this unconventional, but by all accounts rather proper Victorian woman, than others. Although she had a series of passionate attachments to other women, and affected a severely tailored style of dress, she did not seek notoriety through brazen defiance of contemporary notions of womanhood as some women of the times did, by flaunting their lesbian intimacy and dressing in shirt fronts and bow ties. Indeed, one acquaintance describes the particular form her androgyny took in terms of her being 'less like a girl and woman than like a marvellous brain clothed as a woman' (quoted in Gunn 174). Therefore, we might expect any expression of her sexuality to be coded. Her adoption of a pseudonym which, while not decisively masculine, was not feminine, when at the age of twenty-one she began to publish in the British periodical press, appears to have been for pragmatic reasons. Her awareness of the sexual politics of authorship is revealed in a letter to a friend in the following year: 'I don't care that Vernon Lee should be known to be myself or any other young woman, as I am sure that no one reads a woman's writing on art, history or aesthetics with anything but unmitigated contempt' (quoted in Gunn 9). Nevertheless, considered in conjunction with other instances of her self-fashioning as a person who inhabits an 'in-between' subject position, her choice of pseudonym suggests that she was required to negotiate not only the gender politics of publishing and marketing herself as a writer, but more profound issues of authorial and personal identity.

Lee's transgressive self-construction, I propose, profoundly affected her representation of art and its histories. Martha Vicinus has recently pointed out that, in the final decades of the nineteenth century, 'A refashioned past ... signalled both learning and an imaginative space where the lesbian imagination might flourish' (Vicinus 91). In Richard Dellamora's collection of essays *Victorian Sexual Dissidence* (1999) both she and Kathy Psomiades explore some of the ways in which 'women drew on the tactics of same-sex desire in male cultural production in order to (re)present women beyond the limits of the bourgeois sexual economy' (Dellamora 8). Psomiades in fact writes about Vernon Lee specifically, finding in her anti-aestheticist novel *Miss Brown* (1884) and in her later collaborative work with Clementina Anstruther-Thompson, 'Beauty and Ugliness' (1897) and *Art and Man* (1924), a re-gendering of aestheticism and a linking of aesthetic experience to desire between women.

We may find such tendencies even in Lee's earliest work. Whilst lesbian desire does not manifest itself directly in *Studies of the Eighteenth Century in Italy* (1880) as it does in these later texts, I suggest that in this her first book, published just four years before the novel in which she tackles both aestheticism and dissident sexuality head-on, she rehearses these themes: in her appropriation of a Paterian vocabulary to conjure a 'delicate and diaphanous' (Lee *Studies* 122), feminised eighteenth century (recalling the 'diaphanous' qualities of Pater's Winckelmann, whose affinity with Hellenism and the 'sexless beauty' of Greek statues was explicitly identified as 'not merely intellectual' [Pater 220, 191]); in her interest in cross-dressing and cross-gender performances, and in unconventional sexual relationships; and above all in her relish for the extravagant performance culture of eighteenth-century Italy, which provided Violet Paget with a stage for her first book-length performance of her self-fashioned sexually indeterminate authorial identity as Vernon Lee. And in fiction published after *Miss Brown*, most notably her first published collection of supernatural tales, *Hauntings*, which appeared in 1890, Lee quite explicitly represents figures 'of doubtful sex' (to borrow Pater's suggestive phrase from his essay on 'Leonardo Da Vinci' [115]) and same-sex desire: a *castrato* singer of the eighteenth century, with a 'sensual, effeminate face', whose singing 'no woman had ever been able to resist' (Lee *Leaves* 207, 202), and who returns to haunt a modern Wagnerian (read 'masculine') composer; and a series of androgynous tempters, powerful historical seductresses and returning gods in exile (such as the mysterious Venus Aphrodite figure Dionea, a reincarnation in female form of Dionysus, whom Lee was later to describe as 'a seducer of women, though little more than a woman himself' [Lee 'Dionysus' 349]), women who symbolise what Catherine Maxwell terms the 'female sublime' (260–7).

In her memorial essay for Pater, 'Dionysus in the Euganean Hills' (1921), Lee meditates on the Heineian theme of 'The Gods in Exile' that so fascinated Pater, and which she herself appropriated and feminised, in ways that have resonance for my own argument: 'Exile like this, implying an in-and-out existence of alternate mysterious appearance and disappearance is ... a kind of haunting' (Lee 'Dionysus' 348). The exiled state of the returning gods, forever condemned to an 'in-and-out' existence, articulates with their sexual indeterminacy, and is oddly suggestive of Lee's interstitial condition, of the hybrid, *becoming* identity she fashions for herself that is not conceived as originary and fixed, but forever in process. In the final pages of the 'Leaves from a Diary' which she collected into a volume entitled *The Spirit of Rome* in 1906, she writes, 'Yesterday morning, while looking through, with a view to copying out, my Roman notes of the last eighteen years, I felt, with odd vividness, the various myselfs who suffered and hoped while writing them' (Lee 204). One of the notes Vernon Lee wrote in her Roman diary was, 'Went to take the English seeds to the gardener at S. Saba, and got in return some plants of border pinks' (Lee *Spirit of Rome* 104). Given her interest in the symbolic possibilities of gardens (she published a volume of essays entitled *Hortus Vitae: Essays on the Gardening of Life*, taking her epigraph from *Candide*), such herbaceous negotiations are suggestive of the cultural exchanges and cross-fertilisation of ideas that are such a feature of her work.

Her very earliest writings reveal her preoccupation with perspective and difference, and with the culturally foreign. She had a lifelong interest in the concept of 'foreignness' that is woven into the very texture of her essays, fiction and cultural criticism, and is symptomatic, I suggest, not only of her own cultural positionality as a 'foreigner' in Italy and England, but of her intellectual positionality as a female intellectual in the business of defining culture, who speaks, as a foreigner, from difference. Her writing arguably participates in wider discourses about gender, hybridity and difference, providing avenues for and legitimising her exploration and articulation of the foreign. She maintained 'that we all of us are the better, of whatever nationality (and most, perhaps, we rather too too solid Anglo-Saxons) for some fusion of a foreign element, correcting our deficiencies and faults, and ripening (as the literature of the Italians ripened our Elizabethans) our own intrinsic qualities' (quoted in Gunn 28). The eponymous heroine of her novel *Miss Brown* (1884), half-Scottish and half-Italian by birth, with Moorish blood thrown in, and having lived all her life in Italy, is decidedly 'better' than the English with whom she associates for her 'foreignness'. She is also a woman with conspicuously masculine presence: her features are 'monumental' (her nose 'massive, heavy', her lips 'thick, and of curiously bold projection and curl', her neck 'round and erect like a tower', and her chest, again, 'massive' [Lee *Miss Brown* 1: 24–5]). It is my contention that Lee's interest in the foreign and the hybrid, and her own occupation of in-between cultural and sexual territories, inflect her ways of seeing and her writing about history, art and place in fundamental and defining ways.

III

In an essay 'On Modern Travelling' in the volume *Limbo* Lee remarks on the rapturous response of foreign tourists to the sights which locals take for granted. 'There is no doubt that wandering about in the haunts of the past undisturbed by the knowledge of the present is marvellously favourable to the historic, the poetical emotion,' she wryly observes:

> The American fresh from the States thinks of Johnson and Dickens in Fleet Street; at Oxford or Cambridge he has raptures (are any raptures like these?) into which, like notes in a chord and overtones in a note, there enters the deliciousness, the poignancy of Chaucer, Shakespeare, Milton, Turner.
>
> The Oxford or Cambridge man, on the other hand, will have similar raptures in some boarding-house at Venice or Florence; raptures rapturous in proportion almost to his ignorance of the language and the people. Do not let us smile, dear friends, who are Romans yourselves, at the foreigner with his Baedeker, turning his back to the Colosseum in his anxiety to reach it, and ashamed as well as unable to ask his way. That Goth or Vandal, very likely, is in the act of possessing Rome, of making its wonder and glory his own, consubstantial to his soul; Rome is his for the moment. (Lee *Limbo* 103)

The awkwardness of the construction 'Do not let us smile, dear friends, who are Romans yourselves', as she moves from the first to the third person, suggests the ambiguity of Lee's own relationship to Rome, a city in which she was particularly conscious of being 'in-between', in more senses than one. As she tries to convey her sense of Rome as the repository of its own rich past, she evokes an extraordinary sense of history in process in this 'organic city' (Lee *Limbo* 44), not least of her own place, in the present, in limbo between the past and the future, of 'all of us, bringing our absurd modernnesses, our far-fetched things of civilisation into the solemn, starved, lousy, silent Past! (Lee *Limbo* 129). From the perspective of the present, she observes:

> It helps one to conceive the fact that life comes everywhere out of death and subdues it; to feel that, as there are centuries in the Past, so there will be centuries and centuries in the Future. It helps the imagination with its remnants of old, used-up theatre scenes, to

guess at all the scene-shifting that will be accomplished, and to take its stand, be it only in the emotion of an instant, as witness of the vague phantasmagoria of the future. (Lee *Limbo* 101)

Always striking is the modernity of Vernon Lee's conceptualisation of history, of her keen awareness of the fact that perceptions of the past are culturally positioned, and that history is a construction, 'only a creation of the present' (Lee *Spirit of Rome* 142). Furthermore, her approach to history, like her experience of art, is framed by a consciousness of visuality that is also distinctively modern in its sceptical questioning of referential fidelity and its ironist awareness of simulation. Indeed, her visual imagination may be said to have shaped her view of Italy and its history, as when she writes of Rome that it is 'a theatre of the ages; a gigantic stage, splendidly impressive to eye and fancy, where Time has strutted and ranted' (Lee *Spirit of Rome* 41–2); that it is a location that 'is all theatre scenes; marvellous *coup d'œils*, into which, advancing (from the Capitol) from opposite the Palatine palms, from the Lateran steps, from the Tiber quays, you find nothing *to go on with*; and in so far it fits, it symbolises, perhaps, its own history – for what is history but a series of such admirable theatrical views; mere delusion. And behind them prose, mere prose?' (Lee *Spirit of Rome* 115–16)

Vernon Lee's observer status regarding Italy and its history and art is, I suggest, determined by her hybrid cultural positionality, which marks her writing about Italian history and art as something between the real and the imaginary that she can reach and touch across time, can mediate and resurrect for the present. We might take as an example her first book, *Studies of the Eighteenth Century in Italy* (1880), written when she was twenty-four. She describes how, as a child, she imaginatively entered and 'really did live in' the eighteenth century; how she 'began to see only the things belonging thereunto; and ... had little or no connection with anything else'. 'The eighteenth century,' she writes, 'existed for me as a reality, surrounded by faint and fluctuating shadows, which shadows were simply the present. Things presented themselves to me only from their eighteenth-century side, real or – very often – imaginary' (Lee *Juvenilia*). *Studies of the Eighteenth Century in Italy*, the fruit of this Orlando-like eighteenth-century reincarnation, is fascinating for its exploration of the unstable boundaries and secret passages between the present and the past, the real and the imaginary, history and art, England and Italy, as well as, like *Orlando* itself, between the masculine and the feminine. Lee describes the moment of eighteenth-century scholarship at which she writes as a pivotal time, when

> The men and things of the Italian eighteenth century have not yet been exhumed and examined and criticised and classified; they have not yet been arranged, properly furbished and restored, like so many waxwork dolls decked in crumbling silk and lace, like so many pretty, quaint, or preposterous knick-knacks in the glass cases of our historical museum.

A citizen of the great age of museum culture notwithstanding, Lee sees a fleeting opportunity to insert herself into the genealogy of eighteenth-century Italy. She continues:

> An old book of cantatas of Porpora, an old volume of plays of Carlo Gozzi, does not affect us in the same manner as a darkened canvas of Titian or a yellowed folio of Shakespeare; these latter have passed through too many hands, been looked at by too many eyes, they retain the personality of none of their owners. But the volume of Gozzi's plays was probably touched last by hands which had clapped applause to Truffaldino-Sacchi or Pantalone-Darbes; the notes in the book of cantatas may last have been glanced over by singers who had learned to sing them from Porpora himself. (293–4)

We have never known the people of the eighteenth century, she says, 'but we have met occasionally men and women who have': the lady 'whose hand, which pressed ours, had pressed the hand of Fanny Burney', and the old musician 'who had sung with boyish voice to Cimarosa and Paisiello those airs which he hummed over for us in faint and husky tones' (294). It is this intense desire for tactile contact with a past world only just out of reach, for the faintest echo of performances which can never again be heard, before its men and women are 'exhumed, restored, put into glass cases and exhibited mummy-fashion in our historical museums' (295) that defines the particular quality of Lee's extraordinary study, from its first page to its last.

But if such writing speaks of an authorial identity suspended between the past and the present, it may also, and relatedly, be said to be framed by the intellectual moment of modernity at which she wrote. There is much in Vernon Lee's prose to support Jonathan Crary's argument in *Techniques of the Observer* about the convergence of 'realism' and 'subjective vision' in the nineteenth century (Crary

Techniques 9), and indeed his broader thesis about the relation between new technologies of vision and ways of seeing seems pertinent to the techniques of conjuration and illusion used by Lee to view the past. She is clearly entranced by the eighteenth century as spectacle, as her many luscious descriptions of carnival and other theatrical pleasures attest, and again and again in *Studies in the Eighteenth Century in Italy* she moves from meticulously observed realistic description to an imaginary scene: passing through the familiar 'rusty gates of the melancholy suburban gardens' she so often walks by, through the 'vast half-furnished entrance', and into a reanimated eighteenth-century Villegiatura, where Giacinta and Lelio whisper 'behind yonder screen', Ferdinando shuffles cards 'on yonder green baize', and Signor Filippo enters through the folded gilded doors calling out, '"What, children! No one playing, no one eating, no one drinking?"' (264); following a resuscitated Goldoni across St Mark's Square, repopulated with an eighteenth-century crowd of masked revellers, gorgeously bedecked nobles, gamblers and painted women, into the narrow streets of the *Merceria*, and thence to the distant wharves and remoter canals, and calling his favourite gondolier, Menego Cainello, to steer her through the remotest Venetian islands, across the shallow open lagoon to the fishing town of Chiozza (265–7). In a prose version of the kind of illusion-generating optical gadgetry that proliferated in the nineteenth century, Lee achieves a *trompe l'oeil* effect. The shift of which Crary writes from the two-dimensional world defined by the camera obscura to the scopic regime of modernity shapes the historical imaginary. 'Is it a reality?' she asks. 'Has Menego rowed us over the lagoon? ... Have we really witnessed this incident of fishing life on the Adriatic?' 'No,' she confesses, 'we have only laid down a little musty volume, at the place marked "Le Baruffe Chizzotte"' (268).

Lee exemplifies in her aesthetic practice, and later theorises in her work on psychological and physiological aesthetics, the psychology and aesthetics of attention that Jonathan Crary has identified as the decisive issue for modern Western theorists of perception in the final two decades of the nineteenth century.[1] Crary titles his book on attention, spectacle and modern culture *Suspensions of Perception*, a formulation which ambiguously suggests at once 'the state of being suspended, a looking or listening so rapt that it is an exemption of ordinary conditions, that it becomes a suspended temporality, a hovering out of time' (Crary *Suspensions* 10) and its interruption. Both senses of 'suspension' may be found in Lee's work, and again *Studies in the Eighteenth Century in Italy* may serve as an example.

The historian of film Tom Gunning has written of a formative technology of 'attraction' at work in the development in the late 1880s and 1890s of a modernised mass visual culture. His discussion of the strategies of early film throws light on Lee's tactics for engaging the attention of her audience: 'From comedians smirking at the camera, to the constant bowing and gesturing of conjurers in magic films, this is a cinema that displays its visibility, willing to rupture a self-enclosed fictional world for a chance to solicit the attention of the spectator' (Gunning 57). Writing of the fairy plays of Carlo Gozzi, Lee observes that they must be, in modern times, 'completed ... by the fancy of the reader' (Lee *Studies* 283). She engages the fancy of the reader of her own book through the kinds of devices and theatricalities identified by Gunning. Again, it is an 'in-between' position that she occupies. Her principal strategy is to reconstruct a particular eighteenth-century individual through whose eyes we may view the period, or whose own history exemplifies something of its characteristics and preoccupations. Italy's music, for example, is approached by way of the published journal of Dr Charles Burney, father of Fanny Burney, which chronicles his musical tour through France and Italy in 1770 (68). '[L]et us try and place ourselves in the position of Burney,' suggests Lee, 'of this intelligent, cultivated, and enlightened traveller of the eighteenth century' (79–80). Roland Barthes' 'realistic effect' is everywhere enacted in her account of the experiences of this 'perfect representative of the educated traveller of the eighteenth century' (81). We watch Dr Burney 'Stepping out of the little cheap theatre' and finding 'music again in the streets' (89); taken by a chance acquaintance to a dilettante concert in a private house and 'introduced into the trim little parlour as a distinguished foreigner ... The company would rise and look with awe at the stranger (perhaps a *milordo* – who knows? – are not the English the most eccentric of beings?), the hostess would meet him, curtsey ...' (90).

Yet at the same time Lee's frequent reflections on her own writing practice, and her frank authorial interventions, refuse to naturalise the telling of history as anything other than a narrative which she can manipulate at will. At one point, for example, she interjects,

> According to a bad but invincible tendency of which the reader may often have to complain, we have taken the opportunity of discussing the church music of the eighteenth century in general, when there was no occasion to speak of any save the trifling performances which Dr. Burney attended; keeping our traveller waiting, standing in some dull little church listening to mediocre music. (85)

And later, having digressed once more from her reconstruction of Burney's experience of Italy to talk about eighteenth-century singers, and her own discovery of Gasparo Pacchierotti's house and garden, she recalls herself to the past of which she is meant to be writing: 'Whither have our fancies carried us? The garden at Padua, the harpsichord, the portrait – are none of them present. Pacchierotti, so far from being a mere faint recollection, is as yet a scarcely noticed reality, an obscure youth with undivined talents. Dr. Burney has never yet heard his name' (122). Such disarming self-commentary designedly foregrounds the fact that she is not only reconstructing but constructing a period; that this is not a transparent window onto the past, but a narrative, the chronological handling of which the author is in control, and in which the very idea of what constitutes 'the past' is unstable, inevitably determined by and imbricated in similarly unstable notions of 'the present'. Through such interventions, she establishes her position in the spaces in-between the reader and the text, the spectator and the spectacle.

IV

For Vernon Lee, vision itself is located on the borderlands – of the physiological and the ontological, of the sensory and the psychological – as is clear from her descriptive and critical writing as well as from her theoretical essays into physiological and psychological aesthetics (Fraser; Maltz). She hankers after 'the delightful semi-obscurity of vision and keenness of fancy of our childhood' (Lee *Juvenilia* 96), and often in her writing vision shades into fancy. For example, visiting Rome in 1902, she looks down from her hotel window, as from a theatre box, at the archaeological excavations in the Forum. She is led from the literal to the metaphorical, and from a particular perspectival view to wholly imaginary vistas:

I look down on a sort of mediæval city of the Trastevere – upon a still stranger imaginary one made by perspective and fancy; the old bridge, with its two double *hermes* leading between towers, and the long prison-like walls of the inland buildings, into an imaginary square – an imaginary city with more towers, more Romanesque belfries. This is a case of the imaginary place due to perspective, to bird's eye view, to some reminiscence. ... This case is an illustration of how large a part illusion, even recognised as such, plays in our feeling.

And similarly as regards the *invisible* view. Here am I, in a house nesting in the theatre of Marcellus, the little orange and lemon garden presumably built actually on to those remaining black arches. (Lee *Spirit of Rome* 123–4)

Lee enters into Rome's multi-layered, dismantled and refabricated history through the ruined archways laid bare before her very eyes, again creating *trompe l'oeil* effects in her own writing. She insists that '*seeing* is a business of the mind, the memory and the heart, quite as much as the eye' (quoted in Charteris 251). That seeing is indeed for Lee 'a business of' the synergy of mind and body, of vision informed by imagination and feeling, is clear not only from her aesthetic experiments with Kit Anstruther-Thompson, but from her *genius loci* essays and critical writings. When she tries to define 'the specially Tuscan mood' (Lee *Laurus Nobilis* 181) for instance, it is in terms of vision and perspective. She describes how, in this country of hills and plains,

there is always a view, definite and yet very complex, made up of every variety of line, but always of clearest perspective: perfect horizontals at one's feet, perfect perpendiculars opposite the eye, a constant alteration of looking up and looking down, a never-failing possibility of looking *beyond*, an outlet everywhere for the eye, and for the breath; and endless intricacy of projecting spur and engulfed ravine, of valley above valley, and ridge beyond ridge; and all of it, whether definitely modelled by stormy lights or windy dryness, or washed to mere outline by sunshine or mist, always massed into intelligible, harmonious, and ever-changing groups. Ever changing as you move, hills rising or sinking as you mount or descend, furling or unfurling as you go to the right or to the left, valleys and ravines opening or closing up, the whole country altering, so to speak, its attitude and gesture as quickly almost, and with quite as perfect consecutiveness, as does a great cathedral when you walk round it. And, for this reason, never letting you rest; keeping *you* also in movement, feet, eyes and fancy. Add to all this a particular topographical feeling, very strong and delightful, which I can only describe as seeing all the kingdoms of the earth. In the high places close to Florence (and with that especial lie of the land everything is a *high place*) a view is not only of foregrounds and backgrounds, river troughs and mountain lines of great variety, but of whole districts – distant peaks making you feel the places at their feet – which you know to be extremely various. (Lee *Laurus Nobilis* 182)

Vernon Lee's fascination with the conditions and the mechanics of vision as a dynamic exchange between observer and observed informs her art criticism. It shapes her discussion of the art of the Impressionists, for example, whom she believes to 'have done more for us by the beauty they have taught us to see in Nature than by the beauty they have actually put before us in their pictures'. She finds, in fact, 'in recent landscape, a preoccupation of technical methods and an indifference to choice of subject, above all, a degree of insistence on what is *actually seen*', a 'terrible over-importance of the act of vision', which is 'doubtless the preparation for a new kind of landscape, which will employ these arduously acquired facts of colour and light, this restlessly renovated technique, in the service of a new kind of sentiment and imagination' (Lee *Limbo* 56). And her interest in ways of seeing also underwrites her stress on the crucial role of the observer of art, on the history and experience of spectatorship. As she contends in *Limbo*, 'the life of all art goes on in the mind and heart, not merely of those who make the work, but of those who see and read it'. 'Nay,' she adds, 'is not *the* work, the real one, a certain particular state of feeling, a pattern woven of new perceptions and impressions and of old memories and feelings, which the picture, the statue or poem, awakens, different in each different individual? (Lee *Limbo* 59).

Maurice Baring wrote of Vernon Lee's magical ability to make one see: 'She lent you a magical glass, like that I read about long ago in an old fairy tale, where an astrologer gave a fairy prince a glass in which he was to look at the stars to find the one bright particular star that was to guide him to the home of an imprisoned princess' (Baring 90). Baring's image of the 'magical glass' leads me to one final example of Lee's interest in the mechanics and the metaphorics of visual experience which seems to capture what I have been attempting to argue about her construction of a cross-cultural, intersubjective identity as an observer and cultural commentator. At the turn of the century, Vernon Lee paid a visit to Patrick Geddes' Outlook Tower on Castlehill in Edinburgh with its camera obscura. As the modern guide explains it, Geddes bought the tower in 1892, and named it thus because he wanted to change people's outlook, using the camera 'to show them life as a whole and the interaction between town and country. ... After seeing the Camera visitors sat in a darkened meditation room – the inlook room – to internalise what they had learned and make it their own. Then visitors went down through the tower – descending through the Edinburgh Room, then down to exhibitions about Scotland, Empire, Europe and finally the World.'[2]

Vernon Lee was spellbound by the Tower, which she named 'The Tower of the Mirrors' and compared to Virgil's tower with its mirrors 'whereby you could see whatever happened in the world's length and breadth' (Lee *The Tower of the Mirrors* 1). She wrote a fascinating essay on it entitled 'The Tower of the Mirrors', and made it the title chapter of a collection of essays exploring some of the themes the Tower suggested to her, interestingly reappropriating the camera obscura, which for Jonathan Crary is paradigmatic of an earlier visual regime that was displaced in the 1820s and 1830s by radically different models of the observer, for modernity, and identifying it with contemporary art practice (Crary *Techniques* 25–66; Lee *The Tower of the Mirrors*, 4–5). First she describes the specular experience itself, and how

> You gradually recognize that what you are gazing down onto is, of all unlikely things, a piece of sky overhead ... But that this thing which is beneath you, and which is at the same time the sky, can also be the sea, becomes apparent only after a far stranger thing has suddenly become visible, throwing its dark jags across the mirror ... It is indeed the inside of a town; roofs looked down upon along their steepness; racks of chimneys, and a wide shining gulf, across which hurry black spots, which are men and women. Men and women! And the gulf is the great castle-terrace, wet with a passing shower, and the whole mediaeval town like the tail of St. George's slain dragon, winding down from it. ... The sea reappears; headlands and rocks. The town has vanished, and hilltops have slid into view, bare, like tops of Alpine passes, misty green after the plum-colour and orange of tiles and slate. The hills subside, and there is nothing once more but weltering cloud with rifts of blue and sudden crape of wind-driven rain. (Lee *The Tower of the Mirrors* 1–3)

Patrick Geddes would surely have been gratified for his camera obscura to be experienced by such a responsive subject. She then descends through the exhibitions of globes, the 'models showing what we should see were the earth to become transparent and display the continents and seas beneath our feet', the geological relief maps, and, after being taken to the centre of the earth, everywhere the signposts to its furthest reaches, showing that 'Alongside that clock-tower is the crow's flight to Paris; a little to the side, by that wind-warped beech-knoll, is Mont Blanc; beyond it Rome, Athens, all the Antique Lands, the Pyramids. And the New World is stretched yonder (like a witch's hour-glass) across those crags, where the afternoon clouds are crimsoned' (3–4). It is a description that recalls some of the wonderful examples of the Victorian museological enterprise of which Barbara Black writes in her recent book *On Exhibit* – James Wyld's massive model of the globe, for example, or the literally named Whalebone Lounge constructed within the skeleton of a vast whale – offering further evidence for her proposition that the nineteenth century witnesses the beginnings of the age of the simulacrum that Baudrillard locates in the twentieth century, that the Victorian period was 'the true age of the emergent hyperreal' (Black 5–6). 'Here,' Lee observes, 'our eye can penetrate through the dimensions of stellar space, and the dimensions also, the manyvista'd planes, of Time'(3); and 'we are given the emotions of looking into the immense distances of geological ages' (5).

Vernon Lee continues to respond to the experience of Geddes' Tower of the Mirrors in a way that he would have approved by herself 'reflecting' inwardly on the optical magic of the camera obscura, and divining its 'symbolical meaning':

> The analogy thereof lets us guess at the universal mirrorings by which all outside things exist as we know them only in the reflecting and refracting mirrors of our memory and our emotions; while yet those mirroring surfaces of our spirit themselves exist, and pivot to receive images, only in that universe which themselves reflect. Nay the symbol may help us to conceive that the mirroring material whereof they are made, is consubstantial with the universe reflected in their facets; and that the very modes of that refraction and deflection of Reality are but one of Reality's own modes of existing and reacting. (Lee *The Tower of the Mirrors* 5)

The image of those reflecting mirrors playing above the city is powerfully suggestive of how, for a travelled and cosmopolitan observer such as Lee, as she herself writes, 'our imaginative emotions, our glimpses of the Genius Loci, multiply themselves like views in opposite mirrors' (Lee *The Tower of the Mirrors* 202). It is an image that also speaks of the dialectical processes by which subjects are made, of the liminal spaces in-between, of the endlessly self-reflecting selves that make up the borderland identity of Vernon Lee in that *fin-de-siècle* 'moment of transit' of which Bhabha writes, 'where space and time cross to produce complex figures of difference and identity, past and present, inside and outside, inclusion and exclusion' (Bhabha 1).

Notes

1 Later, in *Beauty and Ugliness and Other Studies in Psychological Aesthetics*, co-authored with Clementina Anstruther-Thompson in 1912, she was to acknowledge the work of the German psychologist Oswald Külpe, whose laboratory at the University of Bonn she visited, and the French psychologist Théodule Ribot, whom she describes as an 'older friend' (*Beauty and Ugliness* viii–ix). Both are significant researchers in the field of attention of which Crary writes.
2 I am grateful to Andrew Johnson, Manager of the Camera Obscura, for providing the information brochure, from which these extracts are quoted.

Works cited

Baring, Maurice, *Lost Lectures, or The Fruits of Experience*. London: William Heinemann, 1932.

Bhabha, Homi K., *The Location of Culture*. London and New York: Routledge, 1994.

Black, Barbara J., *On Exhibit: Victorians and Their Museums*. Charlottesville and London: University Press of Virginia, 2000.

Charteris, The Hon. Evan, *John Sargent*. London: William Heinemann, 1927.

Crary, Jonathan, *Techniques of the Observer: On Vision and Modernity in the Nineteenth Century*. Cambridge, Mass. and London: MIT Press, 1990.

——— *Suspensions of Perception: Attention, Spectacle, and Modern Culture*. Cambridge, Mass. and London: MIT Press, 1999.

Dellamora, Richard, ed., *Victorian Sexual Dissidence*. Chicago and London: University of Chicago Press, 1999.

Field, Michael, *Work and Days: From the Journal of Michael Field*, ed. T. and D.C. Sturge Moore. London: John Murray, 1933.

Fraser, Hilary, 'Women and the Ends of Art History: Vision and Corporeality in Nineteenth-Century Critical Discourse', *Victorian Studies* 42 (Autumn 1998/99), 77–100.

Gunn, Peter, *Vernon Lee: Violet Paget, 1856–1935*. London: Oxford University Press, 1964.

Gunning, Tom, 'The Cinema of Attractions: Early Film, its Spectator, and the Avant-Garde', in Thomas Elsaesser, ed., *Early Cinema: Space, Frame, Narrative*. London: BFI, 1990, pp. 56–62.

Hall, Stuart, 'New Cultures for Old', in Doreen Massey and Pat Jess, eds, *A Place in the World? Places, Cultures and Globalization*. Oxford: Oxford University Press, 1995, pp. 175–213.

Lee, Vernon, *Studies of the Eighteenth Century in Italy*. London: W. Satchell and Co., 1880.

——— *Juvenilia: Being a Second Series of Essays on Sundry Aesthetical Questions*. 2 vols. London: T. Fisher Unwin, 1887.

——— *Miss Brown*. 3 vols. Edinburgh: William Blackwood and Sons, 1884.

——— *Hauntings: Fantastic Stories*. Second edition. London: John Lane, The Bodley Head, 1906.

——— *The Spirit of Rome: Leaves from a Diary*. London: John Lane, The Bodley Head, 1906.

—— *Limbo, and Other Essays, to which is now added Ariadne in Mantua*. London: John Lane, The Bodley Head, 1908.

—— *Laurus Nobilis: Chapters on Art and Life*. London: John Lane, 1909.

—— *The Tower of the Mirrors, and Other Essays on the Spirit of Place*. London: John Lane, The Bodley Head, 1914.

—— 'Dionysus in the Euganean Hills: W. H. Pater in memoriam', *Contemporary Review*, 120 (September 1921), 346–53.

Maltz, Diana, 'Engaging "Delicate Brains": From Working-Class Enculturation to Upper-Class Lesbian Liberation in Vernon Lee and Kit Anstruther-Thompson's Psychological Aesthetics', in Talia Schaffer and Kathy Alexis Psomiades, eds, *Women and British Aestheticism*. Charlottesville and London: University Press of Virginia, 1999, pp. 21–9.

Maxwell, Catherine, 'From Dionysus to "Dionea": Vernon Lee's portraits', *Word & Image* 13 (July–September 1997), 253–69.

Pater, Walter, *The Renaissance: Studies in Art and Poetry*. Library Edition, London: Macmillan, 1910.

Psomiades, Kathy, '"Still Burning from this Strangling Embrace": Vernon Lee on Desire and Aesthetics', in Richard Dellamora, ed., *Victorian Sexual Dissidence*. Chicago and London: University of Chicago Press, 1999, pp. 21–41.

Rushdie, Salman, *Imaginary Homelands*. London: Granta, 1991.

Vicinus, Martha, 'The Adolescent Boy: Fin-de-Siècle Femme Fatale?', in Richard Dellamora, ed., *Victorian Sexual Dissidence*. Chicago and London: University of Chicago Press, 1999, pp. 83–106.

7
A Woman Poet Angling for Notice: Rosamund Marriott Watson

Linda K. Hughes

The triple invention of the photograph, cheap methods of graphic reproduction and the celebrity interview in the nineteenth century can be said to have changed authorship forever.[1] Authors have always been tied as visual images, as visible bodies, to their bodies of work through frontispieces and public appearances before courts or salons. Byron's legendary good looks and sensational life, moreover, turned fascination with biography and personal appearance into something of a cult – so much so that, as Andrew Elfenbein suggests, Byron's example rather frightened away succeeding Victorians from pegging their own poetic careers to personal display and revelation (Elfenbein 8–11 and *passim*).

With the saturation of newspapers and magazines – the Victorian mass medium – by illustrations, photographs and interviews, Victorian authors had no choice but to consider how best to manage their publicity and promotion, including self-promotion (Shires 199). If, as Pierre Bourdieu asserts, competition in the field of cultural production is ultimately competition for the authority to determine what counts as art (36, 42), pressure to establish literary authority in the late nineteenth century became inseparable from managing the angle of vision through which an aspiring or famous author was glimpsed by readers and fellow authors. As Nigel Cross remarks, the 1880s brought a new and 'direct equation between publicity and sales', forcing serious artists as well as Grub Street regulars to seek (or at least permit) photographs and gossip of themselves to be published (219).

The pressures to achieve such publicity affected men and women authors like. *Spy* cartoonist Leslie Ward remarked of Thomas Hardy, 'In appearance he did not present the idea of a typical literary man'

134

(Gibson 34); Ward in fact admired Hardy, but his remark indicates that a tacit assumption about how literary men *ought* to look and dress was in circulation. The best-selling novelist Marie Corelli, as Annette Federico has shown, resisted the circulation of photographs as long as possible and, when forced to counter an unflattering photograph taken surreptitiously and published in *Sketch*, she gave the public touched-up photographs. Erasing the signs of age and stoutness created a successful simulacrum of the feminine image expected of a romance fiction writer and was also consistent with Corelli's general privileging of romance over realism (Federico 14–52). In this essay I want to look at cultural production and publishing in the career of poet Rosamund Marriott Watson (1860–1911), who first established her reputation under the signature Graham R. Tomson.[2] Tomson/Watson was highly regarded in her day for her lyrics celebrating urban pleasures (e.g. 'London in October') and ballads of the uncanny, as well as for impeccable crafts-manship. She is of interest today as an occasional female decadent who more often wrote as a female aesthete, discoursing with élan and playful wit about poetry, fashion .and the decorative arts in the *Academy, Athenaeum, Scots Observer, Pall Mall Gazette* and other periodi-cals. Her case history illuminates three specific conditions under which competition for prestige, publicity and hence agency with publishers might be carried out: the situation of the author who attains *succès d'estime* but whose sales are modest; the dangers of physical beauty for a woman seeking critical success as a poet; and the strategies available to a woman writer whose breach of permissible behaviour diminished her symbolic capital.

There was a schism of sorts between the needs of the late Victorian publishing world and aspiring authors. The two parties collaborated in so far as the aspiring author needed to attain citation and hence visibil-ity before a reading public and publishers needed new information (including material on new authors and their new works) to sustain readership and subscriptions. Book reviews and literary gossip columns, which might announce forthcoming volumes, call attention to fugitive pieces in periodicals, or even hail a rising poet or novelist, all served to promote the aspiring author while providing copy for newspapers and magazines and assisting publishing houses' sales. But when it came to publishing sketches or photographs of aspiring authors, the needs of authors and editors diverged. Personal images inserted into papers and magazines literally made new authors visible to the public, but there was little benefit to editors. Only when the work of an author had already sold widely or offered the prospect of fame was it worth an editor's while to expend reproduction costs and precious space within an issue's layout.

This condition helps explain the relative paucity of images of poets compared to novelists in the late Victorian press (excepting a figure like Tennyson, whose *Idylls of the King* and *Enoch Arden* produced substantial profits). As Andrew Lang remarked in *How to Fail in Literature*, published in 1890 after initial presentation as a public lecture, 'in poetry to-day a man may succeed, as far as his art goes, and yet may be unread, and may publish at his own expense, or not publish at all. He pleases himself, and a very tiny audience: I do not call that failure' (18). Besides confirming the high cultural prestige that poetry continued to enjoy into the last decade of the nineteenth century, Lang's remark also acknowledges that, relative to novels that might be bought by a circulating library whether highly meritorious or not, poetry sales as a whole generated relatively little capital in the late Victorian literary world (see Erickson 3, 10–11; Feltes 24–7). Even though poetry's vogue in the early 1890s created an increase in market share, its sales were still modest (Eliot 50). John Lane made a successful career out of publishing a wide list of poets, but he did so less through high-volume sales than through cutting publishing costs and capitalising on the appeal of 'limited editions' (Stetz *passim*).

Graham R. Tomson's early career certainly conformed to the pattern Lang identified. Her first volume of poems, *Tares*, was published anonymously by Kegan Paul in 1884, when the poet was still in her first marriage to a wealthy Australian landholder. A slender collection of technically accomplished lyrics that traced the dissolution of a couple's love, *Tares* registered the influence of Dante Gabriel and Christina Rossetti, Swinburne and Jean Ingelow. It attracted a single laudatory notice in the *Academy*, but this was not enough to generate substantial sales, and after only twenty-three copies were purchased in three years, most remaining copies were sold as waste paper at the end of 1887.[3] Meantime the poet's first marriage failed, resulting in legal separation; late in 1886 she eloped with the painter Arthur Tomson and promptly adopted the pseudonym Graham R. Tomson. She was soon successfully placing poems in *Longman's Magazine* and *St. James's Gazette* as well as prestigious American periodicals such as *Scribner's Magazine*, *Harper's* and *Atlantic Monthly*. In the course of submitting her work she attracted the notice of Andrew Lang, who was impressed with the talent of what he assumed was a new young man on the literary scene. Even while the woman behind the pseudonym was waiting to finalise her divorce, hastily marrying when nearly eight months' pregnant, and giving birth to her son, she was steadily being networked into important literary circles by Lang, who mentioned 'Mr. Graham R. Tomson' and printed 'his' poems in 'At the Sign of the Ship', Lang's well-known monthly causerie in *Longman's*.

In the late 1880s Lang enjoyed an unusual degree of influence – what Bourdieu terms 'symbolic capital' – in the British publishing world. As Marysa Demoor remarks, Lang had the ability to 'make or destroy a new author', power also evident in the assessment by Lang's contemporary, the publisher Grant Richards: '"No man alive, no newspaper, has all that power ..."' (Demoor *Dear* 11, n. 42). Lang was markedly generous to Graham R. Tomson, placing a Tomson poem, 'Ballade of Nicolete', next to his own introductory ballade in the translation of *Aucassin and Nicolete* he published in November 1887 (Tomson 'Ballad'). Such networking and promotion also assured that a dozen French verse forms by Tomson were included in an important landmark in British aestheticism, *Ballades and Rondeaus* (1887), edited by Gleeson White, who likewise assumed that the talented new poet was a man. Under such circumstances – the scandal of a divorce reported in *The Times* and *News of the World* early in 1887 versus the generous promotional efforts extended by Lang to a rising young poet – Graham R. Tomson had every reason to inhibit the visibility of her person in favour of the publicity given her name and texts.

Eventually (when Lang invited her to the all-male Savile Club [Waltman 405]) she was forced to reveal herself as a woman, by which time she was safely married and able, by virtue of her new name, to distance herself from the scandal of divorce. Lang had no reason to retract his sponsorship; indeed, cutting off the connection merely because the 'new young man' turned out to be a woman could have been an embarrassment to him and his critical acumen. Lang, moreover, was promoting another woman poet, May Kendall, in these years and collaborating with her on some projects. Thus he continued to feature Tomson's work in his causerie, introduced her to other literary acquaintances in London, and connected her to a publisher (Longman's) for her first volume under signature, *The Bird-Bride. A Volume of Ballads and Sonnets*, published in 1889. This volume announced its author's allegiance to aestheticism through sections devoted to French verse forms, the sonnet, and poems about books; but like other female aesthetes (Schaffer 3–5), Tomson also adapted devotion to poetic beauty to unconventional ends, as in the title poem's appropriation of the Pre-Raphaelite ballad to explore marriage as a form of female imprisonment.

When the way into visibility as a reputable poet had been made so smooth by Lang, Tomson did not need to exert herself unduly to gain a foothold in the publishing world. She was ambitious, however, as the publication of four books in two years – two editions of Scottish ballads (1888), another of translations from the Greek Anthology (1889) and *The Bird-Bride* – might indicate. She was also rarely beautiful, a further complication for her literary career as well as her marital history. In sending along a new poem of hers in a letter to James Russell Lowell in early 1888, Lang termed her 'a new Muse, and more like a Muse than most' (Demoor *Friends* 213–14). Elizabeth Robins Pennell, who became Tomson's close friend, described her as 'beautiful, reminiscent of Rossetti in her tall, willowy slimness, with her long neck like a column and her great halo of black hair and her big brown eyes, appealing, confinding [*sic*], beseeching'(157–8). Such beauty might have been parlayed into a highly effective publicity campaign. But she again chose to limit the angle of vision permitted on her physicality. Why might she have done so?

One reason had to do with ideology and symbolic capital, the other her particular history. The early nineteenth-century tradition of the poetess encouraged the construction of images of women poets as sylph-like, beautiful creatures whose lyric outpourings could be conceptualised as the effusions of beauty by embodiments of beauty (Armstrong 321–4). Laetitia Landon not only published long narrative poems with great success, but also edited Heath's *Book of Beauty*, and not coincidentally an image of her as a dainty, virginal, lovely young poet was printed in an 1833 issue of *Fraser's Magazine* (Casteras and Peterson 37). As Coulson Kernahan later recalled, in the 1890s Oscar Wilde inscribed gifts to more than one woman poet (including Tomson herself), 'To a poet, and a poem' (Mikhail 2: 302). It was precisely this literal equation between feminine beauty and poetic beauty, however, that could be used to circumscribe the seriousness and power of a woman poet's verses. Wilde himself had used this trope in the dedicatory lyric 'To My Wife *with a copy of my poems*': 'As a prelude to my lay; From a poet to a poem / I would dare to say' (Wilde 809). As Dorothy Mermin notes, such an equation of woman with poem denied poetic agency, for if beauty was an achievement in itself, there was no need to pen verses as well; if one did write under the aegis of the poetess, the results were often represented less as a consequence of artistic craft than emotional effusions issuing from the singer's pure womanhood (Mermin 200–2). That women might craftily embrace the 'identity' of poetess to develop careers was of little help to younger women who, like Tomson, wanted recognition as *poets*. Over-reliance on circulating images of herself as an object of beauty subject to the gaze of the reading public would have fixed Tomson as a product rather than creator of beauty. Oscar Wilde, who published Tomson's two-part essay on female 'Beauty, from the Historical Point of View' and reviewed her 1889 poems in *Woman's World* ('one of our most artistic workers in poetry' [Rev. 448]), could himself capitalise on popular images of him as an aesthete.[4] Women novelists and journalists were assailed if they were not sufficiently (that is, femininely) pretty (Federico 22, 35). But the ideology surrounding the poetess made the woman poet's connection with personal beauty a troublesome strategy. And in Tomson's case, display of a markedly attractive female body would have intensified her link with sexuality, already problematical because of her divorce and second marriage, and provoked investigations into her past that she was anxious to suppress.[5] In 'Dorinda's Mirror', her poem of 1891, the only trace of a long-dead eighteenth-century beauty is her tarnished antique mirror; the poet may imagine Dorinda's ghostly image staring back at her but in fact would see only her own reflection. The poem troped the past's unknowability; it also usefully glosses Tomson's public image relative to her poems of 1889: readers may have projected an image of the poet, but her body was nowhere visible and her only trace was the printed page.

Though two sketches of Tomson appeared in the *Daily Graphic* and *Queen* in conjunction with her part in the annual dinner of the Literary Ladies, a group founded in 1889 to promote women writers, these were not of her own making. Nor was she shown alone but as part of a group, and in a setting that had little to do with poetry. Moreover, these papers had limited prestige, one a woman's paper and the other a less literary, more ephemeral version of the weekly *Graphic*. The 'advanced' magazine *Woman*, edited by Arnold Bennett (Ballaster et al. 46–7), did feature her in one of a series of illustrated celebrity interviews in 1892, which profiled such figures as the prominent novelist, Mrs Humphry Ward; the Queen of Holland; the feminist leader Mrs Fawcett; the political activist and linguist Maud Gonne; and Oscar Wilde himself ('"Woman" Portaits'). Besides the attraction of joining such distinguished company, Tomson may also have consented to the feature on the basis of friendship, if (as I speculate) the 'P.E.R.' who regularly contributed an art column to *Woman* was Tomson's close friend Elizabeth Robins Pennell. In any case, Tomson took care to thwart any implication that she was a 'poetess'; after the interviewer suggested that poets were born rather than made, she replied, 'Poetry, like everything else, is no more written without hard work and years of training than a trade is learnt or a picture painted. The technique must be acquired, the craftsmanship perfected, and then the soul has its body, the mind its tools for work' (U. 5). Even in the context of a celebrity interview in *Woman*, moreover, Tomson did not appear, like most other interviewees, in a photograph but in an artist's drawing 'assisted by a photo by Mr. Hollyer' (U. 4).

Only once, so far as I know, did a photograph of Graham R. Tomson appear in a widely circulating magazine, and then again only under specific conditions. The photograph, taken by the fine art photographer Frederick Hollyer, was part of a group illustrating an article on 'Woman-Poets of the Day' by Richard Le Gallienne in the April 1894 *English Illustrated Magazine*. Le Gallienne directly addressed the issue of the 'poet' versus the 'poetess'. He noted lingering assumptions that sexual difference affected poetic quality and that women's poetry was defined by 'an excess of feeling over form, a lack of authority and distinction' (651). But he countered that these last qualities were merely the sign of immature poetry written by men as well as women and asserted that 'The barbarous word "poetess" is seldom employed by any one with a literary character to lose' (650). Le Gallienne declared his allegiances in the deliberateness with which his title used the word 'poet',[6] and it seems no coincidence that where women were called 'poets' rather than 'poetesses' the leading women poets of the day were willing to contribute photographs of themselves. Some of the images, moreover, flouted the association of the woman poet with youthful, virginal beauty. Though youthful beauty was indeed apparent in the images of E. Nesbit and Dora Sigerson, Christina Rossetti was depicted realistically as an older woman affected by Graves' disease; Jean Ingelow was decorously feminine but clearly middle-aged; and Alice Meynell's photograph was feminine but austere as to dress and expression. Tomson's photograph, showing her seated and in profile, depicted an attractive, highly confident woman whose sensuality emerged in the echoing 'S' curves of her cocked elbow and torso liberally displayed. This was a worldly, 'advanced' woman rather than a virginal singer.

In addition to Tomson's appearance among other women as a poet rather than poetess, her visibility here is also due to the prestige and cultural authority she had gained by this point. *The Bird-Bride* of 1889 had not sold particularly well (roughly 250 copies in a year in Britain and America)[7] but was widely and well reviewed. After publishing a

Photo by F. F Hollyer, Pembroke Square, W.

GRAHAM R. TOMSON (MRS. ARTHUR TOMSON).

2. 'Mrs Arthur Tomson', *English Ilustrated Magazine*, April 1894. Reproduced courtesy of the Bodleian Library, Univeristy of Oxford, Per. 2705 s.223, p. 65

number of poems in W.E. Henley's prestigious *National Observer* (which also published poems by Kipling, Yeats, Meynell, Nesbit and Henley himself), she published another well-reviewed volume in 1891, *A Summer Night, and Other Poems*, which demonstrated her new command of urban impressionism (e.g. 'In the Rain') and continuing experimentation with ballads (see Hughes 'Fin-de-Siècle' 108–11). That same year she contributed signed reviews of volumes by Henley and the late Amy Levy to the *Illustrated London News*; and by 1892 she was also tapped as a regular contributor of signed reviews of poetry by the *Academy*, the journal that had praised *Tares* eight years earlier and enjoyed high prestige because of its long-standing association with university men. In 1892 and 1893 she reviewed several important volumes, including the first *Book of the Rhymers' Club, Song of the Sword* by Henley, *Lachyrmae Musarum, and Other Poems* by William Watson (then considered a brilliant new poet on the scene) and *Poems* and *The Rhythm of Life* by Meynell. In her reviews, Tomson exercised considerable authority, delivering crisp judgements of poetic merit while extending her aesthetic writing through analysis of the decorative qualities of books. Given her prestige, the circulation of her photographic image (even with its faintly seductive pose) could do her little harm and potentially a great deal of good.

In contrast to the glaring display of images in newspapers and magazines, the less public world of salons and networking offered different strategies to women; here a woman's personal attractions could prove useful in securing the attentions, and cooperation, of powerful male mentors and editors who controlled access to publication. Robert Scholnick has recently documented the role of erotic attraction in the mentoring of American poet Lizette Reese by the critic, editor and man of letters E.C. Stedman; after Reese and Stedman corresponded for three years, the unmarried Reese sent a photograph to her married sponsor, adopting a flirtatious tone in her accompanying letter: '"I shall be very careful in wrapping it so that it won't reach you with a mark across the eyes, or the impress of a United States stamp on some other part of the body"' (Scholnick 26). Graham R. Tomson had no need to send photographs to the publisher T. Fisher Unwin, who knew her, nor did she adopt so forthrightly flirtatious a tone in her correspondence with him. But she did use charm and obliquely seductive playfulness to veil and mediate her assertive professional negotiations with him.

In 1891 she and her husband were finalising a work for Unwin's Cameo series *Concerning Cats* (1892). This tome, for which Graham R.

Tomson selected and introduced the letter press and Arthur Tomson, a member of the New English Art Club, contributed original drawings, managed to be decadent and domestic at once, encompassing children's verse, untranslated poems by Baudelaire and Verlaine, and Tomson's own Hellenistic 'Arsinoë's Cats' (adapted from the Greek Anthology) and decadent paean 'To My Cat' – these last memorable enough to be quoted with pleasure by the jazz age critic Carl Van Vechten in *Tiger in the House* (20, 257). In early July, after updating Unwin on the progress of contributions and requesting that he intervene with a publishing house that had denied permission to reprint a poem, she praised the most recent volume in Unwin's Pseudonym series and invited him to join her and Arthur in Sussex, glancing at his name in the process: 'It is very jolly here – you must come down to us soon – and bring a fishing rod – the pond is just teeming with fish.'[8] A subsequent letter first playfully laughed at her discomfiture caused by weather, then pointedly proposed herself as a prospective house reader for Unwin:

> it pours still and fills up the intervals with gales that threaten to sweep one with all one's belongings (and everything else to boot) from the face of the earth. So don't be surprised if you hear that your friend the Minor Poet (that's me) has shared the same fate as Flying Robert of Struwelpeter fame.
>
> When you feel inclined send me any M.S. you like, to read (any, I mean, that you care to send whether you like them or not).[9]

On 25 September she was again writing amicably following a visit Unwin had paid, telling him, for example, about her new Belgian hares ('they … eat everything I offer them, which shows their innate amiability of character'). Three days later, she wrote again, furious at the shoddy quality of proofs that had arrived, all charm instantly vanished:

> The proofs have just arrived, and we are appalled by the monstrous caricatures of the illustrations. Even if, eventually, they look ninety-nine per cent better than this they will still be unworthy of publication … it does seem such a terrible pity, to have money and pains (as it were) wasted, by printing so utterly unintelligent as this: I feel distressed very nearly, if not quite, as much on your account as on my own – or the artist's … I do not know what can be done, but feel sure that you will be able to arrange something, and that you will

feel how important 'for all our own goods' is the proper rendering of the illustrations. The very first proofs of the blocks were so excellent that I could not have imagined that clumsy printing could have so degraded them.

Her protestations and expectation of redress worked, and with her desires satisfied she immediately reverted to the playful tone of prior letters: 'Many thanks for your reassuring letter; "thou has comforted me marvellous much" – But you have mistaken what I said about the proofs – I meant that the block-maker's proofs were excellent – not the big sheet of cats – I thought <u>them</u> horrid! So <u>there</u>, M'sieur le Pecheur!'[10] Here she is 'angling for notice' in rather different terms than in the public world of print. The letters disclose a highly assertive and ambitious woman who assumes she has literary authority and is entitled to consideration, yet who tends to cloak aggressive contention in feminine playfulness and charm that defuse potential conflict.

Two months after the photograph of 'Graham R. Tomson (Mrs. Arthur Tomson)' appeared in the *English Illustrated Magazine*, the poet left her husband and son Tommy to elope with Australian-born novelist H.B. Marriott Watson, one of Henley's 'young men' who had co-written the drama *Richard Savage* with J.M. Barrie in 1891 and was steadily gaining repute as a fiction writer. If her elopement was in personal terms an unrestrained indulgence in transgressive sexual desire, professionally it was an act of extravagant sacrifice. Indeed, it might be termed suicidal sacrifice, since she effectively killed off Graham R. Tomson. She also put paid to her forthcoming volume of poems, *After Sunset*, which had been announced in the press by her publisher Elkin Mathews and John Lane[11] and was so far advanced in production that R. Anning Bell's frontispiece design was complete. But *After Sunset* was by Graham R. Tomson, and from the time of her elopement she redubbed herself Rosamund Marriott Watson.

This *volte-face* in erotic attachment and nomenclature had several results, all of which squandered the symbolic capital that Graham R. Tomson had so carefully accumulated over several years. First, she was now associated with an unruly female body rather than cultural authority. Prior to the elopement she had represented dangerous beauty only to associates, a woman with a past who had managed to overcome this obstacle through sheer talent and hard work, attaining a respected position within the world of letters. She had even been awarded the editorship of her own women's magazine, *Sylvia's Journal*, which she had remade into an outlet for aestheticism and progressive views, as in its feminist literary analyses of poets' heroines by Katharine Tynan, articles on women's colleges, and emphasis on decorative arts anchored by Anning Bell's black and white art (Hughes 'Female'). Now she was hopelessly tainted by scandal, clearly excluded from any possibility of a celebrity interview that might advance her literary reputation and name recognition with readers.

Second, she had destroyed much of her literary network through her elopement. Though Henley and many of his set stuck by the Marriott Watsons, she shocked and alienated many of her prior associates. Lang, her first mentor and sponsor, never mentioned her again, and in fact took care to publish a new edition of *Aucassin and Nicolete* without the accompanying ballade by Graham R. Tomson.[12] She had also damaged her standing with her publisher, since Mathews and Lane now had to scrap production despite the expenses they had already invested.

Third, and most crucially, she had destroyed perhaps the most important means by which authors become and remain familiar to audiences and purchasers: name recognition and citation. No one could now mention Graham R. Tomson and Rosamund Marriott Watson without narrating the cause of the change, and this was at least awkward and at most inconsistent with minimum standards of respectability still demanded of mass publications in the 1890s. Literary insiders might know who 'Rosamund Marriott Watson' was, but readers in periodicals and magazines did not, nor did editors have any reason to help the poet who had dealt so fast and loose with her marriage and professional interests.

At this point it might be useful to contrast the different cases of Graham R. Tomson and Oscar Wilde, whose arrest, trials, and ultimate conviction roughly a year after Tomson's elopement were handled so differently in the press. The difference in part goes back to the same factors as those discussed above regarding photographs of respected but less famous authors. Wilde did not win his fame primarily (perhaps very little) from his poems but from his performances as a public personality, from his fiction (ranging from *The Happy Prince* to *Picture of Dorian Gray*), and above all from his immensely successful dramas. Wilde's work generated capital on a scale that was out of reach for a respected 'high culture' woman poet. Wilde's trial, moreover, was tied to the long-standing practice of extensive reporting of scandalous trials, whether in highly contested divorce cases (e.g. that of Lady Colin Campbell in 1886) or the contested identity of the Tichborne Claimant in 1871–72. Trials and newspapers had developed symbiotically, so that the trial itself, not just the scandalous charges against

Wilde, intensified his notoriety as well as public interest in the case. In contrast, private elopements were left unreported unless succeeded by a divorce trial of sufficient interest to gain public attention.

Gender ideology, however, also had a role in the differing reactions to the two scandals. The notorious male body could be contemplated and discussed. Whether the notorious female body might be similarly contemplated and discussed depended on the woman's class: the long-standing tradition of aristocratic licence permitted liberties, as did working-class status, whether the woman involved was an actress, music hall performer or prostitute. But the notorious middle-class female body was a contradiction in terms and most often was simply suppressed altogether. Significantly, just when Graham R. Tomson had given gossip writers ample material for copy, mention of her in the contemporary press virtually disappeared overnight.

The merits of her work, as well as the increasing symbolic capital of her new 'husband',[13] meant that she still readily found a place for her poems in important literary magazines such as the *Yellow Book*, *Pageant* and *Pall Mall Magazine*. Rosamund Marriott Watson also published three volumes of poems with John Lane, as well as a collection of (for-tuitously) unsigned columns on interior decoration she had contributed to the *Pall Mall Gazette* while still named Graham R. Tomson in 1893–94 (*Art of the House* 1897), and another book of essays and poems inspired by her garden in Turnham Green, where she lived with Marriott Watson and their son Richard after 1895 (*Heart of a Garden* 1906). As Marysa Demoor has recently shown, Marriott Watson also found a new post as poetry critic with the *Athenaeum* (*Fair* 123–6). Tellingly, however, after 1895 she retreated from decadence in her poetry; her aesthetic writing on gardens elided rather than provoca-tively glanced towards the female body, as did Tomson's fashion and interior decoration columns; and her literary criticism was predomi-nantly anonymous, denied the publicity and accumulating symbolic capital of Tomson's signed reviews.

Not surprisingly, no further photographs of the poet appeared in the press after her elopement, though William Archer reproduced a woodcut engraving of her (as for all the others profiled in the book) in *Poets of the Younger Generation* (1902) (Archer 471); and an American avant-garde magazine, *Chap Book*, published engravings of her and H.B. Marriott Watson in separate volumes.[14] Neither Archer nor the *Chap Book* editor (nor most periodicals to which she contributed) identified her link to Graham R. Tomson. This practice continued up to and immediately after her death: even the *Athenaeum* obituary by the editor, her friend Vernon Rendall, made no mention of her four children or her prior marriages.

Under such unpropitious conditions, how did Rosamund Marriott Watson angle for notice and negotiate with publishers? Surprisingly, she remained assertive and confident, and perhaps the importance of adopting that strategy is one of the major conclusions to be drawn from her unusual circumstances. To have acquiesced in public judgements of her would have meant complicity in her own erasure. Only by performing the role of someone whose work demanded respect and consideration was she likely to achieve either. And though she continued to reject seduction as a negotiating ploy, she could still exert charm with considerable success, as her correspondence with John Lane demonstrates.

Lane, a long-time friend to her and her brother, the painter-etcher Wilfrid Ball,[15] was extraordinarily generous after her elopement with Marriott Watson. Not only did he publish her 1895 volume (*Vespertilia and Other Verses*), he also reissued her 1891 volume, ripping off the old covers and frontispiece (a painting by her husband Arthur) and replacing them with a new cover and title-page identifying the author as Rosamund Marriott Watson. Giving her another chance despite the abortive *After Sunset* and its expenses, he also provided the best opportunity she had of recouping some of the symbolic capital of 'Graham R. Tomson' by associating her new name with the earlier poems.

He also helped her recoup the title of her earlier, abortive volume in 1904. She had begun to contemplate another collection of poems by 1902. Rather than humbly asking Lane to consider the new venture, she assumed the stance of a valued commodity who could easily place her work elsewhere when writing to Lane at the beginning of the year:

> You will remember that we discussed, some two years ago, the subject of your publishing my new book of verses. Since then it has been greatly added to and improved, and, I think, contains far the best work I have done.
>
> For the sentiment of old times' sake I should much prefer that you should publish it; but, at the same time, I should not like you to do so if you could not see your way with it. I thought of either this late spring, or the early autumn, as a suitable time. I should like you to let me know your views, as I want to be in a position to make arrangements in case you did not care to have it.
>
> I received a very kind letter from Mr. Archer yesterday, sending me the enclosed, which perhaps you may have seen already.

Her enclosure was a blatant piece of self-advertising designed to bolster her negotiating position with Lane. This was a circular announcing William Archer's second series of lectures on 'Latter-Day Poets' at the Women's Department, King's College, University of London; his concluding lecture, on 12 March, was to be devoted to 'Poetesses of Culture': Alice Meynell, Rosamund Marriott-Watson and Margaret L. Woods (Archer had addressed the work of Katharine Tynan and Moira O'Neill the prior week in a lecture on 'Poetesses of Nature').[16]

For unknown reasons she wrote a few weeks later to ask for the manuscript to be returned and to postpone publication until she had completed further revisions and rearrangement of the material. Even after taxing Lane's patience she still included a veiled threat to change publishers in her letter to him a year later, when she enquired about the status of her proposed volume and remarked, 'I hope, however, that I shall not have to change my publisher.'[17]

As with Fisher Unwin, she was gracious and charming, even somewhat flirtatious, once she had achieved her ends, writing thus to Lane after he proposed to bring out her new volume on 6 October, her birthday,

> Here is your birthday gift to me – rather an Ugly Duckling in its present form; but, under your auspices, I hope a Swan in the making. I have done a good deal of addition, and a certain amount of subtraction, and think both processes an improvement. By the way, Dick [her son] will share in the festivities; for his birthday is identical with mine – Oct. 6.th – He is feeling rather grand about it. I'm sending you his last portrait, and wonder whether you will still think him like me?[18]

She did not send Lane her own photograph, but did include one of her son, asking Lane to compare it to the boy's attractive mother.

Her method of negotiating with (male) publishers, then, comprised an alternating rhythm of charm and strenuous assertion. She was equally persistent, even pushy, about the details of publication itself: 'Are you thinking of publishing "After Sunset" in America, as well as in England, this autumn?' she inquired of Lane. 'I merely ask, as (if you were not) I had thought of making arrangements with Scribner's.' Lane acquiesced to her request yet again.[19] In June she was writing about the aesthetic format of the volume and requesting that she be included in all decisions: 'I wonder, (when the time comes), whether it would be possible for me to see the cover? If it were, I should so very much like to; for, as you know, covers are rather a weakness of mine (especially your covers).' When she had no lever (such as a rival publisher) to exert pressure on Lane, she was still assertive but now folded flattery into her negotiation and adopted a slightly more subordinate stance. Two days later, with partial concession granted her by Lane, she mixed overt assertion (in her remark about Meynell's volume) with deference and self-effacement:

> I think I had better leave the cover to the admirable taste that pre-sides over the <u>Buchkleider</u> of the Bodley Head – but I must own to an especial enthusiasm for the delightful <u>green</u>, <u>ribbed</u>, bindings wherewith the Works of the Poet Phillips were so gloriously arrayed. Could I, do you think, have something of the same? The only cover of yours that I precisely didn't like was that of Mrs. Meynell's <u>Later Poems</u>.[20]

Appearing to relinquish control at the outset, she next stated precisely what she wanted, and clearly hoped to link her volume, through visual association, to the volumes of Stephen Phillips and the prestige he enjoyed at the time (Grushow 464).

Despite appearances to the contrary, clearly, this woman poet had not thrown away all her professional acumen when she discarded her second marriage for the companionship of H.B. Marriott Watson. Though some earlier avenues enjoyed by Graham R. Tomson were closed to Rosamund Marriott Watson (it would have been unthinkable, for example, to turn over a woman's magazine, often a source of advice to unmarried girls, to such a woman), she retained mastery of a number of strategies for self-promotion. Though the wide dissemina-tion of photographs had never been feasible because of her genre, gender, and status as divorcee, she could still draw on the assertiveness and charm she had learned to exert so effectively with T. Fisher Unwin and earlier publishers.

Her efforts were not entirely successful, in part because her 1904 volume was less accomplished than earlier collections, even more because she had lost so much name recognition due to her confusing change of signature. The results can be seen in two different contexts. Some time after 1895 Elkin Mathews wrote to a collector to explain, 'All the Rosamund Marriott Watson volumes you ask for were written while she was still Mrs. Arthur Tomson <u>before</u> she married Mr. Marriott Watson.'[21] Clearly Mathews' customer knew the poet Marriott Watson but was unclear about Tomson. The opposite situation arose in a literary causerie by A. T. Quiller-Couch in the 23 July 1898 *Speaker.* Wishing to counter Alice Meynell's recent assertion that all verse forms except the sonnet were now *passé,* Quiller-Couch rejoined, 'Discarded by whom? By the mass of poets, no doubt; but not, for instance, by Mr. Swinburne. Mr. Henley, Mr. Dobson, Mr. Lang, Mr. Gosse, Mme. Graham R. Tomson may, for aught I know, have repented that they ever experimented in formal verse .... But Mr. Swinburne ... is impenitent' (110–11). Mme. Rosamund Marriott Watson was not consulted or even recalled.

When she was assailed by increasing illness and obscurity after 1904, her energies and ability to promote her career dissipated. But neither literary careers nor the field of cultural production tend to proceed unidirectionally, and an unexpected quarter provided the advertising and publicity she could not: musical settings based on her poems. She had met the British composer Cyril Scott, an early associate of Percy Grainger and Edward Elgar, in the Surrey village of Shere, to which she and her family retreated after she suffered a nervous breakdown. Responding to the subtle rhythms and dream states of her lyrics (e.g. 'Fata Morgana), Scott set fifteen of her poems to music between 1904 and 1924; 'Blackbird's Song', composed in 1906, became a staple of concerts for years (Banfield 1: 91, 2: 503–6).[22] Perhaps Scott's precedent inspired composer William Henry Bell, Professor of Harmony at the Royal Academy of Music from 1903 to 1912 (before he emigrated to South Africa), to tackle the more demanding adaptation of the swan maiden myth in Graham R. Tomson's 'Ballad of the Bird-Bride' (1889).[23] Bell's setting had its premier performance in a London Symphony Orchestra concert in 1909 that also featured Berlioz, Strauss, Weber and Beethoven. Credit for the Tomson poem, reintroduced to the public in the validating context of high art, was now transferred to Rosamund Marriott Watson in publicity and reviews. The poet was only two and a half years away from death at this point, but her readiness to promote her work prevailed. First suggesting that enough poems had accumulated for yet another volume in a 23 January 1909 letter to Lane, she followed up on 4 February by telling Lane about the tribute still being paid to her verse: 'W.H. Bell has set my "Ballad of the Bird-Bride" – It is to be given on March 1st at Queen's Hall by Sr Richter, with full orchestration, and Charles Clarke will sing the voice part.'[24]

In many respects the story of Rosamund Marriott Watson's attempts to control public perception of her while 'angling for notice' is one of disaster and failure. By surrendering her 'brand name' as a poet after her 1894 elopement she very nearly disappeared altogether. Her career as both Graham R. Tomson and Rosamund Marriott Watson, however, illuminates many of the challenges peculiar to women poets in an era of gossip, celebrity and photography. And her authorial history also reveals the surprising number of resources at her disposal when her career was most vulnerable and tenuous – and her active disposition to use them.

Notes

1 See Altick 134–5; Salmon passim; Schalck 75, 79–80; and Wiener *Papers* 52, 61, 'Yates' 260, 269.
2 The work of poet Rosamund Marriott Watson, one of several significant women writers of the 1890s whose work later suffered eclipse, has received increasing notice in the past decade. Her work appears in a number of recent anthologies of Victorian women poets (Reilly 102–3, Leighton and Reynolds 581–9, Armstrong and Bristow 746–54, Blain 257–82) and is the subject of scholarly analysis in studies devoted to women and aestheticism (Schaffer 113–18, 87–102; Hughes 'Fashioning'), women's literary salons (Vadillo), and women reviewers (Demoor *Their Fair Share* 123–6). My own additional essays on this provocative *fin-de-siècle* poet and journalist are listed in the Works Cited.
3 Account Book, Kegan Paul, Trench, Trübner Archive, Item 168, f. 146, University College London.
4 Wilde also devoted the cover of his penultimate issue of *Woman's World* to an illustration of Tomson's 'In Picardy' (September 1889). As Jennifer Wicke remarks, Oscar Wilde was the '*locus classicus* for the confluence of advertising and literature' until he became 'a literary totem capable of conjuring up a fervent world of celebrity and aesthetic rapture' (83).
5 The danger to which her beauty and sexual past might expose her is evident in Arthur Symons' letter of 15 June 1889 to James Dykes Campbell: 'Graham Tomson was there [at the home of William and Elizabeth Sharp] too, in an antique peplum of red, looking very handsome, but I was only introduced to her husband (he is No. 2 and they both look about three and twenty) – *not* a fascinating person, which makes Bunand [the French journalist who accompanied Symons to the gathering] anticipate the chance of some day offering himself as "le troisième"!' In contrast to this reductive representation of Tomson, Symons shares a respectful account of his chat with Alice Meynell, who was also present: '*Preludes* ... is some of the most truly poetical poetry any woman has ever written ... she talks really like a poet' (Beckson and Munro 50).
6 In his critical judgements, however, Le Gallienne favoured 'spontaneous' emotional verse by women rather than strong intellectual work. Thus he preferred Augusta Webster's lyric rispetti over her dramatic monologues and found Mathilde Blind's *Ascent of Man* interesting only when it abandoned philosophy for the lyric mode. He faulted Tomson for too much form and culture, too little 'blood' and emotional vitality in her work.

7 Ledger R1, f. 517, Longman Archive, University of Reading.

8 Graham R. Tomson ALS to T. Fisher Unwin 10 July 1891, T. F. Unwin Papers, Harry Ransom Humanities Research Center, The University of Texas.

9 Graham R. Tomson ALS to T. Fisher Unwin Wednesday, n.d., T.F. Unwin Papers, Harry Ransom Humanities Research Center, The University of Texas.

10 Graham R. Tomson ALS to T. Fisher Unwin 25, 28, 30 September [1891], T. F. Unwin Papers, Harry Ransom Humanities Research Center, The University of Texas.

11 The title was announced both in the *Bookman* March 1894: 175, and in the *Yellow Book* 2 (July 1894): 12. *After Sunset*, announced as 'In preparation' in the *Yellow Book*, was to have been offered in both duodecimo and a limited large paper edition.

12 The edition of 1905, published by Routledge in London and E.P. Dutton in New York, featured twelve photogravures after drawings by Gilbert James and was retitled *Aucassin & Nicolette, done into English by Andrew Lang*. An earlier American edition under Lang's signature, *Aucassin et Nicolette: being a love story tr. out of the ancient French*, replaced Graham R. Tomson's introductory poem with one by American poet and critic E. C. Stedman, 'Provencal Lovers' (East Aurora, NY: The Roycrofters, 1899).

13 The Marriott Watsons never legalised their union with a marriage ceremony, though by the time of Rosamund Marriott Watson's death in 1911 they had achieved the status of common-law husband and wife.

14 *Chap-Book* 15 March 1896: 419 (H. B.); 15 June 1896: 120 (Rosamund). Only when the poet was safely dead did a photograph appear (as a frontispiece) in her posthumous poems of 1912.

15 Wilfrid Ball and John Lane met through the Sette of Odd Volumes, a club formed in 1877 by antiquarian bookseller Bernard Quaritch. Ball was active in the group at least by 1885 and was elected vice president in 1891; Lane was an active member by 1889. See 'Notes and News', *Academy* 14 October 1893, p. 318; *Black and White*, 12 December 1891, p. 774; 'Tatler', 'Books and Bookmen: "Tatler's" Literary Notes', *Star* 12 March 1891; and Whittington-Egan and Smerdon 124n.1.

16 Rosamund Marriott Watson ALS to John Lane 17 January 1902, John Lane Papers, Harry Ransom Humanities Research Center, The University of Texas.

17 Rosamund Marriott Watson ALS to John Lane 2 February 1903, John Lane Papers, Harry Ransom Humanities Research Center, The University of Texas. Her earlier letter was dated 11 February 1902.

18 Rosamund Marriott Watson ALS to John Lane 3 March 1903, John Lane Papers, Harry Ransom Humanities Research Center, The University of Texas.

19 Rosamund Marriott Watson ALS to John Lane 16 April 1903, John Lane Papers, Harry Ransom Humanities Research Center, The University of Texas. Her 25 April 1903 letter to Lane from the same collection began, 'I am very pleased that you are going to publish "<u>After Sunset</u>" in America, as well as here'.

20 Rosamund Marriott Watson ALS to John Lane, 16 June 1903, 18 June 1903, John Lane Papers, Humanities Research Center, The University of Texas.

21 Elkin Mathews ALS to Philip D. Sherman n.d., Special Collections, John Hay
    Library, Brown University.
22 In her 1946–47 recitals in the US, Lotte Lehmann included 'Blackbird's
    Song' as part of her repertoire. See the Lotte Lehmann Foundation web-site
    at www.lottelehman.org.
23 R.F.M. Immelman, letter of transmittal (typescript) to British Museum
    Librarian 7 February 1949, bound into L. E. Taylor, comp., *Catalogue of the
    Music Manuscripts of William Henry Bell, 1873–1946* (Cape Town: U. of Cape
    Town Libraries, 1948), British Library copy.
24 Rosamund Marriott Watson ALS to John Lane, 4 Feburary 1909, MS
    Walpole d.19, f. 107–108, Bodleian Library, Oxford University.

Works cited

Altick, Richard D., *Lives and Letters: A History of Literary Biography in England and America*. New York: Alfred A. Knopf, 1965.

Archer, William, *Poets of the Younger Generation*. 1902. Rpt. New York: AMS Press, 1970.

Armstrong, Isobel, *Victorian Poetry: Poetry, Poetics and Politics*. London and New York: Routledge, 1993.

Armstrong, Isobel, and Joseph Bristow, with Cath Sharrock, eds., *Nineteenth-Century Women Poets: An Oxford Anthology*. Oxford: Clarendon Press, 1996.

Ballaster, Ros, Margaret Beetham, Elizabeth Frazer and Sandra Hebron, *Women's Worlds: Ideology, Femininity and the Woman's Magazine*. Basingstoke: Macmillan, 1991.

Banfield, Stephen, *Sensibility and English Song: Critical Studies of the Early Twentieth Century*. 2 vols. Cambridge: Cambridge University Press, 1985.

Beckson, Karl, and John M. Munro, eds., *Arthur Symons: Selected Letters, 1880–1935*. Iowa City: University of Iowa Press, 1989.

Blain, Virginia, ed., *Victorian Women Poets: A New Annotated Anthology*. Longman Annotated Texts ser. Harlow: Pearson Education, 2001.

Bourdieu, Pierre, *The Field of Cultural Production*. Ed. Randal Johnson. New York: Columbia University Press, 1993.

Casteras, Susan P., and Linda H. Peterson, *A Struggle for Fame: Victorian Women Artists and Authors*. New Haven, Conn.: Yale Center for British Art, 1994.

Cross, Nigel, *The Common Writer: Life in Nineteenth-Century Grub Street*. Cambridge: Cambridge University Press, 1985.

Demoor, Marysa, *Their Fair Share: Women, Power and Criticism in the Athenaeum, From Millicent Garrett Fawcett to Katherine Mansfield, 1870–1920*. Aldershot: Ashgate, 2000.

—— ed., *Dear Stevenson: Letters from Andrew Lang to Robert Louis Stevenson with Five Letters from Stevenson to Lang*. Leuven: Uitgeverij Peeters, 1990.

—— *Friends Over the Ocean: Andrew Lang's American Correspondents 1881–1912*. Gent: Rijksuniversiteit Gent, 1989.

Elfenbein, Andrew, *Byron and the Victorians*. Cambridge: Cambridge University Press, 1995.

Eliot, Simon, *Some Patterns and Trends in British Publishing 1800–1919*. Bibliographic Society Occasional Papers No. 8. London: Bibliographical Society, 1994.

Erickson, Lee, *The Economy of Literary Form: English Literature and the Industrialization of Publishing, 1800–1850*. Baltimore and London: Johns Hopkins University Press, 1996.

Federico, Annette R., *Idol of Suburbia: Marie Corelli and Late-Victorian Literary Culture*. Charlottesville and London: University Press of Virginia, 2000.

Feltes, N. N., *Modes of Production of Victorian Novels*. Chicago and London: University of Chicago Press, 1986.

Gibson, James, ed., *Thomas Hardy: Interviews and Recollections*. Basingstoke: Macmillan, 1999.

Grushow, Ira, 'Phillips, Stephen (1864–1915)'. *The 1890s: An Encyclopedia of British Literature, Art, and Culture*. Ed. G.A. Cevasco. New York and London: Garland, 1993, pp. 463–4.

Hughes, Linda K., '"Fair Hymen Holdeth Hid a World of Woes": Myth and Marriage in Poems by Graham R. Tomson'. *Victorian Poetry* 32.2 (Summer 1994), 97–120. Rpt. *Victorian Women Poets: A Critical Reader*. Ed. Angela Leighton. Oxford: Basil Blackwell, 1996, pp. 162–85.

—— 'A Female Aesthete at the Helm: *Sylvia's Journal* and 'Graham R. Tomson', 1893–1894'. *Victorian Periodicals Review* 29.2 (Summer 1996), 173–92.

—— 'Feminizing Decadence: Poems by Graham R. Tomson'. *Women and British Aestheticism*. Ed. Talia Schaffer and Kathy Alexis Psomiades. Charlottesville: University Press of Virginia, 1999, pp. 119–38.

—— 'A Fin-de-Siecle Beauty and the Beast: Configuring the Body in Works by Graham R. Tomson (Rosamund Marriott Watson)'. *Tulsa Studies in Women's Literature* 14.1 (Spring 1995), 95–121.

—— 'Rosamund Marriott Watson'. *Dictionary of Literary Biography 240: Late Nineteenth- and Early Twentieth-Century British Women Poets*. Ed. William B. Thesing. Detroit: Gale, 2001, pp. 308–20.

Lang, Andrew, *How to Fail in Literature: A Lecture*. London: Field and Tuer, 1890.

Le Gallienne, Richard, 'Woman-Poets of the Day'. *English Illustrated Magazine* April 1894, 648–57.

Leighton, Angela, and Margaret Reynolds, eds., *Victorian Women Poets: An Anthology*. Oxford: Blackwell, 1995.

Mermin, Dorothy, 'The Damsel, the Knight, and the Victorian Woman Poet'. 1986. Rpt. *Victorian Women Poets: A Critical Reader*. Ed. Angela Leighton. Oxford: Basil Blackwell, 1996, pp. 198–214.

Mikhail, E. H., ed., *Oscar Wilde: Interviews and Recollections*. 2 vols. London and Basingstoke: Macmillan, 1979.

Pennell, Elizabeth Robins, *Nights: Rome and Venice in the Aesthetic Eighties, London and Paris in the Fighting Nineties*. Second edition. Philadelphia and London: J.P. Lippincott, 1916.

Reilly, Catherine, ed., *Winged Words: Victorian Women's Poetry and Verse*. London: Enitharmon Press, 1994.

Rev. of *Tares. Academy* 21 March 1885, 203.

Salmon, Richard, 'Signs of Intimacy: The Literary Celebrity in the "Age. Of Interviewing"'. *Victorian Literature and Culture* 25 (1997), 159–77.

Schaffer, Talia, *The Forgotten Female Aesthetes: Literary Culture in Late-Victorian England*. Charlottesville and London: University Press of Virginia, 2000.

Schalck, Harry, 'Fleet Street in the 1890s: The New Journalism'. In Wiener 73–87.

Scholnick, Robert J., '"The last letter of all": Reese, Stedman, and Poetry in Late-Nineteenth-Century America'. *American Literary Mentors*. Ed. Irene C. Goldman-Price and Melissa McFarland Pennell. Gainesville: University Press of Florida, 1999, pp.14–33.

Shires, Linda M., 'The Author as Spectacle and Commodity: Elizabeth Barrett Browning and Thomas Hardy'. *Victorian Literature and the Victorian Visual Imagination*. Ed. Carol T. Christ and John O. Jordan. Berkeley, Los Angeles and London: University of California Press, 1995, pp. 198–212.

Stetz, Margaret, 'Sex, Lies, and Printed Cloth: Bookselling at the Bodley Head in the Eighteen-Nineties'. *Victorian Studies* 35 (1991), 71–86.

Tomson, Graham R., 'Ballade of Nicolete'. *Aucassin and Nicolete*. Tr. Andrew Lang. London: David Nutt, 1887, pp. xix–xx.

—— 'Beauty, from the Historical Point of View'. *Woman's World* 2 (July, August 1889), 454–9, 536–41.

—— *The Bird-Bride. A Volume of Ballads and Sonnets*. London: Longmans, Green, and Co., 1889.

—— ed. *Ballads of the North Countrie*. London: Walter Scott, 1888.

—— *Border Ballads*. London: Walter Scott [1888].

—— *Selections from the Greek Anthology*. London: Walter Scott [1889].

U., 'Notes on Notables: Graham R. Tomson.' *Woman* 17 August 1892, 4–5.

Vadillo, Ana I. Parejo, 'New Women Poets and the Culture of the *salon* at the *fin de siècle*'. *Woman: A Cultural Review* 10.1 (1999), 22–34.

Van Vechten, Carl, *The Tiger in the House*. New York: Alfred A. Knopf, 1920.

Waltman, John L., 'The Early London Journals of Elizabeth Robins Pennell'. PhD dissertation, The University of Texas, 1976.

White, Gleeson, ed., *Ballades and Rondeaus, Chants-Royal, Sestinas, Villanelles, &c.* London: Walter Scott, 1887.

Whittington-Egan, Richard, and Geoffrey Smerdon, *The Quest of the Golden Boy: The Life and Letters of Richard Le Gallienne*. Barre, Mass.: Barre Publishing Company, 1962.

Wicke, Jennifer, *Advertising Fictions: Literature, Advertisement, and Social Reading*. New York: Columbia University Press, 1988.

Wiener, Joel H., ed., *Papers of the Millions: The New Journalism in Britain, 1850s to* New York: Greenwood Press, 1988.

—— 'Edmund Yates: The Gossip as Editor'. *Innovators and Preachers: The Role of the Editor in Victorian England*. Ed. Joel H. Wiener. Westport, Conn. and London: Greenwood Press, 1985, pp. 259–74.

Wilde, Oscar, *The Complete Works of Oscar Wilde*. New York: Harper & Row, 1989.

—— Review of *The Bird-Bride*, by Graham R. Tomson. *Woman's World* 2 (July 1889), 447–8.

'"Woman" Portraits'. Advertisement. *Woman* 20 October 1892, iii.

8
Arnold Bennett's Other Selves
Robert Squillace

Ideas of self-fashioning are as various and as contradictory to each other in the Edwardian period as general concepts generally are at any time and place. Indeed, they tend to inconsistency in the work of any individual author one might choose to examine, a phenomenon for which Arnold Bennett provides spectacular confirmation. For that matter, it is unlikely that anyone has ever held an entirely coherent idea of self, let alone of self-fashioning – considered, that is, in abstraction from the particular contexts in which their various constructions of self come into use. Within the economy of a particular kind of exchange, however, the manner in which a writer (or a larger linguistic community) delineates the self against some named, implied or suppressed other often reveals coherent motives and produces extra-discursive consequences. The disparate attitudes towards a concept like self-fashioning voiced by the same author according to the perceived needs of different sorts of literary exchange can thus reveal more than the fault-lines in the concept itself. Examining the relation between the incommensurable models of self-fashioning Arnold Bennett provided for readers of his pocket philosophies and of his literary fiction clarifies the imagined consequences that distinguished literature from other forms of discourse for Bennett himself, for his period and perhaps for the novelistic tradition itself.

Declarations of the soul's plasticity, its capacity to assume whatever shape a disciplined will imposed upon it, grew plentifully on the Edwardian landscape. The term 'self-made man', initially a product of an American determination to establish its democratic credentials by contriving to judge character against the yardstick of wealth rather than birth, had rooted itself in the mother country's lexicon by 1860.[1] The phrase, of course, equates self-formation with economic success,

the romance of which dubious formula inspired a considerable literature in the second half of the nineteenth century, from the self-help
books of Samuel Smiles to the novels of Horatio Alger. As a novelist
with the highest artistic aspirations, Bennett was an unlikely but dedicated inheritor of this tradition. No writer of any period even a fraction
so highly regarded as Bennett wrote a single self-help book, let alone
the six or eight Bennett produced; no Edwardian beat the drum of self-
improvement more insistently than he.[2]

Never so crass as to pretend that the accumulation of wealth beto-
kened high moral fibre – the light play *What The Public Wants* (1909)
takes virtually the opposite position, implying that a blindness to scruples was indispensable to creating a financial titan of the Northcliffe
mould – Bennett nevertheless preserved an association between
making money and making oneself in his guides to self-improvement.
These self-help books, slender volumes Bennett half-accurately called
his 'pocket philosophies', clearly imagine their audience as the striving
class. In his most popular self-help book, *How to Live on 24 Hours a Day*,
Bennett plucks from the admitted multitude of possibilities for repre-
senting his typical reader 'a Londoner who works in an office ... and
who spends fifty minutes morning and night in travelling between his
house door and his office door' (42). In other words, a suburban, non-
industrial worker. The book's title is itself a budgetary metaphor: the
great majority of people, Bennett proclaims, 'cannot arrange that an
income of twenty-four hours a day shall exactly cover all proper items
of expenditure' (26). Perceiving that the desire for self-improvement
would be strongest in those for whom work was neither an expression
of personal desire nor a physically exhausting necessity, Bennett
explicitly identifies his putative reader as someone whose job is a
matter of personal indifference, a way to make a living rather than a
way of life. The self-help books assume a reader employed for salary in
someone else's business. Satisfaction and self-realisation for this office
worker must come in leisure hours if they are to come at all.

Bennett's vision of self-fashioning as a process divorced from and
even antithetical to ordinary working life embedded itself immediately
and deeply in the mass mind. *How to Live on 24 Hours a Day*, by its
author's own accounting in his *Journal 1929*, sold more copies than
any other book he had written, surpassing even the far more aggres-
sively publicised novels of the 1920s.[3] The book's place in popular consciousness may be gauged by the iconic role it played in the fiction of
those who remembered its impact. When Maud Hart Lovelace, for
instance, reconstructed the world of Mankato, Minnesota in 1912 for

her young adult novel *Emily of Deep Valley* (1950), an unusually detailed psychological portrait of an adolescent's conscious formation of her adult self, she slyly cited *How to Live on 24 Hours a Day* as a model for her heroine's disciplined struggle toward self-possession (and cited Bennett's book with a brevity that suggests she assumed her own readers would still be generally aware of the book's contents). In the novel, the orphaned Emily Webster, a bright young woman constrained to live at home by her grandfather's infirmity while classmates with little intellectual curiosity trip thoughtlessly off to sleepwalk through their collegiate studies, sinks for a time into a paralytic despair; 'Life,' she feels along with the unsatisfied readers who populate Bennett's self-help books, 'was passing without love or work' (108). Finally taking herself in hand, she visits her High School English teacher, Miss Fowler, to begin a self-directed and self-empowering programme of reading. While her mentor makes tea, Emily absorbs the lessons of the apartment's furnishings, which imply that an unmarried woman might find satisfaction in art and thought, and picks a single volume, not from the teacher's bookshelf, but from those laid conveniently on her table: '*How to Live on 24 Hours a Day*, by Arnold Bennett' (132). While Emily later gives the book only jocular credit for the focus and energy she subsequently achieves, for her determination to define a self almost literally independent of her daily circumstances,[4] the main arc of her progress closely resembles the trajectory Bennett envisaged in his pocket philosophies. *Mental Efficiency*, for instance, imputes to those readers eager for self-improvement the fundamental conviction that 'it needs only an impulse, an effort, a system, in order gradually to cure the mind of its slackness ... and to enable it to grapple with the splendours of knowledge that await it!' (11). *How to Live on 24 Hours a Day* invokes the totem of system as well; when recommending a course of self-improvement to those with an inchoate fondness for music, for instance, Bennett assures them that 'The foundations of a genuine, systematic knowledge of music might be laid' (81) in a few hours a week spare time so long as they follow a regular and coherent plan of study. Emily begins to transcend her crippling consciousness of limitation when she systematises her empty hours: '"I'll start taking [piano] lessons again," she planned. "Another thing I can do, of course, is read – not the way I've been doing, but to some purpose"' (129). Emily starts her programme by taking advantage of the hours she must read aloud to her grandfather, choosing a biography of Lincoln, that American icon of heroic self-education, titled *The True Story of a Great Life*. Bennett's declaration in *Literary Taste* that 'The aim of literary study is not to amuse the hours of leisure; it is to awake oneself, it is to be alive, to intensify one's capacity for pleasure, for sympathy, and for comprehension' (12) applies in every particular to Lovelace's hero. That Lovelace may well never have read *Literary Taste* or *Mental Efficiency* demonstrates how influential a model of self-help Bennett had hit upon.[5] As Emily persists in her effort to exercise the faculties she hasn't the chance to develop at college, she learns that life everywhere has equal value and interest, that she has no less opportunity to live meaningfully, to live consequentially, confined to Deep Valley than her friends do at college – indeed, hers is the fuller life, because she has recognised her own responsibility for the direction it takes and for the quality of every hour composing it. 'Nothing in Life is Humdrum', the title of a chapter in *How to Live on 24 Hours a Day* proclaims. Happiness, Bennett avers, 'does not spring from the procuring of physical or mental pleasure, but from the development of reason and the adjustment of conduct to principles' (71). Lovelace's construction of self-formation in *Emily of Deep Valley* helps illuminate the appeal of Bennett's pocket philosophies. That he initially links the process of self-formation with that of accumulation, harking back to the familiar equation of social arrival and self-realisation with wealth, reassures his readers that they are not on ground too unfamiliar to them, too psychologically slippery. Money is no longer the object to be accrued, however; Bennett instead promises aid in slaking 'the disturbing thirst to improve one's self – to increase one's knowledge' (HTL 33), making self-improvement and the stockpiling of facts interchangeable processes.[6] The self thus improved – as by Emily's reading programme – seems construed as a sum of experiences. Such a conception promises a return of value on one's investment – committing the time and effort to learn coordinated facts unfailingly procures a better self – that suits the distinctly middle-class audience to whom Bennett addressed these books.

And yet, for all his emphasis on systematic improvement by concentrated study, Bennett ultimately leaves his readers with an equally comforting image of the self as something that is not formed, but formative, the director of activities above which it stands untouchable: 'My sense of security amid the collisions of existence lies in the firm consciousness that just as my body is the servant of my mind, so is my mind the servant of *me*' (ME 113). Inconsistent as these two constructions may appear (or actually be), both spring from a single root. In Bennett's pocket philosophies, the concepts of self and self-formation are defined strictly in relation to personal happiness. In the context of giving advice on how to be happy to people whose work is neither physically exhausting nor personally fulfilling (being undertaken largely under someone else's direction for the abstract benefit of a 'company', it offers selfhood no role), 'self' becomes that which is separate from material circumstances. In the economy of self-help discourse, the control absent from working life is balanced by a complete autonomy in self-formation, the 'I' developing in the manner most pleasing to itself, in the direction it alone chooses. Nowhere does Bennett address the possibility that following his advice to greater self-possession might change one's relation to the world of work. As Peter McDonald establishes in *British Literary Culture and Publishing Practice, 1880–1914*, Bennett's own burgeoning artistic aspirations required him to negotiate a complex system of what might constitute acceptable and unacceptable work for a serious writer. But in his self-help books, he assumes a readerly self bounded, like Emily, by circumstances at once inalterable and incapable of permeating the envelope of self. The autonomy of self-formation from circumstances simultaneously asserts its powerlessness before them; self is precisely that which, unlike what lies beyond its boundaries, can be controlled. What can't be controlled isn't 'self'.

Privileging happiness, however, has the curious side-effect of ruling emotion and desire outside the land of disciplined and mature selfhood: 'Nearly always, when the heart opposes the brain, the heart is merely a pretty name which we give to our idleness and our egotism' (HM 118). He rules out natural abilities and their absence, writing in *Mental Efficiency* that 'I hear you say that kindliness of heart can be "cultivated". Well, I hate to contradict you, but it can only be cultivated in the botanical sense. You can't cultivate violets on a nettle' (ME 38). Even his obsession with the external facts of cause and effect – attention to which, he claims in *How to Live on 24 Hours a Day*, gives life its spice – surreptitiously advances the case for the autonomous self; such detailed contemplation serves to confirm the self's discontinuity from the physical world. The intended consequence of enabling a happy adjustment to limitation controls all facets of Bennett's definition of self in his self-help books; as he writes in *The Human Machine*, 'If we regard ourselves as free agents, and the personalities surrounding us as the puppets of determinism, we shall have arrived at the working compromise from which the finest results can be obtained' (78). Under these terms, self-formation is not a gradual or sudden differentiation of one's own behaviour from alternative ways of acting, but a process of continual adjustment of inward attitude to outward circumstance.

The relation of self to other that Bennett enacts in the pocket philosophies demonstrates the economy of his discourse of self-formation even more tellingly than the advice he gives. Bennett adopts a voice in these works so strongly marked as to border on self-parody. Anyone with the least talent for pastiche could mimic it. You address your reader in second person, exactly as if he sat opposite you in the compartment of a second-class railway carriage. Specify the class of the railway carriage! You must maintain the illusion of physical presence at all costs; the atmosphere of plain speech betwixt man and man might otherwise dissipate like fog. Besides, you must show an intimate acquaintance with the world of bright particulars that your auditor so often sums up to himself in a blind cliché; your purpose, after all, is to acquaint him with that stranger, his own mind, which requires training above all in the art of observation. Invent questions and objections to fill the mouth of your reader, speaking not only to but for him. Leave no abstraction to float nebulously before the man's eternal but quite possibly bored or tired consciousness, instead producing a pungent anecdote or metaphor to illustrate every large statement you make about remorse or judgement or success or what have you. Your mood must be declarative and imperative, never interrogative. You are the authority, the man who does.[7] The job of thinking is not your reader's; it is yours, and ought to be effectually hidden. Cultivate the aphoristic touch. Slogans give the man opposite you a chance to take stock, to assure himself that 'Yes, I see what the chap's getting at. I shall remember that.' Your grammar, than which nothing more securely marks your authority, should flaunt its impeccability just enough to establish your superior standing without making you seem overbearing. Pitch your vocabulary, too, just an inch or two above the height of daily speech so as to look ever so slightly downward into your reader's eyes, while maintaining an overall impression of colloquialism.

Such a prose style, like a finger poked repeatedly against one's chest, serves to measure the distance between the pocket philosopher and oneself. Whatever else Bennett might be telling a reader of his self-help books, he simultaneously remarks the fact of difference between himself and that reader. He never allows himself to be caught in the act of reasoning his way towards his aphorisms, despite his emphasis on the sovereignty of reason, for the process of thinking involves equivocation and uncertainty, ifs and buts. Instead, he simply informs his readers how to build wiser and happier selves. Indeed, readers enter the texts, only to be found wanting. In the first of the series of columns that became *Mental Efficiency*, Bennett invites his audience to explain their own systems for achieving the goal his title identifies. In the second column, though Bennett disavows any ambition 'to play the role of the Sandow of the brain' (14), he proceeds to judge the advice of his correspondents from a position of absolute authority, ending by co-opting their voices: 'Let me take your case, O man or woman of thirty, living in comfort, with some cares, and some responsibilities, and some pretty hard daily work, but not too much of any! The question of mental efficiency is in the air. It interests you. It touches you nearly. Your conscience tells you that your mind is less active and less informed than it might be' (20). Less, that is, than the mind of the man who wrote *Mental Efficiency*. Bennett thus constructs himself in direct and almost truculent contrast to his readers as the man who knows what they don't, who has trained himself to perceive clearly what they at best hazily apprehend, who has achieved the self-discipline they covet. He is an author because he is an authority; we are readers because we are not.

To draw a boundary, though, is to acknowledge the possibility that it might be crossed or even to invite such passage. The distinction between the masterful author and the incapable reader has such prominence in the self-help books because self-help is the process of crossing from incapacity to mastery. In fact, the 'I' and 'you' of Bennett's imaginary conversations with his reader finally emerge as mirror images of each other, separate only by reason of their positions on opposite sides of the text. 'I have not the pleasure of your acquaintance,' Bennett writes in *Mental Efficiency*, 'But I know you because I know myself' (21). The apparent fatuity of this claim lessens when one recognises that the essential idea of self-formation these books advance exiles individuality from the realm of selfhood. To know oneself in Bennett's 'philosophical' view is to recognise one's independence from internal event as fully as from external, to depersonalise experience as much as possible. At the end of *Mental Efficiency*, in fact, Bennett intimates that his readers might achieve his own Olympian calm by meditation on the mystic identity of selfhood: 'The same Force pervades my razor, my cow in my field, and the central me which dominates my mind: the same force in different stages of evolution. And that Force persists for ever' (114). Everyone's case is identical in Arnold Bennett's self-help clinic; he never subdivides his patients into discrete diagnostic types. Indeed, the pocket philosophies offer absolutely no advice on the *culti-*

vation of difference – self-fashioning seems to involve the erasure of personal distinctions.

So, adorning his chatty treatises with a smattering of stoic formulas from Epictetus and Marcus Aurelius, Bennett insisted on the absolute freedom, within very narrow boundaries, of self-formation. However useful his concept of self may have been within the confines of the self-help game, however much his vision of autonomy may have assuaged dissatisfaction with a life of unfulfilling work and undirected leisure, Bennett's model simultaneously comprehends far less attractive consequences. By avowing that all selves are cut from essentially the same stuff, he implicitly denies any vital relation of individual to community, any communal role in self-formation, other selves offering nothing in the search for purpose that one may not already find within. One element of Emily Webster's transformation into her adult self emphatically not inspired by *How to Live on 24 Hours a Day* is her devotion to local social causes. Further, for all the cloudy indeterminacy of its status as essential being, 'self' tends to operate as a kind of mechanism in the pocket philosophies. Indeed, the titles of these books read like a collection of technical manuals: *Self and Self-Management, Mental Efficiency, The Human Machine, How to Live on 24 Hours a Day, Literary Taste: How to Form It, How to Make the Best of Life.* Even if one takes Bennett at his word and regards the self as the director of the machinery and not the gears and fly-rods themselves, the process of self-formation remains not only curiously divested of emotion, it requires an almost Boethian escape from emotion. Bennett admits as much in *Mental Efficiency*: 'I freely grant that such meditation [on the self's impersonality], while it "casts out fear", slowly kills desire and makes for a certain high indifference' (116). So attached is Bennett to locating ultimate selfhood in an impersonal unity that he gravely and laughably informs his readers that 'science' confirms his claims (ME 114). 'Science', of course, was and remains a mass cultural emblem of the impersonal.

One ultimately wonders if the whole apparatus of self-formation as conceived in the pocket philosophies is meant to box and control, in effect to exterminate, what it purports to perfect. The self-help books invariably abstract selfhood from personal, emotional experience in greater and greater measure as they progress. Early in *The Human Machine*, for instance, Bennett scorns the idea that the brain – shorthand for the life of the individual intellect – acts as the seat of selfhood: 'Do you love your mother, wife, or children with your brain? Do you desire with your brain? Do you, in a word, ultimately and essentially live with your brain?' (28). By the last instalment of the series, however, Bennett has reversed field: 'When the reason and the heart come into conflict,' he declares, 'the heart is invariably wrong' (117). To feel it seems, makes one guilty of the crimes of individuality and subjectivity, for Bennett insists that the final step in realising selfhood is to reduce oneself to a disinterested observer of external phenomena: 'And this habit of originally examining phenomena ... fosters reliance on one's self and courage to accept the consequences of the act of reasoning' (123). The price of autonomy is the very desire originally identified as the essence of life.

Of course, Bennett had made himself into an author of imaginative fiction, a literary taste-maker, and a public figure who found his own portrait staring at him from the sides of hundreds of London busses by just such self-abnegating discipline as he advocates in his pocket philosophies. He completed his first novel by rising early every Sunday morning for a year and writing for several hours, replacing one sort of religious observance with another. Throughout most of his career, and particularly while establishing himself as a name, Bennett maintained time schedules as inviolable as an English railway's. He lived, in fact, like a human machine; as Dorothy Cheston Bennett commented, 'that machinery which Arnold had set up around, and in support and defence of, his existence, did, for one who lived with it, intervene between the spontaneous and necessary expression of that person's individual and private soul' (D.C. Bennett 54). He tallied his score of written words in each year's final journey entry, thus locating his identity as a writer in objective fact. Indeed, McDonald points out that, as Bennett transformed himself from editor to author, he showed an unusual consciousness of the fact that 'To acknowledge his new position and prospects fully, he required not only the sanction of "fellow artists" ... but also the *imprimatur* of the right cultural intermediaries, including critics and above all, publishers' (72). Frank Swinnerton commented that Bennett 'never spoke of his own books, though often of the number of words he had written that day' (CH 525), while André Gide, after one of his earliest encounters with the Englishman's intimidating industry, marvelled in his journal that 'he writes without stopping every day from six a.m. to nine a. m., then gets into his bath and doesn't think of his work again until the next morning' (329). Thus, both Bennett's own self-formation and the image of it he presented to his fellow writers were founded upon a vigilantly maintained distance from the subjective. His self-help books, it seems, projected his own need for mental discipline onto his readers. The premise of

How to Live on 24 Hours a Day, after all, dovetails precisely with Bennett's private habit of word-counting; the idea that one must compartmentalise time so as not to 'waste' it follows from an assumption that some objective measure of accomplishment is the truest test of success. Bennett even insists in *The Human Machine*, again universalising his personal experience, that the course of history has been ruled by just such feats of self-control as his own: 'If you admit that [human nature] has changed, let me ask you how it has changed, unless by the continual infinitesimal efforts, upon themselves, of individual men, like you and me' (81). If Bennett is not the Sandow of the brain, it is only because we all are.

As one would expect of a man intent on circumventing the snare of purely personal experience, Bennett wrote relatively little about his transformation of self from provincial law clerk to cosmopolitan novelist. When he did, he found opportunities to strike the triadic chord of discipline, impersonality and observation. In 'The Making of Me', written for his friend Lord Beaverbrook's *Daily Express*, which ran a series of such pieces by well-known authors, Bennett offered only a few lightning sketches of the more distinctive figures he had observed in childhood. About his own interior life, he commented only, 'I spent large portions of time in being bored' (S 5). But he admitted – or, perhaps, boasted – that his childhood had impressed upon him the values of work and silence: 'I grew up in an atmosphere of sustained effort, of grim "sticking it," of silent endurance, of never being beaten by circumstances. I am now glad of it' (5). A few years later, Bennett slipped into his fact-drenched account of 'How I was Educated' a description of his recent proud discovery that the iron constitution of his mentality allowed him to digest scraps of time too bony for more sensitive souls: 'Since then, in odd half-hours suddenly thrown to me by the vagaries of men and circumstance, I have considerably advanced even long books, which many authors will not touch unless they feel sure of at least three uninterrupted hours' (S 12). Most strikingly of all, in *The Truth About an Author* (1903; reprinted 1911 (US) and 1914 (UK)), Bennett presents the origin of his literary life not in irresistible desire but in happy accident. He repeatedly ascribes the impetus for his work, and even the origins of his mature self-conception, to outside forces. He begins to consider his temperament 'artistic' only when an established artist informs him from his privileged, exterior perspective that '"You've got it as badly as any of us, if you only knew it"' (6); only recognises his own sensitivity when a doctor diagnoses him as '"one of the most highly-strung men I have ever met"'

(48); only writes his first novel when yet another wise observer asks '"Why don't you write a novel on Sundays?"' (49). Even the book's title, by its reference to *an* author, suggests the impersonality of the sort of artistic identity Bennett was willing to claim for himself. Indeed, Bennett so habitually ruled personal desire out of the narrative of his self-formation that he insisted of his acknowledged masterpiece, *Riceyman Steps* (albeit in the midst of a contractual dispute), that 'I wrote the book at the special instigation of [Newman] Flower' (L I 328).[8] Little wonder that Bennett repeatedly stressed detachment as one of the identifying marks all true novelists displayed.

That Bennett might have performed the romance of his artistic self-discovery far differently throws into even sharper relief his presentation of his literary career as the result of external circumstances acting on a core of native talent, virtually unaffected by any desire for self-expression. As in the prevailing modernist myth of self-formation, his emergence as a writer involved parricide. Born Enoch Arnold Bennett, the novelist was saddled with the first name of his father, a self-made man of the old variety who had passed the law exams his son failed without the benefit of nearly so much educational preparation. Enoch Bennett died in January 1902; at the end of that year, when Arnold discontinued the column he had written for 'Hearth and Home' since October 1900, he had signed a piece 'E.A. Bennett' for the last time. He did continue to sign himself 'EAB' in letters to such old friends as H.G. Wells, as close to a surrogate father as Bennett had among his own generation, until 23 November 1908 – about a week after publication of *The Old Wives' Tale* had in Wells' own words 'at least doubled your size in my estimation' (AB/HG 154). Thereafter, Bennett usually signed letters to friends, including Wells, as 'A.B.' thus appropriating the first two letters of the alphabet as his initials and so betokening his transformation from lawyer's son to man of letters.[9] In 1920, when the agent J.B. Pinker refunded part of a loan 'E.A. Bennett' had made to D.H. Lawrence back in the grim year of 1915, Lawrence had to ask 'And who is E.A. Bennett' (DHL L I 621).

In accordance with another modernist myth, Bennett might have narrated the creation of his authorial self in the language of journey and escape. Fleeing the geographic and symbolic middle of industrial England, he made himself a Londoner in the early 1890s, then became a Parisian about the same time as Picasso and Joyce. But Bennett never publicly assigned his exile any vital role in the formation of his artistic identity. Instead, 'The Man Who Does' commonly wrote his travel pieces in the same reader-centred manner as his pocket philosophies, taking his English audience inside the casinos of Monte Carlo or atop a Swiss mountain and snappily moralising the landscape for them. He remains a detached observer, explaining and judging foreign usages for a specifically English audience, but never entertaining the possibility that dislocation from the Potteries might relate to his own achievement of an authorial self. Joyce for one performed his exile far differently, implicitly claiming the superior perspective of distance by composing his fullest statement on the identity of Ireland in Italian, 1907's 'Irlanda, Isola dei Santi e dei Savi', which he delivered as a lecture, not to an Irish audience, but to a polyglot group in Trieste (see Mason/Ellman 153–74). Nor did Bennett choose to portray himself as a temporal exile, a Hugh Selwyn Mauberley out of joint with his time, even though he shared the modernist attitude that the industrial era failed to nurture artistic appreciation as past epochs had. Indeed, he explicitly refuses this option in a piece, 'Morning and Evening in Florence', that he wrote for *The English Review* shortly after Ford Madox Ford had flared out of its editorship. Alighting in Florence for the first time, Bennett compares the condition of the arts in the great Florentine age of public support and recognition with the current period of mass public indifference. Rather than offering the typical Poundian lament at this state of affairs, he declares,

> There is an agreeable bitterness, an exquisite tang, in the thought of the loneliness of artists in an age whose greatness and whose epic quality are quite divorced from art. And when I think of the artist in this age, I think of the Invisible Man of H.G. Wells, in the first pride of his invisibility ... I like to be that man ... there is something beyond happiness, and that is, to know intensely and painfully that you are what you are. (reprinted in *Paris Nights* 128–9)

Maybe Bennett could afford to dismiss the importance of a readership only because he had already acquired one, but in any case he acts as he might advise a reader of *Mental Efficiency*, taking refuge from outward circumstances in a vision of contact with an essential, inward selfhood much like that ultimately envisioned in the pocket philosophies: a central identity (in this case, artistic) that is not formed but formative. Although Bennett noted in his Journal that 'the sight of this district [the Potteries] gave me a shudder' (J 983) when he passed it on a train bound from Manchester to London in 1927, he never publicly ascribed his achievement of an artistic career to his escape from its narrow perspectives.

Finally, for all his self-discipline, Bennett had almost as strong a claim to self-victimising artistic sensibilities as Kafka or Proust. A 'nervously organised' insomniac, he suffered all his life from a severe and incurable stutter, an incapacity to control the most basic means of delivering himself to others. He might well have located the source of his artistic identity in his sensitive inner being's *inability* to fashion itself, his helplessness before the onslaught of sensations and emotions callously deflected by the thicker skinned and less discerning. Instead, he crowed in *The Truth About an Author*, 'What a fine thing to be highly-strung, nervously organized!' (48), thus immediately reassuring his audience that no peculiar suffering accompanied his sensitivity – nothing that would touch the core of his being. In fact, he claimed to remain unaware of his condition until a physician informed him of it. He similarly turned his insomnia into a public performance of dynamic energy, a sign of his indefatigable interest in life, announcing in the preface to *How to Live on 24 Hours a Day* that 'I am convinced that most people sleep as long as they do because they are at a loss for any other diversion' (xii). His journal tells a different story. Bennett charted the advances and retreats in his life-long war with Morpheus as assiduously as he tallied the number of words he wrote: 'Of course I did not have a very good night' (10 November 1903; 127), 'Considerable inconvenience from sleeplessness' (2 June 1908; 303), 'I awoke at 2 A.M. and after then scarcely dozed' (2 June 1910; 376), 'Slept at R.T.Y.C. [Royal Thames Yacht Club] Very good. I finished *The Lion's Share* on Wednesday night and slept very ill and was really too fatigued for London, but I took a tonic, which did me good' (4 December 1915; 575), 'He [Edward Elgar] seldom talks to me without mentioning his poverty and my riches. I suppose this is natural, and I expect I should do it in his place. I have a grievance, and it is that I sleep badly, and I am always mentioning it' (10 May 1924; 177–8), 'Fair night, vitiated by over-smoking. However, at the end I received from God just over $2\frac{1}{2}$ hours of unbroken sleep, and at 5:45 accordingly felt restored to health' (26 March 1927; 942). Even in our own caffeine-drenched days, few but new parents would regard two and a half hours of sleep as a godsend. Perhaps finding his stammer impossible to interpret as evidence of self-control, Bennett never mentioned it in public documents except so murkily that only intimate friends might conceivably have recognised it through the fog of abstraction, as in *The Truth About an Author's* reference to 'intellectual complaints' (48). The problem was so severe, according to Somerset Maugham, that 'it was painful to watch the struggle he had sometimes to get the words out. It was torture to him' (R. Pound 31). And yet, the idea that his exceptional facility in print originated in his difficulty with conversation seems not to have occurred to the author of *Self and Self-Management*.

Why, then, did Bennett write weakness and desire out of the story of self-formation he concocted for his Edwardian public? The vogue for neurasthenia, of course, followed the First World War, by which time the public snapshot of Bennett had long since been dipped in its fixative bath. One might also argue that Bennett constructed a persona that flattered the hope of a positivist age for free self-formulation – the idea that consciously reasoning from careful observation might allow a perfect understanding and control of both self and state had great appeal at a time when the authority of hierarchical traditions of obedience seemed in retreat everywhere and Freud had yet to be translated. But such arguments do not touch the particularity of Bennett's self-presentation, so different from those of such equally pre-modernist, pro-rationalist figures as H.G. Wells and George Bernard Shaw. Only Bennett strove to make himself transparent; so enraptured did he purport to be with the romance of having an audience, of earning a living by writing, that he baulked at suggesting his essential self might be shaded differently from the souls of his readers.[10] Promising on the first page of *The Truth About an Author* 'to trace as well as I can the phenomena of the development of that idiosyncrasy [authorship] from its inception to such maturity as it has attained' (5–6), Bennett instead describes a series of objective events, from the earliest narrative he recalled reading (significantly, a story of success by objectified transformation, 'The Ugly Duckling') to the moment when his 'brain was visited by a Plot' (51) and he wrote his first literary story (which appeared in *The Yellow Book*), to his removal from London to the land of rural inspiration, where, the author having at last escaped the world of exterior circumstances to that of his own mind, the book promptly ends, foretelling death.[11] Only a writer so determined to define 'self' as an impersonal essence practically identical in all its singular manifestations could have written as variously as Bennett did. Bennett, that is, might comfortably write whatever he perceived would fit a market because he did not refer his authorial impulse to his own desires or to the necessities of unconscious conflicts. The staggering contradictions between pieces like *The Grand Babylon Hotel* and *Anna of the Five Towns* (both 1902), between *How to Live on 24 Hours a Day*, *The Old Wives' Tale* and *Buried Alive* (all 1908), between *Mister Prohack*, *Riceyman Steps* and *How to Make the Best of Life* (1922, 1923 and 1923, respectively) troubled critics even while

Bennett was alive; the first major posthumous study, Geoffrey West's revealingly titled *The Problem of Arnold Bennett* (1932), concerns itself largely with the question of Bennett's unevenness. West's titular 'problem' arises from the expectation that an author – or, at least, a great author, a serious author – writes out of his or her individuality, out of the most personal and private regions of the self, creating what he or she most wants to create. By seeming to escape the demands of self, by maintaining and advertising his schedules and his discipline, Bennett managed a pyrrhic victory. He created an appealing if shallow version of self-formation that a very large audience evidently found useful for overcoming lassitude or hopelessness, and he made himself the illustration of his programme's success, greatly to the detriment of his reputation with fellow artists and taste-makers.

Equally, though, Bennett's inclination to write the same book of 'practical philosophy' over and over and to arrange his day by its com-partmentalist principles suggests that he may himself have been the primary audience for his many volumes of hearty encouragement. One may read his declaration of identity with the readers of *Mental Efficiency* as an admission that he, as much as they, needed to hold himself to his chosen course by an almost violent exertion of will. The expense of so much energy on the maintenance of self-possession pre-supposes the existence of a self always ready to rebel or, perhaps, to fly apart. It is true that in his pocket philosophies Bennett conceives the impulses of desire as exterior to an impenetrable core of selfhood, to an 'I' that may choose freely whether to yield to the blandishments of pleasure and the menaces of fear or to transcend them. Self-formation in such books is the disciplinary process by which the self discovers and sustains its utter independence from internal promptings as well as external stimuli. It does so by constant vigilance, becoming its own panopticon, in Foucault's terms, though Bennett found his philosoph-ical sanction in Herbert Spencer's *First Principles*, which he often cited as the book that most influenced his thinking.[12] In Bennett's serious fiction, however, a different economy rules the usage of his concepts of self and self-formation.[13] The very impulses ruled outside the bound-aries of selfhood appear from this perspective as its essence, while self-control resembles an externalised Blakean 'governor'. Such a model problematises the whole concept of self and turns self-formation at every level into an expressive rather than a repressive process. Not only did Bennett depict the process by which his central characters formu-late their adult selves as a blossoming forth of infolded desire, but the story of his own self-formation, as retold in the person of his more autobiographically inspired heroes and heroines, contradicts the version of publications like *The Truth About an Author* or 'The Making of Me'. And the relation he constructs between narrative self and reader actively undermines that established by the bantering hector of *The Human Machine* and its like.

One finds the most tightly focused depictions of self-formation in Bennett's intertwined Bildungsromans, *Clayhanger* (1910) and *Hilda Lessways* (1911). Both novels do connect the establishment of a mature, independent identity with a power of self-direction very similar to that advocated in the pocket philosophies. Bennett's title characters, Edwin Clayhanger and Hilda Lessways, stand out from their human and physical environments by their uniquely developed senses of the superiority of rational organisation. Edwin, indeed, bears 'the holy flame of the desire for self-perfection' (C 28) like a halo over his curly-haired head, while Hilda in her 'youthful passion for order and efficiency' (HL 38) recognises, like the frustrated clerks and house-bound wives at whom the pocket philosophies are aimed, that 'domesticity was not life itself, was at best the clumsy external machinery of life' (HL 49).[14] In other words, either would make an ideal reader for *Mental Efficiency* or *How to Live on 24 Hours a Day*. And yet, they would find little useful guidance from their creator in those texts, for the distractions of impulse do not prove the enemy of self-direction in the novels as in the self-help books. Rather, the conventions of patriarchal authority, the systematic assertion of privilege to create relationships of grossly unequal power, chiefly impede Hilda and Edwin in their quest for self-possession, often obstructing their wishes even within the apparent privacy of their own minds. Self-formation appears, not as an escape from desire into impersonality, but as a struggle to express the desires that the forces of a coercive conventionalism would suppress. Further, Edwin and Hilda achieve some degree of self-possession, of freedom from the exterior influences of social programming, only by a series of impulsive leaps into the waters of uncharted behaviour. Edwin falters in his youthful attempt at directing his own life when he quails at the opposition of his authoritarian father to his desire to become an architect; he fails, that is, to choose how he will live in accordance with his own impulses, instead accepting the strictures imposed upon him by the ancient tradition that the son must, Telemachus-like, reiterate the identity established by his father. He eventually takes over the printing business Darius has created. Throughout the rest of the novel, Edwin struggles to assert an independent self against the formative influence of his social position, often nearly succumbing to the image of himself the world expects to see. He finds himself inordinately impressed by fellow members of The Felons Club, an ostensibly social organisation of affluent men that in fact holds the reins of local government securely, if unofficially, in its hands. Though Edwin recovers his political senses, we soon find him, a few years past the age of thirty, beginning to calcify in attitudes he does not consciously approve: 'Bit by bit he was assuming the historic privileges of the English master of the house' (C 419). Hilda, who 'had always dreamt vaguely of an enlarged liberty, of wide interests, and of original activities – such as no woman of her knowledge had ever had' (HL 415), also loses the battle of individual desire against social expectation, falling before a conventionally glamorous show of mastering masculine force. Marrying the dashing George Cannon, she winds up confined to domestic drudgery: first, to help maintain his business and personal pretensions; later, to maintain herself and her son after Mr Cannon's still-living first wife has had him hauled off to prison for bigamy. Edwin and Hilda ultimately clear a space for self-possession, not by any planned opposition to (or even reasoned understanding of) the forces that press upon them, but by expressing their mutual desire. Having finally learned that Hilda is living in poverty after the dissolution of her illegal marriage, Edwin irrationally, impulsively, emotionally and surreptitiously goes to Brighton to find her. The whole trip is a plunge into the void: 'His brain was a maze of anarchy ... "What am I doing here? ... What's my object? Where's the sense of it? I'm nothing but a damned fool. I've got no plan. I don't know what I'm going to do"' (C 437–40). Having no plan saves Edwin's life. He and Hilda admit their love, severing themselves irrevocably from the oldest values of patriarchy: female virginity, the legitimacy of the male heir, the submergence of personal desire to community standards. They achieve their adult selves by the very impulsiveness that the self-help books condemn.

In making themselves, however, Hilda and Edwin attain nothing like the Olympian detachment their author defines as ultimate self-discovery in his pocket philosophies; none of Bennett's characters do, at least in the novels he regarded as his truest fiction. And yet, the protagonists of these novels are all moulded in the image of their creator, animated by the breath of his life in their nostrils. Though Bennett gently mocked the pretensions of his first novel, *A Man from the North* (1898), in which 'in obedience to my [aesthetic] philosophy, I made myself a failure' (T 65), he persisted in rewriting himself into corners he had successfully avoided in his own life, investing his fictional selves with little of the easy mastery and wise authority that marked the spruce figure of 'Arnold Bennett' that he presented to his various publics. Early and late, his author-surrogates embody all the anxiety about self-fashioning that his other publications suppress. Indeed, the fact that Bennett invariably remade himself as a failure suggests a perception, conscious or not, that his own concept of self might be deeply flawed.

Indeed, Bennett more often rehearsed the dissolution of his surrogate selves than their formation. *The Old Wives' Tale's* Sophia Baines and *Riceyman Steps'* Henry Earlforward provide the two finest examples. Each consistently reflects the creator's image, particularly in regard to the aspects of his character most emphasised by the pocket philosophies. Sophia, like Bennett, flees the provincial strictures of the Potteries and frankifies herself, at last finding scope for her 'gifts of organization, foresight, common sense and tenacity' (OWT 419). And, like Bennett, Henry Earlforward is 'highly strung and "highly nervously organized"' (63). According to Dorothy Cheston Bennett, Arnold's response to any suggested disarrangement of his time was 'I must know where I am' (D.C. Bennett 67); both Sophia and Henry express their needs for safe predictability in the same phrase (OWT 514; *Riceyman Steps* 96, 275, 286). But the death of each symbolises a collapse of self, a challenge to the very idea of a stable nucleus of selfhood, unthinkable in the discourse of *Mental Efficiency*. Indeed, physical causes are curiously absent in Sophia's case, given Bennett's zeal for medical accuracy. She declines and dies rapidly after claiming the body of her long-estranged husband. Her epiphany over his wasted figure teaches her the universality of being, the essential identity of every seemingly separate human self, but the perception that crowns the pocket philosopher in comfort wreathes the author's fictional self in despair. Her husband's death, Sophia recognises, will be hers; life offers only one story: 'She turned to the veiled window and idly pulled the blind and looked out. Huge red and yellow cars were swimming in thunder along Deansgate; lorries jolted and rattled; the people of Manchester hurried along the pavements, apparently unconscious that all their doings were vain' (OWT 578). The unity of self and other is found not in reference to eternity, but to the effects of time, equal for everyone. That Bennett provides little physical excuse for Sophia's immediately subsequent death makes it seem that she expires from her own perception of the unsure basis of her unique selfhood. Indeed, the scene caps a series of intimations of impersonality threaded throughout the novel, Sophia repeatedly adopting new identities that contradict the old, becoming in turn a prospective schoolteacher, an eager sensualist, a helpless invalid, a sharp hotelier who distrusts all emotion, a domineering sister, a proud but ineffectual dowager, and a helpless victim of fate, changing so deeply that Bennett can only describe her selfhood in contradictory terms: 'It did really seem to her ... that another Sophia had come into her body: so intensely conscious was she of a fundamental change in herself under the stress of continuous experience. And though this was but a seeming, though she was still the same Sophia more fully disclosed, it was a true seeming' (OWT 360). How does one make sense of 'a true seeming' of difference that is simultaneously identity? Reading this passage is like stepping into the middle of a family argument, except that both voices belong to Bennett, the philosophising Man Who Does insisting that experience merely burns away the impurities obscuring an essential selfhood, while AB, the novelist, suggests that identity might be discontinuous, the mutable function of time and place. The whole rhetoric of the novel, with its emphasis on replacement and oblivion, on forgetful generations succeeding to each other in semi-wilful ignorance of the shared story that robs each of any unique identity, opposes the philosopher.

Or suggests, at least, that in Bennett's novels he indulged his own fear of coming apart, of failing to hold the mighty engine of his mentality to some unified course. Henry Earlforward represents Bennett's most garish nightmare of the failure of his daytime philosophy: suffocation by the very tightness of the grip in which he held himself. In fact, Earlforward serves as the particular surrogate for the prophet of lofty impersonality who wrote *How to Live on 24 Hours a Day* and *The Human Machine* in letters of fire; 'a very great practical philosopher' (16) Henry exemplifies his creator's precepts of self-discipline, 'always so polite!' (218). Unlike the putative acolytes of Bennett's pocket philosophies, Henry makes no effort to interest himself in butterflies or urban planning or literature. He shows little inclination to read the thousands of books that fill his second-hand shop. But such lethargy is precisely the point: in *Riceyman Steps*, Bennett identifies the Aurelian impersonality he regards as the summit of self-formation in his pocket philosophies with a deadly inertia, a fatal incapacity for self-expression. Henry, as Bennett continually recommends in his self-help books, renders himself nearly immune from experience. 'He was now better. A little pain in the old spot – no more,' he convinces himself the evening of his wife's death; though he himself is mortally weak from cancer, he manages to transcend his mere feelings and walk unaided down the stairs to resume his neglected work (286). Such repression, constructed in the pocket philosophies as rising above attachment for the unworthy objects on which we might fix our affections, does not allow Henry a comforting vision of the immortality of his soul-stuff. It kills him. When he briefly succumbs to desire, marrying his new neighbour, he '[feels] himself to be exalted into some realm of romance surpassing his dreams' (91). Even before the single day of his honeymoon has ended, though, he has returned to his self-denying philosophy; he pares his meals down to the minimum, he spends less and less money, and he apparently stops spending himself in bed (219). When his wife dies, he transcends his grief before he even begins to plan a funeral, in a parody of the strictures against mourning from *Mental Efficiency* (42ff). Unlike the Bennett who chortles over the intense romance of composing 'facetious comments while my grandfather is dying upstairs!' (T 29), the callous hide of Henry Earlforward does not finally protect him from grief. Rather, he holds so much inside that he finally implodes. Shocked by his servant's pilfering of sixpence from his safe, he instantly expires, as if convinced at last that he cannot preserve his inward equanimity from the contamination of experience. Stoicism dies, not with a bang, but a whimper.

The situation of the self thrown back upon its own devices, in fact, always read as nightmare in Bennett's serious novels. The moments of truth invariably come in locked rooms, behind drawn blinds, or in the dark, the character's carefully tended self-image dissolving into nothingness in the absence of the objective contexts that have held it together. Samuel Povey begins to lose the stable self he has built around his roles as father, husband and draper when he literally sees into the dark rooms of his cousin's life; Sophia begins to fall apart in the curtained twilight of the room where her husband's body lies and totally dissolves while alone in the back of a car driving through the dark between Manchester and Bursley; Edwin Clayhanger discovers his father sitting on dim stairs after the funeral of his boyhood idol, his own old self smashed to pieces; Henry Earlforward meets his end alone in a carelessly unlocked room deep at night.[15] The status of the characters in the novels thus inverts the presumed situation of the readers to whom Bennett addressed his self-help books. According to *How to Live on 24 Hours a Day*, one best achieves the mood of detachment from present hopes and fears that allows the highest self-possession in the very evening hours that witness the dissolution of self-control in the novels (75). While Bennett advocated the systematic acquisition of expertise in a narrowly defined field as a path to self-improvement, he defined his identity as a novelist in a completely opposite way: 'in the whole of my life I have not devoted one day to the systematic study of literature,' he confessed in *The Truth About an Author* (36), and affirmed in 'How I Was Educated' that 'the novelist, who has to deal with everything in life, has a great privilege. He is permitted to have no exact knowledge of anything in life – except his craft, and not always that' (S 13). Such a contrast even suggests an inversion of performed gender in the narrative strategy of the novels from the masculine show of certainty – the George Cannon tone – of the pocket philosophies. In *Paris Nights*, Bennett describes a Parisienne who also 'had no exact knowledge of anything' (S 62). Like a novelist, as described by Bennett at the start of *The Truth About an Author*, she 'had no purpose in life; she was perfectly futile and useless' (62). And, like a novelist, she reads character: 'But she was acquainted with the secret nature of men and women; she could judge them shrewdly' (62). In the self-help books, there are no secrets; all motives are transparent and virtually universal.

Perhaps most startlingly of all, the author's creation of self by his (bridgeable) distance from the anti-self, his reader, changes radically in the novels. Bennett does not abandon second person and the imperative in his fiction, much as one sometimes wishes he had.[16] Rather, he uses these techniques in order to undermine them, to question his claim to a special authority denied readers. Bennett, for instance, informs his readers that the Potteries district 'gets up at six a.m., winter and summer ... that you may drink tea out of a teacup' (OWT 39), thus initially seeming to construct an audience that misperceives the world his characters inhabit, a world he may authoritatively explain. Such moments recur frequently, tempting readers to assume both the narrator's capacity to see to the core of each character and his willingness to explain them so fully that we need only listen passively. Late in *The Old Wives' Tale*, the narrator almost belligerently demands that we 'see Constance, stout and bowed ... See that face whose mark is meekness' (*OWT* 561). He then penetrates beneath what any mere observer, let alone we readers, could possibly see: 'you would not think that that placid soul could, while submitting to it, only rage against the imposed weight of Sophia's individuality' (561).

However, unlike the self-help books, whose premise is the possibility of climbing to the author's summit, in the novels we are offered no means by which to attain the narrator's expertise. Indeed, he must tell us what's in Constance's mind precisely because it shows itself by no outward sign. Consciousness is a sealed box. The narrator thus reveals his own ability to read minds, to be many selves simultaneously, as a fiction, a device by which to expose the inadequacy of any outward signs to manifest fully the self that inhabits them, if any such unitary creature indeed exists. Side by side with his imperative declarations of what we readers must recognise about a character or situation, Bennett plants quiet observations that ultimately whisper far greater secrets than the narrator shouts. That Constance feels a quasi-erotic attachment to her son Cyril, for instance, is established only by such third person observations as 'She liked to feel him and to gaze at him, and to smell that faint, uncleanly odour of sweat that hung in his clothes' (*OWT* 235) or that '[Cyril] was a far more brilliant, more advanced, more seductive being than his homely father' (*OWT* 303). In fact, only the subtlest hints had marked the progress of Constance's courtship with Mr Povey in the first place. The narrator even occasionally asserts falsehoods from his position of apparent privilege, as when he declares early in *The Old Wives' Tale* that 'the time will never come when the other towns ... will not pronounce the name of Bursley as one pronounces the name of one's mother' (*OWT* 40). By the end of the novel, Hanbridge having already siphoned off most of Bursley's trade, is fostering a federation of the Five Towns that will rob Bursley of its very name. The novel's structure itself – it is divided into long sections on Sophia's life in Paris and Constance's in Bursley – admits innumerable comparisons between the sisters, to none of which the narrator draws readerly attention, a technique even more spectacularly repeated in the first two novels of the *Clayhanger* trilogy, in which scenes originally narrated from Edwin's point of view are revisited from Hilda's with no comment on the significance (or even the existence) of the numerous discrepancies between the two. When the narrator observes toward the end of *The Old Wives' Tale* that 'No one but Constance could realise all that Constance had been through, and all that life had meant to her' he reverses, a little clumsily but definitively, the claim the author of *Mental Efficiency* had made to 'know you because I know myself' (21).

The point is not that Bennett's philosophy of self was, in the abstract, any less pocked with contradiction than anyone else's. Rather, the inconsistencies ultimately illuminate the nature of the exchange between writer and reader demanded by Edwardian fiction and ultimately by representation itself. Fictitious representation of the sort Bennett did understand himself as writing out of the deepest personal convictions made very different demands on his treatment of self and self-formation than those of the self-help market; the economy of the exchange, more than personal slipperiness, accounts for the difference. To represent self-formation is no more like telling someone how to form a self than depicting the piloting of a ship in a narrative is like giving actual instructions on how to pilot one. Such, of course, was the foundation of Plato's antipathy towards Homer; why read poets when they explained nothing so usefully as those engaged in the real activity, whether that was combat, the search for moral truth or, in fact, piloting a ship (*Ion*)? Plato has had sufficient answer over the centuries, so I shall pass to the differences between spinning fictions of self-formation and furnishing advice on the same subject. In part, Bennett's representation of self contradicts his advice on self-formation precisely because it is a representation. In fictitiously depicting self-formation (and dissolution), Bennett need not consider them in relation to the efforts of individual readers to make themselves happier; rather, the depiction's effect derives from its relation to other patterns of representation that it alternately supports or subverts, thus creating a recognisable voice or style, without which success as an author of fiction was and remains impossible. Bennett defines self-formation in his novels by relation to the idea of historical release from patriarchy on which they are constructed.[17] That is, when he is defining self-formation without the express aim of improving middle-class lives, the selves Bennett represents become signs; they serve to undermine the ideals of external authority that the novelist liked to imagine were coming apart in his own time, the depiction invoking the desired reality in the manner of all traditional magic. The desires these selves express are not constructed as the self-defeating whims against which readers of the pocket philosophies are encouraged to guard themselves; they represent an evolving personal autonomy asserting itself against the strictures of a culture of inherited privilege, a culture by which the desires of a few have long been indulged at the expense of the restraint of those felt by thousands of others.

At the same time, the difference between Bennett's journalistic and novelistic versions of self-formation typifies a strongly Edwardian sense of novelistic significance, of what makes a serious novel serious. For all their world's public confidence in the human soul's infinite plasticity, Edwardian novelists in their private imaginations told and retold stories of fatally partial self-awareness, of the invariable failure of any attempt to consciously direct an interior life that could not be finally known. Virtually every novel one thinks of as characteristically Edwardian turns on the problem of a secret self – *Nostromo*, *The Secret Agent*, *A Room with a View*, *The Golden Bowl*, *The Wings of the Dove*, *Howards End*, *The Good Soldier*. Like their contemporaries in the visual arts, authors from the 1890s to the 1920s were discovering the impossibility of collapsing a variety of perspectives into a single truth about anything; hence, their emphasis on the faulty perception of reading outward clues to discover inward character. Such a focus may have béen necessary to preserve belief in the significance of fictitious representation itself. Were it possible to know and to shape ourselves with scientific precision, fictional characters might be dispensable as mere imperfect replicas of our actual selves. The apparent triumphs of Edwardian science in lighting the dark, reproducing sound and motion, and mapping the criminal skull gave such a Platonic position surprising new life; indeed, as late as 1934, H.G. Wells wrote that completely honest autobiography, had anyone the temerity to write it, would render the novel obsolete.[18] Few other artists entertained similar convictions. Instead, they asserted the impossibility of disentangling what is being represented from the conditions of its representation, thus reinterpreting the self we fashion as a kind of fiction and so affirming that only fiction can adequately represent the life of the self.

And, perhaps, the versions of self and self-formation promoted in *Mental Efficiency* or *How to Live on 24 Hours a Day* sort ill with the enterprise of the novel itself. The pocket philosophies, after all, ultimately envision other as self; that is, they consider selfhood an inherent and featureless essence alike in all its manifestations, regardless of the accidental variations in its individual instances. But novels commonly work from the opposite direction, fictionalising the (authorial) self as other, subjecting it to the semblance of an exterior perspective by removing it from the actual circumstances of its formation, detaching alter-ego from ego. Thus Dickens remakes himself as David Copperfield and Joyce as Stephen Dedalus, Woolf as Lily Briscoe and Lawrence as Rupert Birkin, Bennett as Henry Earlforward and Charlotte Brontë as Jane Eyre. 'First-class fiction is, and must be, in the final resort autobiographical,' Bennett wrote in *The Author's Craft* (AC 24); equally, to fictionalise autobiography requires an author to imagine seeing him or herself from the outside. Even the first-person novel reconfigures self as other in that the author must achieve some separation from the narrator if the work is to be regarded as fiction at all. That the reader makes a similar leap, seeing the fictional other as a version of her or himself, has been narrative's recurrent dream, even when no shadow of autobiography or even of psychology falls across the page. When Eumaios hears the disguised Odysseus tell a story of the loan of a cloak on a cold night, he does not examine its reality; he understands himself as the narrating other, and gives the man a cloak, perceiving his own experience of want in the other's words. The suitors, by contrast, refuse to find themselves in beggar's tales. Indeed, the distinction between real and imaginary contact between self and other was the work of centuries. The ancient heroes of narrative took shape, not as fictions, but as ancestors, as gods or as intermediaries between the two.[19]

Notes

1 The OED quotes an English source from 1858 that uses the phrase with no apparent suspicion that its audience might find it unfamiliar; the OED Supplement cites 1832 as its earliest known American appearance.

2 Eight if one includes *Journalism for Women* (1898) and *How to Become an Author* (1903) as self-help texts; otherwise, six.

3 Bennett recorded that Lord Beaverbrook spent £5,000 to launch the serialisation of *Lord Raingo*; he also noted his distaste at seeing 'My physiog ... on the walls of London, horribly revolting' (L III 274).

4 Emily remakes herself chiefly on her free evenings. The Browning Club she forms with Miss Fowler meets at night, as does the Americanisation class she forms to integrate the town's mistreated Syrian immigrants into its customs and language. Such assimilation, of course, privileges European culture, but it also represents in public life the same process of programmatic self-improvement by study (in the face of adverse circumstances) that one finds in Emily's private life.

5 In fact, one may currently find three laudatory reviews of *How to Live on 24 Hours a Day* from satisfied customers on Amazon.com's web-site, the oldest dated 1998. All have awarded it five stars of a possible five.

6 In fact, Bennett routinely mocked books promising the key to worldly success (see *Self and Self-Management* 60 and *Mental Efficiency* 92–5).

7 'The Man Who Does' was Bennett's byline for the 'Savoir-Faire Papers', which ran in *T. P.'s Weekly* from November 14, 1902 until 6 November 1903.

8 Newman Flower was the head of Cassell, which was insisting that Bennett had deluded them into thinking that *Riceyman Steps* would be suitable for serial publication. Bennett gives a rather different account of the novel's inspiration in the privacy of his Journal (see Pound 301), but the point is that he publicly refused to attribute his novel's origin to personal desire. It won the James Tait Black Memorial Prize, the only literary award Bennett ever received.

9 Only once before 1908 did Bennett use 'AB' as the salutation in a letter to Wells (26 March 1902; AB/HG 79). He occasionally slipped back into the old 'EAB' usage, as on 21 March 1912 (AB/HG 181), in a letter addressed 'Dear Father'.

10 Regarding Bennett's romanticisation of living by the pen, see *The Truth About an Author*, 5–6. Bennett was, of course, perfectly willing to acknowledge as vast a gulf in talent between himself and his readers as one would like; on the more elusive matter of selfhood, however, he perceived only identity.

11 Bennett interrogates himself:
    'You have no real satisfaction to look forward to except the satisfaction of continually inventing, fancying, imagining, scribbling ... Is it good enough?'
        And I answered: 'Yes.'
    But who knows? Who can preclude the regrets of the dying couch?' (154).
12 Spencer goes even further than his follower in repudiating desire, foreseeing a future in which 'the individual has no desires but those which may be satisfied without exceeding his proper sphere of action' (512–13).
13 By 'serious fiction', I refer to the novels Bennett regarded as his best efforts.
14 The Penguin edition reads 'self-protection', mistakenly following the American rather than the British edition.
15 In *Riceyman Steps*, as in *Lord Raingo*, Bennett adds the detail of lurid electrical illumination, which paradoxically emphasises the surrounding darkness.
16 In charging himself with 'forcing the effect', Bennett perhaps recognises his tendency to dictate a reader's response at the knife-point of an imperative or by writing it into the text itself.
17 Most directly in the Five Towns fiction; in the London novels, Bennett focuses on the internalised expectations of patriarchy and on the men hamstrung by them, identifying rationality and system themselves among patriarchy's cultural products rather than as the means to subvert it. The release of desire remains the foundation of self-realisation, to the extent it is ever achieved in the later works, which concentrate much more on the impediment of self-restraint.
18 *Experiment in Autobiography* 423.
19 Odysseus and Penelope, Abraham and Sarah, Gilgamesh; Inanna, Osiris, Huhnapu and Xbalanque; Rama, Krishna, Jesus.

Works cited

Quotations from Arnold Bennett's works are cited in the text by the abbreviations listed below. I have quoted Bennett's novels from the Penguin editions (where they exist), since they are by far the most easily available.

AB/HG: *Arnold Bennett and H. G. Wells, A Record of a Personal and Literary Friendship*. Ed. Harris Wilson. Urbana: University of Illinois Press, 1960.
AC: *The Author's Craft and other Critical Writings*. Ed. Samuel Hynes. Lincoln: University of Nebraska Press, 1968.
C: *Clayhanger*. 1910. New York: Viking Penguin, 1954.
CH: *Arnold Bennett: The Critical Heritage*. Ed. James Hepburn. London: Routledge and Kegan Paul, 1981.
DHL: Lawrence, D. H. *The Collected Letters of D. H. Lawrence*. Ed. Harry T. Moore. London: Heinemann, 1962.
HL: *Hilda Lessways*. New York: E. P. Dutton and Company, 1911.
HM: *The Human Machine*. New York: George H. Doran Company, 1909.
HTL: *How to Live on 24 Hours a Day*. Garden City, NY: Doubleday and Company, 1910.

J: *The Journal of Arnold Bennett, 1896–1928*. New York: Viking, 1933.

L: *Letters of Arnold Bennett*. 4 volumes. Ed. James Hepburn. London: Oxford University Press, 1966–86.

ME: *Mental Efficiency*. New York: George H. Doran Company, 1911.

OWT: *The Old Wives' Tale*. 1908. New York: Penguin Books, 1983.

RS: *Riceyman Steps and Elsie and the Child*. 1923. Ed. Edward Mendelson and Robert Squillace. London: Penguin, 1991.

S: *Sketches for Autobiography*. Ed. James Hepburn. London: Allen and Unwin, 1979.

T: *The Truth about an Author. New Edition with Preface*. New York: George H. Doran Company, 1911.

Bennett, Arnold, *Anna of the Five Towns*. London: Chatto and Windus, 1902.

—— *The Author's Craft and other Critical Writings.*Ed. Samuel Hynes. Lincoln: University of Nebraska Press, 1968.

—— *Buried Alive*. London: Chapman and Hall, 1908.

—— *The Card*. London: Methuen, 1911.

—— *Clayhanger*. 1910. New York: Viking Penguin, 1954.

—— *The Evening Standard Years*. Ed. Andrew Mylett. Hamden, Conn.: Archon, 1974.

—— *The Grand Babylon Hotel*. London: Chatto and Windus, 1902.

—— *Hilda Lessways*. New York: E.P. Dutton and Company, 1911.

—— *How to Become an Author: A Practical Guide*. London: C. Arthur Pearson, 1903.

—— *How to Live on 24 Hours a Day*. Garden City, New York: Doubleday, 1910.

—— *How to Make the Best of Life*. London: Hodder and Stoughton, 1923.

—— *The Human Machine*. New York: George H. Doran Company, 1909.

—— *Imperial Palace*. Garden City: Doubleday, Doran, 1931.

—— *Journal 1929*. London: Cassell, 1930.

——*The Journal of Arnold Bennett, 1896–1928*. New York: Viking, 1933.

—— *Journalism for Women: A Practical Guide*. London: John Lane, 1898.

—— *Letters of Arnold Bennett*. 4 vols. Ed. James Hepburn. London: Oxford University Press, 1966–86.

—— *Literary Taste: How to Form It*. New York: George H. Doran Company, 1910.

—— *Lord Raingo*. London: Cassell, 1926.

—— *A Man from the North*. New York: John Lane, 1898.

—— *Mental Efficiency*. New York: George H. Doran Company, 1911.

—— *Mister Prohack*. London: Methuen, 1922.

—— *The Old Wives' Tale*. 1908. New York: Penguin Books, 1983.

—— *Paris Nights*. New York: George H. Doran Company, 1913.

—— *Riceyman Steps and Elsie and the Child*. 1923. Ed. Edward Mendelson and Robert Squillace. London: Penguin, 1991.

—— *The Savour of Life*. London: Cassell, 1928.

—— *Self and Self-Management*. New York: George H. Doran Company, 1918.

——*The Truth about an Author*. New Edition with Preface. New York: George H. Doran Company, 1911.

—— *What the Public Wants*. London: Duckworth, 1909.

Bennett, Arnold and H.G. Wells, *A Record of a Personal and a Literary Friendship*. Ed. Harris Wilson. Urbana: University of Illinois Press, 1960.

Bennett, Dorothy Cheston, *Arnold Bennett: A Portrait done at Home*. London: Jonathan Cape, 1935.

Drabble, Margaret, *Arnold Bennett*. New York: Knopf, 1974.

Foucault, Michel, *Discipline and Punish*. Trans. Alan Sheridan. New York:Vintage-Random, 1979.

Gide, André, *The Journals of André Gide*, vol. 1. Ed. and trans. Justin O'Brien. New York: Alfred A. Knopf, 1947.

Greenblatt, Stephen, *Renaissance Self-Fashioning*. Chicago: University of Chicago Press, 1980.

Hepburn, James, ed., *Arnold Bennett: The Critical Heritage*. London: Routledge and Kegan Paul, 1981.

Lawrence, D.H., *The Collected Letters of D. H. Lawrence*. Ed. Harry T. Moore London: Heinemann, 1962.

Lovelace, Maud Hart, *Emily of Deep Valley*. New York: HarperCollins, 1950.

McDonald, Peter, *British Literary Culture and Publishing Practice, 1880–1914*. Cambridge: Cambridge University Press, 1997.

Mason, Ellsworth and Richard Ellmann, *The Critical Writing of James Joyce*. Ithaca: Cornell University Press, 1989.

Miller, Anita, *Arnold Bennett: An Annotated Bibliography*. New York: Garland, 1977.

Pound, Ezra, *Literary Essays of Ezra Pound*. Ed. T.S. Eliot. Norfolk, Conn.: New Directions, 1954.

Pound, Reginald, *Arnold Bennett: A Biography*. New York: Harcourt, Brace and Company, 1953.

Spencer, Herbert, *First Principles*. Third edition. London: Williams and Norgate, 1870.

Squillace, Robert, *Modernism, Modernity, and Arnold Bennett*. Lewisburg: Bucknell University Press, 1997.

Wells, H.G., *Experiment in Autobiography*. Boston: Little, Brown, 1934.

West, Geoffrey, *Arnold Bennett*. London: Joiner and Steele, 1932.

9
Perpetuating Joyce

Edward Bishop

In 1933, on the occasion of the American publication of *Ulysses TIME* declared, 'Arrogant Author Joyce gives them no help, lets them sink or swim', and characterised the 51-year-old writer as a 'shy, proud private citizen with a worldwide reputation' (49).

In 1901, a month after his nineteenth birthday, Joyce wrote to Ibsen, on the occasion of Ibsen's seventy-third birthday. The real occasion was Ibsen's mentioning to William Archer that he had 'read or rather spelled out a review in the *Fortnightly Review* by Mr James Joyce which is very benevolent and for which I should greatly like to thank the author if only I had sufficient knowledge of the language' (*LI* 51). Joyce seized the occasion to write what amounts to a small essay in thanks. After telling the playwright how much he was moved, Joyce asks rhetorically, 'What shall I say more?' and proceeds to say a great deal more.

> I have sounded your name defiantly through the college where it was either unknown or known faintly and darkly. I have claimed for you your rightful place in the history of the drama. I have shown what, as it seemed to me, was your highest excellence – your lofty impersonal power. Your minor claims – your satire, your technique and orchestral harmony – these, too, I advanced. Do not think me a hero-worshipper – I am not so. And when I spoke of you in debating societies and so forth, I enforced attention by no futile ranting.

We see as quickly as Ibsen did that this is more about the young writer than about his addressee. And sure enough, the letter lapses into confidence:

But we always keep the dearest things to ourselves. I did not tell them what bound me closest to you. I did not say how what I could discern dimly of your life was my pride to see, how your battles inspired me – not the obvious material battles but those that were fought and won behind your forehead, how your wilful resolution to wrest the secret from life gave me heart and how in your absolute indifference to public canons of art, friends and shibboleths you walked in the light of your inward heroism. And this is what I write to you of now. Your work on earth draws to a close and you are near the silence. It is growing dark for you. Many write of such things, but they do not know....

As one of the young generation for whom you have spoken I give you greeting – not humbly, because I am obscure and you in the glare, not sadly, because you are an old man and I am a young man, not presumptuously nor sentimentally – but joyfully, with hope and with love I give you greeting.

Joyce has single-handedly defined Ibsen for Ireland (and perhaps beyond – 'I have claimed for you your rightful place in the history of the drama'), but he is more than a critic. We believe Joyce when he says, 'Do not think me a hero-worshipper' – for it is clear he sees himself as Ibsen's heir. The parallelism builds and the cadences rise towards the close (the ecstatic rise that will distinguish the endings of both *Portrait* and *Ulysses*) and Ibsen is almost forgotten as the young man – not humbly, not sadly, not presumptuously nor sentimentally, but joyfully – contemplates his own career.

Joyce rather unkindly reminds Ibsen that his writing is pretty much over and that he will die soon (Ibsen would die within five years, and had in fact written his last play), but if Ibsen is 'near the silence', if for Ibsen 'it is growing dark', it is not for Joyce. Joyce will carry on, and he will do so in 'absolute indifference to public canons of art, friends and shibboleths'; like Ibsen he will walk 'in the light of [his] inward heroism'. He will become, as *TIME* proclaims, 'arrogant' and 'proud' with a 'worldwide reputation'. The letter is self-dramatising, self-aggrandising, and above all self-conscious. Joyce knew, or at least hoped, that his letter would be saved, and he is already constructing a public persona. Remarkably, for at this point he had published nothing except the review Ibsen read, Joyce not only remained true to his 'wilful resolution to wrest the secret from life' for his art, he constructed for himself the myth of the artist sketched here as a young man.

The salient features of this myth as he adapts it to himself are rejection, conspiracy, and exile. We see all three in an early letter to Lady Gregory:

> I have a degree of B.S. from the Royal University, and I had made plans to study medicine here. But the college authorities are determined I shall not do so, wishing I dare say to prevent me from securing any position of ease from which I might speak out my heart. ... I intend to study medicine at the University of Paris supporting myself there by teaching English. I am going alone and friendless – I know of a man who used to live somewhere near Montmartre but I have never met him – into another country, and I am writing to you to know can you help me in any way ... though I seem to have been driven out of my country here as a misbeliever I have found no man yet with a faith like mine. (n.d. [November 1902], *LI* 53)

He is alone and friendless (the man who *used* to live somewhere near Montmartre is a nice touch), driven into exile. We see here the beginning of the conspiracy to suppress him in his role of scourge and minister (he has just turned twenty). He might have studied medicine in Dublin, but the authorities are determined to prevent him from speaking out 'his heart'. Even allowing for the congenital malice of college administrators this seems extraordinary. A decade later when Joyce complains to Elkin Mathews about the problems with *Portrait* – 'The later history of the book seems to be open to one interpretation only and that is, that there was a deliberate conspiracy of certain forces in Ireland to silence me. I can scarcely be accused of egoism in coming to this conclusion in view of the facts' (Easter Day 1913, *LI* 73) – it sounds as if he has already been accused of egoism. But the important point is that the conviction of conspiracy was in place long before the book had been written.

And Joyce trumpets rejection. Where most writers, especially those starting out and writing to potential publishers, would accentuate their successes, Joyce introduces himself with his failures. To Yeats he details his sparse public:

> I am sending the typescript of my play *Exiles* (which has already been rejected in Zurich, Berne, Turin and by the stage Society in London .... Besides this I am writing a book *Ulysses* which however will not be finished for some years. Possibly the novel and play will

engage the attention of my six or seven readers (7 copies of *Dubliners* were sold in the last six months) until it is ready. (14 September 1916, *LI* 95)

In a letter providing biographical information for Huebsch, his American publisher, Joyce notes how the *Dubliners* stories were rejected by the *Irish Homestead* because 'readers had complained'. Of *Portrait* he notes that he offered an introductory chapter to the editors of *Dana* but 'it was rejected,' and that having been 'refused by all the publishers' it would, if not for Weaver and Ezra Pound, 'be still unpublished' (to H.S. Weaver, 8 November 1916, *LI* 98–9). Did Joyce seriously think that Huebsch customarily used lists of rejections to promote his authors? Not likely. But Joyce (apart from his compulsion to dwell on the injustices done him) knew that this would contribute to his aura of the author unjustly rejected.

To John Quinn, an important patron, he writes,

[*Dubliners*] was rejected by 40 publishers; three times setup, and once burnt. It cost me about 3,000 francs in postage, fees, train and boat fare, for I was in correspondence with 110 newspapers, 7 solicitors, 3 societies, 40 publishers and several men of letters about it. All refused to aid me, except Mr Ezra Pound. (10 July 1917, *LI* 105)

The numbers balloon – 40 publishers, 110 newspapers, seven solicitors. It is an epic trial. As for *Portrait*, 'Financially it is, like my other books, a fiasco – 450 copies sold to date in the United Kingdom, equivalent to a sale of about 28 copies in all Switzerland' (*LI* 105). It is as if he realises that 450 copies does not sound bad enough, so converts it into an equivalent that will drive home how paltry the sales are. In the same letter he details the multiple rejections of *Exiles*:

I sent it to Turin. It was refused as 'being of local interest'.... I sent it then to London ... it was rejected as unfit for their repertory. I offered it here .... I then sent it to Berne .... It was then sent to Chicago .... I then sent it to my agent .... Then it was sent to the Stage Society, London .... Then it went to the Abbey Theatre .... (*LI* 105)

Most authors, whatever they thought privately, would fear that such persistent rejection – by so many publishers and managers – might be taken by a potential patron as a reflection on the quality of the work itself, not proof of the universally debased judgement of the editorial classes. Not Joyce. To critic Thomas Sturge Moore he writes:

> Mr Ezra Pound told me that you were so kind as to speak well of my play *Exiles* and to suggest to the Stage Society to put it on. The Society, however, kept the typescript for a year and sent it back without comment. Perhaps you could give me the name of some other society which would be likely to consider it or the name of some manager. (26 October 1917, *LI* 108)

Joyce then adds, 'I find it very difficult to get what I write printed or produced and this is my excuse for troubling you' (*LI* 108). Later, when Herbert Gorman is preparing his biography, Joyce provides him with seven sample rejection letters for *Portrait* (233–4). In 1919 he introduces himself to Carlo Linati thus:

> The story of my books is very strange. For the publication of *Dubliners* I had to struggle for ten years. The whole first edition of 1000 copies was burnt at Dublin by fraud; some say it was the doing of priests, some of enemies, others of the then Viceroy or his consort, Countess Aberdeen. (19 December 1919, *LI* 132)

And so on, with the saga of *Portrait* and *Exiles*. We note too that the circle of conspirators has widened.

These grievances go beyond personal correspondence, beyond guidance to willing biographers; they become part of the para-text of *Ulysses*. For the 1926 Shakespeare and Company edition (the eighth impression, what is known as the second edition) the type was entirely reset and the front matter now included an account of the adventures of the previous editions:

> 1st printing (Shakespeare and Company, Paris): February 1922.
> (1,000 numbered copies).
> 2nd printing (Egoist Press, London): October 1922.
> (2,000 numbered copies, of which 500 copies burned by New York Post Office Authorities).
> 3rd printing (Egoist Press, London): January 1923.
> (500 numbered copies of which 499 seized by Customs Authorities, Folkestone).

Joyce's case may have been extreme, but D.H. Lawrence was being banned at the same time; he too had to be published privately on the continent, and he is just as irascible as Joyce, but he does not make his publishing ordeals a prominent part of the texts themselves.

Reviews and promotion

Like all authors, he felt that his work would do better if only better promoted: of his little book of lyrics, *Chamber Music*, he writes to publisher Elkin Mathews in 1910, 'I am very much surprised at the fewness of the copies sold and think the book could have been pushed more in view of the good notices it got on all sides' (*LI* 68). He goes on:

> My proposal ... was that the printing should be charged to me (if necessary, in advance), that 100 copies be taken by me at sale price and that my preface (which, of itself, should suffice as a striking advertisement) should be printed. (73)

(Gilbert notes that this is an account of Joyce's difficulties in getting the book published. So the saga of *Ulysses* the book is not unique to that volume.) Joyce became a tireless promoter of his own work. He writes to Weaver (16 September 1916) with two suggestions for promoting *Portrait*, first to insert review slips 'containing a few extracts from the press notices of *Dubliners*', second, to place books at influential sources; he wants to buy for himself 'ten extra copies which I intend to present to some writers and critics who have lately befriended me and expressed a favourable opinion of the book. Possibly they might write something about it and no doubt that would be an advantage: but even if they do not I feel that I ought to make some return for their kindness' (*LI* 96).

While considering the reviews of *Ulysses* Joyce notes of one, 'For the purposes of sales [this] article is not very useful as it does not give the name and address of the publisher. I always look for this first of all in an article, then at its length and finally at its signature' (to H.S. Weaver 16 May 1922, *LI* 184). This testifies to Joyce's commercial instincts. He wanted – needed – to make money, and he wanted readers. He was not interested in having his books languish on a collector's shelf; he wanted to be read.

Yet I wonder if this emphasis on sales does not serve a strategic purpose: it allows Joyce to be obsessive about reading and collecting reviews while maintaining his pose of indifference to the opinions of the scribblers who wrote those reviews. The correspondence shows Joyce working behind the scenes: 'I sketched a letter for Miss Beach to send to the critic of the *Quarterly*,' he tells Weaver (*LI* 189), and later notes, 'The extract from Leslie's article was all right, I think .... Did it contain the phrase "U has yet to take its place in the thought and script of mankind"?' This long letter goes into detail about the arrangements, and also acknowledges the strains that are developing: Sylvia Beach 'replied that she was not interested in a third edition of *Ulysses* and thought that the "hustling to boom the book" out to be done by the person or persons interested' (*LI* 194–5). (Beach was already annoyed that Weaver's cheaper Egoist Press edition had been advertised before her edition from Shakespeare & Co. had sold out. Joyce had his royalties long before she recovered her costs.) Ironically, part of Joyce's image today is precisely that of a behind-the-scenes manipulator. Gerard Genette uses him as an example of what he calls the 'semiofficial epitext' – a 'critical article that is somewhat 'remote-controlled' by authorial instructions that the public is not in a position to know about' (348):

> We know today, thanks to Richard Ellmann [in *Ulysses on the Liffey*], that the parallels between Joyce's *Ulysses* and Homer's *Odyssey* (parallels that were put forward by Larbaud in a 1921 lecture, were later spelled out by Stuart Gilbert, and ... have continued ever since to govern our reading of the novel) were prompted by Joyce himself, clearly anxious both to circulate them and to evade any direct responsibility for making them public. (350)

To circulate yet to evade responsibility: 'Here we find ourselves,' says Genette, 'in the presence of what in politics is typically called a system of "leaks" organized at the source and maintained through unofficial channels.' He ends with a Gallic shrug, 'In theory the author has said nothing ...But, if the job does not wind up getting done .... What are friends for?' (350)

The same game was played out a decade later with the American publication of *Ulysses*. Bennet Cerf at Random House wanted to use the chart that Joyce had prepared for Larbaud on the dust jacket of the book. On 13 October 1933 Cerf wrote to Joyce's secretary, Paul Leon:

> It is my earnest belief that if we can reprint this chart in our edition of ULYSSES (provided, of course, that we ever do get the right to the edition) we will be rendering a tremendous service to the reading

public. I honestly believe, also, that the inclusion of this chart will result in a tremendous number of additional sales. Furthermore, we can copyright this chart, and it will make one more feature of our own edition that cannot possibly be pirated.

On 21 October 1933 Joyce, through Paul Leon, wrote back refusing, saying the chart 'might just as easily deter the reader as it can according to you bring new ones. Imagine an American reader seeing the chart and concluding that since he has to study it before reading it is not worth while reading the book. It may defeat its purpose.' Then he moves on to the real issue:

> On the one hand we should not forget that Ulysses is a piece of belles lettres i.e. pure littérature [Joyce used the French spelling], if it needs explanations these belong to the class of critical and historical writings not to the book itself. If it is destined to remain a classic in English literature which I have no doubt it will, this work and many others will come and it does not behoove the authors to give this indication – it should be the work of the free critic. (Moscato and LeBlanc 233, 278)

Cerf's exchange of letters with Joyce (through Joyce's secretary Paul Leon) highlights the delicate relation between cultural capital and real capital.

Pierre Bourdieu argues that cultural products function as instruments of 'cultural capital', yielding 'a profit in distinction proportionate to the rarity of the means required to appropriate them' (*Distinction* 228). This puts serious artists who yet want to sell their work in a bind: the cultural product depends for its distinction upon its exclusiveness, and any increase in the number of possessors decreases its rarity; with popularity comes the threat of vulgarisation. He quotes with approval Valéry Larbaud who sees the whole enterprise in quasi-religious terms:

> Cultural objects, with the subtle hierarchy, are predisposed to mark the stages and degrees of the initiatory progress which defines the enterprise of culture, according to Valéry Larbaud. Like 'Christian's progress towards the heavenly Jerusalem,' it leads from the 'illiterate' to the 'literate,' via the 'non-literate' and 'semi-literate' or the 'common reader' (*lecteur*) – leaving aside the 'bibliophile' – to the truly cultivated reader (*liseur*). (*Distinction* 229)

But at the same time as the objects represent *cultural* capital they also represent *real* capital, and the authors obviously want to benefit from this. Thus, says Bourdieu, because artists are

> divided between ... winning a market by widening their audience ... and concern for cultural distinction ... their relationship to everything concerned with the 'democratization of culture' is marked by a deep ambivalence which may be manifested in a dual discourse on the relations between the institutions of cultural diffusion and the public. (*Distinction* 229)

The Paul Leon letters make it clear that Joyce knew exactly how to execute this 'dual discourse' (even down to dictating letters for Leon's signature), carefully preserving the hierarchy of distinction while yet expanding the distribution.

Cerf did not get the chart but he did get a letter from Joyce. The letter 'Reprinted ... by permission of the author', as part of the front matter to the American edition, was in fact demanded by Cerf as a condition of publication: he required 'not less than 300 words, by which he will authenticate the publication' (Moscato and LeBlanc 102, 105). Joyce did authenticate it, three times in three pages, but he also rehearsed 'the difficulties I found in publishing anything I wrote from the very first volume of prose I attempted to publish' (xv).

Shaping the biography

In the 1916 letter with biographical information for Huebsch mentioned above, Joyce notes under *Early Publications* 'Parnell' a pamphlet on Parnell's death written when Joyce was nine, 'It was printed and circulated in Dublin. I do not know if any copy is to be found today' (*LI* 99). Most writers do not list their juvenilia in promotional blurbs, especially juvenilia that is unavailable. Joyce also notes in the same section,

> (2) An article on Ibsen in the *Fortnightly Review* written when I was seventeen. Ibsen was so kind as to send me a message of thanks for it.
> (3) *The Day of the Rabblement* (a pamphlet on the Irish Literary Theatre). This was written for the University Review but refused insertion by the censor as was also an essay on co-education by my

fellow student, the late Mr Skeffington. We published the essays together in pamphlet form. (*LI* 99)

So the portrait of the author as a young genius is sketched.

As the furore surrounding *Ulysses* increased – the *Little Review* had lost the court case and been convicted of obscenity in February 1921 for publishing 'Nausicaa' – Joyce wrote to Weaver (24 June 1921):

A nice collection could be made of legends about me. Here are some ... that I enriched myself in Switzerland during the war by espionage work ... . that I am a cocaine victim .... that I could write no more .... that I was the owner of several cinema theatres .... that I was an austere mixture of the Dalai Lama and sir Rabindranath Tagore .... that I was a crazy fellow who always carried four watches and rarely spoke except to ask my neighbour what o'clock it was[...]that I was extremely lazy and will never do or finish anything. (I calculate that I must have spent nearly 20,000 hours in writing *Ulysses*) ... that I was gradually going mad .... that I am a crafty simulating and dissimulating Ulysses-like type, a 'jejune jesuit', selfish and cynical. (*LI* 165–6)

He admits there may be something in the last charge, but claims, 'it has been my habit to apply this alleged quality to safeguard my poor creations. Really, he insists, 'The truth probably is that I am a quite commonplace person undeserving of so much imaginative painting' (*LI* 166). In fact, Joyce never thought of himself as commonplace, and the collection of legends in this often-quoted letter that he says 'could be made' is in fact first made by Joyce himself.

In the same letter he notes, 'Here now is an example of my emptiness. I have not read a work of literature for several years. My head is full of pebbles and rubbish and broken matches and lots of glass picked up "most everywhere"' (*LI* 167). We do not need Gifford or Thornton to know that *Ulysses* is a book full of literature, but what is being constructed here is the myth of the artist *sui generis*. He speaks in the next sentence of 'The task I set myself technically in writing a book from eighteen different points of view and in as many styles, all apparently unknown or undiscovered by my fellow tradesmen' (*LI* 167): a statement that argues for an encyclopaedic knowledge of books (how would he know the techniques were unknown to his fellow tradesmen unless he had read them?). Yet the charming 'pebbles and rubbish and broken matches' are what stay with us. Joyce was not only lonely but alone, aloof, creating his own world.[1]

His technique of self-aggrandisement through self-deprecation continues in the next paragraph, in which he speaks of not knowing Greek:

> I don't even know Greek though I am spoken of as erudite .... I spoke or used to speak modern Greek not too badly (I speak some four or five languages fluently enough) and have spent a great deal of time with Greeks of all kinds from noblemen down to onion-sellers, chiefly the latter. I am superstitious about them. They bring me luck. (*LI* 167)

Speaking four or five languages is not bad. Joyce reminds Weaver he is learned, yet anything but pedantic: he spends his time, it seems, constantly with onion sellers – no one who could have had a literary influence on *Ulysses*. He closes with another protean statement: 'I now end this long rambling shambling speech, having said nothing of the darker aspects of my detestable character' (*LI* 167). We are supposed to read through this, to see his foibles are not detestable at all, while at the same time we are reminded he is no teddy bear; dark currents swirl beneath the surface. The letter is, in short, a brilliant performance, revealing, concealing, advancing the image of the dark genius only to deny it, constructing the enormously learned writer only to dissolve it into the image of just plain folks. I draw attention to it here because portions of it are so often taken up uncritically. Rereading it for this essay I realised that the undergraduate lectures I received on Joyce presented almost every point in this letter. Joyce was not writing to a friend, he was writing to a patron and more importantly a publisher. He knew this letter would be preserved; he was writing to posterity as much or more as he was writing to Weaver, and posterity listened.

The difference between the letters to Weaver and those to Budgen strike the reader: Joyce is more upbeat in his complaint and what he wants to do is write about writing. These letters contain some of the most often-quoted comments by Joyce on his work:

> *Nausikaa* is written in a namby-pamby jammy marmalady drawersy (alto là!) style. (3 January 1920, *LI* 135)

> As I told you a catchword is enough to set me off. *Moly* is a nut to crack. My latest is this. Moly is the gift of Hermes, god of public ways, and is the invisible influence (prayer, chance, agility, *presence*

of mind, power of recuperation) which saves in case of accident.
(Michelmas 1920, *LI* 147)

I am writing *Ithaca* in the form of a mathematical catechism. All
events are resolved into their cosmic physical, psychical etc. equiva-
lents, e.g. Bloom jumping down the area, drawing water from the
tap, the micturition in the garden, the cone of incense, lighted
candle and statue so that not only will the reader know everything
and know it in the baldest coldest way, but Bloom and Stephen
thereby become heavenly bodies, wanderers like the stars at which
the [*sic*] gaze. (End February 1921, *LI* 159–60)

It is no accident that one of the most attractive portraits we have of
Joyce comes from Budgen's *James Joyce and the Making of Ulysses* (1934).
What emerges in the letters is the image of a writer engaged with his
craft, enthusiastic and energetic, and if the now famous episode from
Budgen's book of Joyce spending all morning arranging the words of
one sentence strikes us as little too consciously done (though this may
be in part from the constant repetition – it reads fresh in the book), the
letters to Budgen validate the portrait. Any letter is of course a performance, but one senses here Joyce letting his enthusiasm leak through.

He is much more genial and congenial to Budgen than his actual
portrait would suggest. He speaks (25 February 1920) of a painting
which the artist's friends refer to as 'Herr Satan' (137). He looks it. And
this is the salacious demon that penned the masturbation scene in
'Nausicaa'; no wonder the young lady in New York was shocked. If you
look at the issue of the *Little Review* where the scene appeared, you find
that while the book version of the episode has the Roman candle
section buried in the middle, in the July–August 1920 *Little Review* it
comes on the second page of the episode – on the right-hand or recto
page where the eye naturally falls if you are leafing through a book.
Joyce, of course, did not arrange this, but the combination of the prose
and the somewhat satanic photograph of the frontispiece contributed
to the slightly demonic aura that he and his writings were acquiring.
As we have seen in his remark to Weaver about his 'detestable character,' Joyce wanted the edge.

To return to the *TIME* article referred to at the beginning, the
reviewer makes it clear that the publication of *Ulysses* is an event in
modernism.[2] In the first paragraph he declares, 'No overt celebration
marked the day with red. Yet many a wide-awake modern-minded
citizen knew he had seen literary history pass another milestone.' And

it is equally clear that modernism is no longer to be identified with the avant-garde. We are reminded of the censorship trial, which had been covered in the issue for 18 December 1933, and told, 'Strictly speaking, *Ulysses* did not so much disembark as come out of hiding, garbed in new and respectable garments.' It is respectable and it is useful. In language that anticipates the philosophy of the Book-of-the-Month Club (discussed later in this essay), we are told, 'For readers to whom books are an important means of learning about life, it stands preeminent above modern rivals.' Further, it comes with a secondary interpretive community:

> Arrogant Author Joyce gives them no help, lets them sink or swim. But thanks to the exploratory works of critics and notably such an exegetical commentary as Stuard [*sic*] Gilbert's *James Joyce's Ulysses* (*TIME*. Jan. 5. 1931) the plain reader can now literally find out what *Ulysses* is all about. (49)

But what of Joyce? We can never find out what *he* is about: he lives in Paris, 'a shy, proud private citizen with a worldwide reputation' (49), a man who has not succumbed to the lure of fame, 'He has proved his hatred of publicity by never granting an interview' (50). Thus Joyce preserves his distinction and the integrity of his work. He declines to explain it, and never grants an interview – but he lets Gilbert explicate it, and he gets his picture on the cover of a magazine with one of the largest circulations in the world; a brilliant negotiation of the forces of the cultural field. When the *New York Times* reviewed *Ulysses* in 1922, they had not been amused:

> A few intuitive, sensitive visionaries may understand and comprehend *Ulysses*, James Joyce's new and mammoth volume, without going through a course of training or instruction, but the average intelligent reader will glean little or nothing from it – even from careful perusal, one might properly say study, of it – save bewilderment and a sense of disgust. It should be companioned with a key and a glossary like the Berlitz books. Then the attentive and diligent reader would eventually get some comprehension of Mr. Joyce's message. (Deming 222)

By 1931, however, it was no longer the self-indulgent work of the avante-garde; it was a work even for the 'plain reader' of *TIME*, and within a few years it would become a coffee-table book for the bourgeoisie. Joyce, it would seem, had perfectly mastered the 'dual discourse' that guaranteed him the status of an uncompromising artist and yet gained him popular appeal.

But what had worked for *Ulysses* would not work for *Work in Progress/Finnegans Wake*. He organized *Our Exagmination round His Factification for Incamination of Work in Progress*, yet, he says to Valery Larbaud (30 July 1929):

> What you say about the Exag is right enough. I did stand behind those twelve Marshals more or less directing them what lines of research to follow. But up to the present though at least a hundred copies have been freely circulated to the press and press men not a single criticism has appeared. My impression is that the paper cover, the grandfather's clock on the title page and the word Exagmination itself for instance incline reviewers to regard it as a joke, though these were all my doing ... (283)

Joyce mentions the *Exagmination* in the Random House letter as well but it did not help the popular response. A letter from H.G. Wells put with devastating frankness the opinion of many readers of *Finnegans Wake* (and indeed of *Ulysses*):

> My dear Joyce: I've been studying you and thinking over you a lot. The outcome is that I don't think I can do anything for the propaganda of your work. I've an enormous respect for your genius dating from your earliest books and I feel now a great personal liking for you but you and I are set upon absolutely different courses. ... Now with regard to this literary experiment of yours. ... I don't think it gets anywhere. You have turned your back on common men, on their elementary needs and their restricted time and intelligence and you have elaborated. What is the result? Vast riddles. Your last two works have been more amusing and exciting to write than they will ever be to read. ... Who the hell is this Joyce who demands so many waking hours of the few thousands I have still to live for a proper appreciation of his quirks and fancies and flashes of rendering?
>
> All this from my point of view. Perhaps you are right and I am all wrong. Your work is an extraordinary experiment and I would go out of my way to save it from destruction or restrictive interruption. It has its believers and its following. Let them rejoice in it. To me it is a dead end. (23 November 1928, LI 274–5)

'Path dependence' and the perpetuation of myth

Yet Joyce's influence remained powerful. Sylvia Beach felt betrayed by him, but found she was trapped by him: no one was interested in her achievement in creating an English- language bookstore and lending library in Paris; she was famous only as the publisher of *Ulysses*. Beach resented being 'enJoycened' and did not want her bookstore remembered as a Joyce factory:

> He had an all-invading way with him, but I resisted to the end anything that threatened to turn the place completely into a Joyce plant. His final attempt to totally en-Joycen me was at the moment when Ulysses was being pirated in the United States. He thought I should abandon my bookshop, probably transplant it to America in order to take up the fight for Ulysses in my country. (Princeton, box 167, folder 2)

She returns to the topic, emphasising the fact that Shakespeare & Co. was her work of art: 'Nobody but Joyce could have written Ulysses, but anybody could have published it. ... Don't forget that my bookshop and Company was already in full swing when Joyce came along' (Princeton, box 167, folder 2). Note the imperative verb. She knows that resistance is futile: we have already forgotten. Though she determined to set the record straight in her memoir, as she revised the work, over a period of fifteen years, she gradually changed it. To take one dramatic example, I want to examine Beach's account of her offer to publish *Ulysses*, which has become part of the mythology surrounding the book.[3]

The drafts of her memoir present at least seven different versions of the story, versions in which Beach incrementally improves upon the event until she has executed a complete *volte face*, transforming herself from Patient Griselda to Joan of Arc.

The first version makes it clear that the idea came from Joyce:

> Joyce discussed the situation with me. Feeling as I did, that Ulysses was the most important and the most beautiful English work of my time, ~~when he suggested that I publish the complete book~~ I accepted with enthusiasm Joyce's suggestion that I publish his book. I felt that my little bookshop was immensely honored.

And Beach is dubious:

> Now I had never imagined Shakespeare and Co would be publishers
> of anything. ... What I took in daily was barely sufficient to cover
> birdseeds – and if my good sister Holly had not kept up her old
> habit of helping me out every month from her hardearned salary,
> and there had not been the cheques from my kind cousins in
> Overbrook ... I could never have kept the business afloat.
> (Princeton, box 168, folder 2; deletion in typescript)

This obviously was not a spur of the moment request; Joyce has kept
Beach abreast of the persecution, the closing down of the venues. It
is he who discusses the situation with Beach; it is she who accepts
the suggestion. Moreover, her initial thought is that she is hopelessly undercapitalized. It is hard to believe that Joyce was not thinking of Shakespeare & Co. as a fall-back position: Harriet Weaver had
already considered producing the book in France, so the idea of publishing in Paris in fact pre-dates Shakespeare & Co.

In the next version, Joyce again gives her the whole sad history of
his troubles but adds another element – guilt:

> He kept me informed of the progress of the persecution of Ulysses ... .
> By this time the Little Review itself was suppressed and the editresses,
> Margaret Anderson and Jane Heap were 'hauled off to court and our
> thumb prints taken' as they described it. When Joyce told me this
> final episode I was ashamed.

Worse,

> Miss Harriet Weaver who had published 'A Portrait of the Artist' and
> a fragment or two of 'Ulysses' in her review 'The Egoist' had by this
> time turned it into a publishing house in order to bring out Joyce's
> books. But she soon perceived that the publication of Ulysses would
> mean trouble and end in disaster.

Anderson and Weaver have done their all for him – what about her?

> In talking with Joyce I saw he would be glad to have me publish
> the book. I said 'what's going to become of it?' – he said 'I think
> you'll have to publish it'. I jumped at the chance, of course. But,

> as usual, I consulted Adrienne about a venture that I saw looming up rather huge. Her advise [*sic*] was 'do it'. (Princeton, box 168, folder 3)

Beach has been placed in a situation where she has to ask the question, but her discomfort is palpable.

The third version makes her look even less enthusiastic: the birdseed appears again, and the reference to Holly's money has an edge:

> Joyce said to me: 'I'm afraid you'll have to do it, Miss Beach'. I was quite willing to accept the honor, though I felt it was going to be rather a huge venture, and consulted Adrienne. ... I had never thought of Shakespeare and Co publishing anything. ... it was kept off the rocks with difficulty. What came in was barely enough to buy birdseed, let alone pay the upkeep of the establishment. My sister Holly, who was getting used to breaking off chunks of her salary for the rest of the family helped me out generously every month. ... (Princeton, box 168, folder 3)

Here we no longer have the set-up question from Beach to Joyce; he simply says, 'you'll have to do it.' In Beach's response, to be 'quite willing' is a long way from 'jumped at the chance' or even 'accepted with enthusiasm'.

But Beach the memoirist obviously seems not to have liked the characters these versions were creating: an entirely self-serving author and a craven bookseller, shamed into doing reluctantly what Margaret Anderson and Harriet Weaver did eagerly. So in a fourth version she rewrites it. Miss Weaver, instead of being cast as the stalwart who has done unasked what Beach has to be prompted to do, becomes a fastidious figure shrinking from the task:

> One might as well expect the angel on Strasbourg Cathedral[,] a very good likeness of Miss Weaver[,] to go wallowing around in the mud.
>
> So there was nothing left to do but for me to bring out 'Ulysses' in France. Immediately I offered to do so, and Joyce accepted – what else could he have done? (Princeton, box 168, folder 6)

Far from feeling pressured, Sylvia takes charge. She makes Joyce an offer he cannot refuse. In the fifth version the fact that Beach has neither money nor experience just makes it all more piquant, and Adrienne cheers her on:

> When Joyce came to tell me the sad news of 'The Little Review' he was in utter despair. I asked him if he would let me have the honor of publishing 'Ulysses' in France. He accepted at once ...
> [Adrienne] ... said by all means go ahead. (Vas-y!)
> So now, without a penny nor any previous experience in publishing I was undertaking to bring out this great book 'Ulysses'. And moreover, I didn't doubt that I would succeed in doing so. (Princeton, box 168, folder 6)

Joyce now is without a plan, in 'utter despair.'

In the first published version of the event, written in French for the *Mercure de France* in 1949, Beach leaves Weaver out, and Joyce too:

> l'éditeur Huebsch refusait de publier le volume ... . De cela, il ne pouvait être question. Ulysses était donc abandonné à la fois par L'Angleterre et l'Amérique. Restait la France ... et moi.
> Je m'offris sans hésiter à faire l'édition et Joyce accepta sans hésiter ma proposition. (Princeton, box 170, folder 1)

Personalities are replaced by nations: England had failed, America had failed, and it rested now with France and Sylvia Beach. The offer itself is made and accepted with neat Gallic parallelism.

By the time she came to publish her memoir in English, her role and Joyce's had been defined, but she decided to deepen the pathos:

> Joyce came to announce the news. It was a heavy blow for him, and I felt, too, that his pride was hurt. In a tone of complete discouragement, he said, 'My book will never come out now.'
> All hope of publication in the English-speaking countries, at least for a long time to come, was gone. And here in my little bookshop sat James Joyce, sighing deeply.
> It occurred to me that something might be done, and I asked: 'Would you let Shakespeare and Company have the honor of bringing out your *Ulysses*?'
> He accepted my offer immediately and joyfully. I thought it rash of him to entrust his great *Ulysses* to such a funny little publisher. But he seemed delighted, and so was I. We parted, both of us, I think, very much moved. (*Shakespeare & Company* 47)

The blow is 'heavy', the discouragement 'complete', the bookstore 'little' and the sighs 'deep'. Beach does not hesitate in the slightest. The birdseed and the sister breaking off chunks of her paycheque are quietly removed. We have come a long way from the commanding Joyce and the timorous but resentful Beach of the earlier drafts.

This is the version that enters the Joyce canon. Ellmann improved it for his biography, making it even more spontaneous than Beach had done:

> [Joyce] went round to Shakespeare and Company to tell Sylvia Beach of this new unhappy development, 'My book will never come out now.' A thought struck her. 'Would you let Shakespeare and Company have the honor of bringing out your Ulysses?' she asked. Joyce was as startled to hear this proposal as she was to make it; he warned her mournfully that no one would buy the book, but at the same time he unhesitatingly accepted. (504)

Here the idea flashes out with no premeditation on either side, but they both embrace it and the deal is sealed.[4]

Uncertainty about the precise nature of The Offer has existed from the outset: we have Joyce's own famous flip-flop in the letter to Harriet Shaw Weaver of 10 April 1921: 'The next day I arranged for a Paris publication to replace the American one – or rather I accepted a proposal made to me by *Shakespeare and Co.*' (LI, 162). And more recently, commentators have expressed doubt about Beach's published version. In 1991 Jean-Michel Rabaté observed, 'Darantiere thus became a logical choice for Sylvia Beach when she needed a printer for the bold idea, suggested by Joyce, to print *Ulysses*' (247); and in 1989 Brenda Maddox quoted Beach's published version of the event, and then corrected it: 'In reality, it was Joyce who took the initiative and suggested the idea' (246). Even Noel Fitch back in 1983 had suggested it is 'difficult to believe ... Joyce ... had not thought of this possibility', and quoted, 'I accepted with enthusiasm Joyce's suggestion ...' from one of the drafts of Beach's memoirs – but she gave pride of place to Beach's published account on the previous page, quoting it in full (77, 78).

And the story lives on: Morris Beja repeated it in 1992, though he qualifies it with, 'According to [Beach's] biography ...'(85); Jeri Johnson used it without qualification in her 1993 introduction to the Oxford World's Classics edition of *Ulysses* (xlii); and in 1994 Senator David Norris and Carl Flint wrote in the widely available *Joyce For Beginners*, 'In April 1921, she proposed publishing *Ulysses* in France, and Joyce agreed at once' (141); Margot Norris's *Companion to James Joyce's 'Ulysses'* quotes Beach's memoir (14). And I have just read a doctoral dissertation that uncritically repeats the anecdote.

Why does this story, and others about Joyce (and other writers) persist?

It is perhaps tempting to dismiss it all as faulty scholarship, to say that scholars keep going back to the same texts and ignore new developments. But this pheomenon occurs with other authors, and in other fields, so that will not do. Perhaps these 'urban myths' of criticism recur because they are factoids, things repeated so often that they are assumed to be true. Perhaps it is that art is stronger than life and that we cannot combat the power of a good story. There may be something in this, Wallace Stevens's 'blessed rage for order' that infects us all. We respond to narrative even as we decry master narratives, and though we value free play and applaud deferral of closure, there is something satisfying in it, and we do long for originary moments.

But there may be a more mundane mechanism at work: what economists refer to as 'path dependence.' Path dependence theory has been used variously to explain the dominance of the QWERTY keyboard, VHS videotape, and private transport over mass transit – cases in which a better alternative clearly exists and is just as clearly ignored (Goodstein 5). The idea is not new. As early as 1915 Veblen was using it to explain why German economic development overtook that of the UK. More recently, it has been used to show how reapers, profitable in the United States, would not have worked in the UK (Arrow 175). Both were situations where the producers were 'locked in'; in the former, the railway system and freight-handling systems at ports were obsolete but complementary, and so the whole system would have had to be replaced at once; in the latter, the soil had been ploughed in ways which made the mechanical reaper inefficient.

The famous case of the QWERTY keyboard (we continue to use a keyboard system designed for mechanical typewriters simply because it has gained wide acceptance) has in fact been disputed. Liebowitz and Margolis painstakingly prove that the Dvorak keyboard, QWERTY's rival, was not clearly superior, that the evidence was tainted, and point out that we could now, because of computers, switch easily and at no cost. 'Yet,' they cry, 'the QWERTY myth continues to be cited as if it were the truth.... And there is no sign of abatement' (14–15). They cite several examples of articles in prestigious journals.

'Apparently,' they conclude, hammering home their point with fierce parallelism, 'the theory of path dependence and lock-in to inferior technologies is in trouble without the QWERTY example. Apparently the cost of giving up this example is greater than the discomfort associated with its illegitimate use. Apparently the typewriter example is of such importance to many writers because it can so easily persuade people that an interventionist technology policy is necessary' (15). But this has nothing to do with 'interventionist technology policy' (this reader doesn't even know what that is), and everything to do with 'path dependence': the QWERTY example is itself an example of path dependence. Academics are consumers as well as producers, and just as with trying to introduce mechanical reapers to nineteenth-century Britain or reclaim the suburbs of Los Angeles with public transport, the issue is not just one of economics but of a complete mental reconfiguration. I am suggesting that there exists a critical and cultural path dependence that is as powerful as any economic one. Wilde, famously, was famous before he had anything to be famous about. Joyce was 'always already' a genius; he laid down the path and we have become his dependants.

'Lock-in' occurs when a system loses 'interpretative flexibility' economists tell us, and the terms seem tailor-made for cultural studies (see Garud 382). In 1443 a cathedral in Florence featured a 24-hour clock that turned counter-clockwise designed by Paolo Uccello; at that time there was no standard format for clocks. But by 1550 12-hour faces, with the hands moving clockwise, were the norm. We have been locked in to that standard analogue face ever since. A more recent example of lock-in is the decision to drive on the left or right hand side of the road. Once made, that decision is very difficult to go back on, and even though there may be a few individuals willing to drive cars in one system designed for the other, they are a rarity, and they do not change the system. Something like lock-in occurs with an influential critical work. We cannot undo *The Pound Era*. There is no going back to a pre-Kenner Pound, however much we may contest Kenner's vision. And there is no un-Ellmannizing Joyce (although Joseph Kelly's *Our Joyce* seriously challenges his portrait).

We are gradually redefining modernism, indeed this volume is part of that work, but there will always be a gap, not just between received wisdom of the general reader and the insights of the scholar, but between the current research and what the scholarly community allows itself to 'know.' Joyce forged in the smithy of his soul the uncreated myth of himself, and we, just by paraphrasing him, participate in that mythologizing. As Joyce recognized, it answers to our need.

Notes

Quotations from James Joyce's letters are cited in the text by the abbreviation LI (see also Works cited).

1 Later, in response to responses to Work in Progress he writes to Weaver (31 May 1927) 'Another (or rather many) says he is imitating Lewis Carroll. I never read him till Mrs Nutting gave me a book, not *Alice*, a few weeks ago, – though, of course, I heard bits and scraps. But then I never read Rabelais either though nobody will believe this' (*LI* 255).
2 This section draws on my article 'Re: Covering *Ulysses*'.
3 This section draws on my article 'The Garbled History of the First-Edition *Ulysses*'.
4 Richard Ellmann, *James Joyce*, revised edition (New York: Oxford University Press, 1982). Also see the *Letters of James Joyce*, vol. III (New York: Viking, 1966): on the first page of his introduction Ellmann writes that Beach 'timidly offered' to publish *Ulysses* (3), and later in a footnote he states that she 'courageously proposed that [Joyce] allow her to publish the book' (40).

Works cited

Arrow, Keith, 'Increasing Returns: Historiographic Issues and Path Dependence'. *European Journal of the History of Economic Thought* 7.2 (Summer 2000), 171–80.
Beach, Sylvia, *Shakespeare & Company*. 1959; Lincoln: University of Nebraska Press, 1991.
—— unpublished papers. Firestone Library, Princeton University.
Beja, Morris, *James Joyce: A Literary Life*. London: Macmillan, 1992.
Bishop. Edward, 'The Garbled History of the First-Edition *Ulysses*'. *Joyce Studies Annual 1998*, 3–36.
—— 'Re: Covering *Ulysses*'. *Joyce Studies Annual 1994*, 22–55.
Bourdieu, Pierre, *Distinction: A Social Critique of the Judgement of Taste*. Trans. Richard Nice. Cambridge, Mass.: Harvard University Press, 1984.
Budgen, Frank, *James Joyce and the Making of Ulysses*. 1934; Bloomington: Indiana University Press, 1973.
Deming, Robert. H., *James Joyce the Critical Heritage: Volume I 1902–1927*. New York: Barnes & Noble, 1970.
Ellmann, Richard, *James Joyce*. Revised edition. London: Oxford University Press, 1982.
Fitch, Noel Riley, *Sylvia Beach and the Lost Generation: A History of Literary Paris in the Twenties and Thirties*. New York: W.W. Norton, 1985.
Garud, Richard and Peter Karnoe, *Path Dependence and Creation*. Mahwah, NJ: Lawrence Erlbaum Associates, 2001.
Gilbert, Stuart, *James Joyce's Ulysses: A Study*. New York: Knopf, 1934.
Goodstein, Eban, 'The Economic Roots of Environmental Decline: Property Rights or Path Dependence.' *Journal of Economic Issues* 29.4 (December 1995), 1029–43 [accessed on-line].
Gorman, Herbert, *James Joyce*. New York: Rinehart & Co., 1939, 1948.

Johnson, Jeri, 'Introduction'. James Joyce, *Ulysses*. London: Oxford University Press, 1993.

Joyce, James, *Ulysses*. Paris: Shakespeare and Company, 1926.

—— *Ulysses*. New York: Random House, 1934.

—— *The Letters of James Joyce*. Volume I, ed. Stuart Gilbert. New York: Viking, 1957, reissued with corrections 1966. Vols II and III, ed. Richard Ellmann. New York: Viking, 1966.

Kelly, Joseph, *Our Joyce: From Outcast to Icon*. Austin: University of Texas Press, 1998.

Liebowitz, Stan and Stephen E. Margolis, 'Typing Errors'. *Reason magazine*. June 1996. 29 January 2002. <http://reason.com/9606/Fe.QWERTY.shtml>.

Maddox, Brenda, *Nora: A Biography of Nora Joyce*. London: Minerva, 1989.

Moscato, Michael and Leslie LeBlanc, eds., *The United States of America v. One Book Entitled Ulysses by James Joyce*. Frederick, MD: University Publications of America, Inc., 1984.

Norris, David and Carl Flint, *Joyce for Beginners*. Cambridge: Icon Books, 1994.

Norris, Margot, ed., *A Companion to James Joyce's 'Ulysses'*. Boston and New York: Bedford Books, 1998.

Rabaté, Jean-Michel, '"Thank Maurice": A Note About Maurice Darantiere'. *Joyce Studies Annual* 1991, 247.

Review of *Ulysses*. *Time*. 29 January 1934, 49.

10
Making Room for the Woman of Genius: Virginia Woolf, Elizabeth Robins and 'Modernism's Other' as Mother

Molly Hite

For we think back through our mothers if we are women.

A Room of One's Own (1929)

But, to make a clearance before I begin, I will suggest that we range Edwardians and Georgians into two camps; Mr. Wells, Mr. Bennett, and Mr. Galsworthy I will call the Edwardians; Mr. Forster, Mr. Lawrence, Mr. Strachey, Mr. Joyce, and Mr. Eliot I will call the Georgians.

'Mr. Bennett and Mrs. Brown' (1924)[1]

Did Virginia Woolf think back through her mothers when she constructed a tradition in which to locate her individual talent? The remark I have taken as my first epigraph became the impetus for a feminist archaeology aiming to recover a female literary tradition, an alternative maternal legacy in which the woman writer could locate herself and from which she could draw sustenance and power. But as my second epigraph indicates, when it came to naming her own peers or immediate precursors, Woolf located herself in a context of novelists, biographers and poets who were exclusively male. In the modernist manifesto 'Mr. Bennett and Mrs. Brown', written five years before the publication of *A Room of One's Own*, she claimed as her 'Georgian' associates 'Mr. Forster, Mr. Lawrence, Mr. Strachey, Mr. Joyce, and Mr. Eliot', and placed them in opposition to a paternal generation of 'Edwardians', exemplified by 'Mr. Wells, Mr. Bennett, and Mr. Galsworthy'. The reiterations of 'Mr.' in these lists insist on a gender uniformity that is never identified as such. The ironically self-effacing narrator ultimately claims the Georgians as 'we', although she never disturbs the homogeneity of the sequence by adding the name of 'Mrs. Woolf'. Her membership in the group is less anomalous for being implicit. Furthermore, in thus 'making a clearance' she clears away other female modernists – and, for that matter, female Edwardians. For Woolf, thinking 'back through our mothers' appears to be a limited project, one that did not (and, I shall suggest, could not) impinge on the enterprise of thinking herself *into* an adversarial community of male modernists committed to exploratory, experimental writing.

On the contrary, Woolf invented herself as a modernist and even as a feminist by thinking back *against* her mothers, defining herself in opposition to some of her most important female precursors and contemporaries. In excluding these literary mothers from her roster of serious writers, she in effect cleared the ground – or to borrow her own metaphor, made room. We see dramatic evidence of this 'clearance' in an early draft of 'Mr. Bennett and Mrs. Brown', in which the list of Georgians includes 'Miss Sitwell' and 'Miss Richardson'.[2] By the time the essay appeared as a Hogarth Pamphlet, however, Edith Sitwell and Dorothy Richardson had left the room of serious modernist innovators. And no Edwardian women were mentioned in any version of this document, although the list could have included the names of Mrs [Alice] Meynell, a poet twice nominated for the laureateship, Miss [Mary St-Legère] Kingsley, who wrote acclaimed novels under the name of Lucas Malet, Miss [Mona] Caird, the author of provocative and successful feminist novels, and the foremother whose work most directly impinged on Woolf's own: Miss [Elizabeth] Robins, the actress, militant suffrage spokeswoman, feminist theorist, and best-selling fiction writer, who followed the example of Henrik Ibsen in her choice and dramatic treatment of provocative social topics.

In this essay I focus on Elizabeth Robins because she is the most obvious example of a potent maternal figure that Woolf could and would not emulate. Twenty years older than Woolf, American-born and extraordinarily beautiful, Robins worked incessantly and exercised considerable charm to penetrate London social and artistic circles, becoming close friends with Oscar Wilde, Henry James, Bernard Shaw, the Ibsen translator William Archer and the legendary actor-manager Beerbohm Tree, among many others. Her memoirs, *Both Sides of the*

Curtain and *Ibsen and the Actress*, indicate how aggressive and tenacious she had to be and how many risks she took in the unladylike business of making a name for herself in a profession still considered shady. Her great suffrage novel *The Convert* and her collection of suffrage speeches, *Way Stations*, show her engaged in street debates, often countering hecklers who impugned her morals as well as her politics. Literally as well as figuratively, she embodied the kind of prominence and the attendant vulnerability to attacks and trivialisation that marked the successful female artist of the immediately preceding generation. Robins herself pointed out the implications of her own status as a public woman: 'To say "a public woman" is, or was recently to say a woman of the streets.'[3]

The substantial tradition of feminist scholarship on Virginia Woolf shows her honouring and deriving support from her literary 'foremothers'. I want to complicate this account by noting that Woolf was more comfortable with past female writers who remained barely known. She had a passionate interest in the 'lives of the obscure', celebrating their letters and diaries as key documents in the history of women's writing. The lives of the famous, however, were a source of unease. For instance, despite her sympathy in *A Room of One's Own* for historical women who tried to write against the social and economic odds, her project in that essay takes for granted their relative failure. Her key question is why there are (as yet) so few great female writers, and why the work of virtually all of them is seriously flawed. An anecdote in an early draft of *A Room* emphasises the asymmetry characterising her comparisons of men's and women's literary accomplishments. Relating how, on one occasion, she was forced to sit through a number of long speeches, all praising famous men, Woolf's narrator reports on a subversive desire to cry out, 'Let us all praise unknown women.'[4] In Woolf's construction of literary history, unknown women counter famous men. In *A Room of One's Own* the great woman who would express her genius completely and take her place among the great male writers of literary history was, rather coyly, yet to come.

Woolf constructed her own writing practice in opposition to the example of immediate female precursors. She was not thereby an antifeminist or an undutiful literary daughter. The evidence indicates, rather, that for Woolf, successful recent female writers were a threat to both her reputation and her productivity. Central to the threat was the idea of being 'in public' in a way familiar to middle-class women: functioning in service of others, sharing space, playing social roles, being available. Many of her writings indicate that for Woolf, a literary room full of women was equivalent to the drawing room, an ostensibly private, domestic space subordinate to the real, public world of men, in which women were nearly interchangeable. Against this threat, Woolf proposed the very small room, just large enough for one woman of genius. For most of the twentieth century, the house of canonical modernist fiction has contained only this one room, inhabited by only one woman, Virginia Woolf.

A room full of women

I have noted elsewhere that for Woolf, immediate foremothers appear to have asserted a model of femininity associated with the female body in society, and that this model of femininity threatened both Woolf's fictional characters and Woolf herself, as an incipiently great writer. One way she represented this vulnerability, especially during her early years when she was shaping her identity as a writer, was through the gendered space of the drawing room. If the hermetic room of one's own is in essence solitary, the matrilineal space of historical women's writing suggests by contrast a room full of women, a quasi-public chamber within the continually violated 'privacy' of the private house, where Jane Austen laid a blotter over her novel-in-progress when callers arrived (*Room* 70) and later where Vanessa and Virginia Stephen assumed the mantle of self-sacrifice from their dead mother and played what Woolf later termed 'the Victorian game of manners' with their father's visitors. The structural metaphor of an impermeable private space as the precondition for great writing thus was at odds with certain implications of the female literary tradition that Woolf discussed in *A Room of One's Own*.[5]

The drawing room is the site of the hostess, whose function is to facilitate the expression of others: to pour tea, pass food, elicit opinions, make general conversation and flatter. In Woolf's writing, the most irresistible guarantor that a young woman will succeed to the role of hostess and assume the mantle of self-sacrifice is the female precursor. After all, it is the charismatic Mrs Ramsay who signals to the painter Lily Briscoe, 'I am drowning, my dear, in seas of fire. Unless you apply some balm to the anguish of this hour and say something nice to that young man there, life will run upon the rocks – indeed I hear the grating and the growling at this minute. My nerves are taut as fiddle strings. Another touch and they will snap.' The result is that incipiently modern Lily has to 'renounce the experiment – what happens if one is not nice to that young man there ...'[6] An eerily similar female figure, the Angel in the House, counsels the fledgling female writer, 'whatever you say let it be pleasing to men. Be sympathetic; be tender; flatter; use all the arts and wiles which I Heaven help me have used till I am sick of the whole thing ... but believe me it is absolutely necessary.'[7] And Woolf's own mother, occupying 'the very centre of that great Cathedral space which was childhood', embodied the role, 'part slave, part angel of sympathy', that the daughters could avoid only by escaping to their own secular Bloomsbury spaces and their radically remade adult lives ('Sketch' 81, 125).

The escape into an anti-familial, anti-Victorian way of life so spatially distinct that it took on the name of its first location, Bloomsbury, was thus a reaction against maternal precedent as much as against more obvious patriarchal strictures. Furthermore, for Woolf the threat of the nurturing and self-sacrificing woman combined with another threat, which Andreas Huyssen describes as the modern feminised genre of 'inferior literature – subjective, emotional and passive', a defining 'other' poised in contrast to a masculinised genre of 'genuine, authentic literature – objective, ironic', produced by a writer 'in control of his aesthetic means'. For Huyssen the most interesting aspect of the feminised modern other is its association with mass culture. But because modernists also defined themselves against the preceding generation, Marysa Demoor notes a more direct and insidious double disparagement of Victorian and Edwardian writers who were women.[8] Indeed, modes like the sentimental or the melodramatic, which were most clearly associated with women writers of the late nineteenth and early twentieth centuries, became the most conspicuous signposts of aesthetic debasement among modernists.

Largely as a consequence of modernist trivialising, the most widely accepted understanding of the British novel from about 1890 to 1910 (the year in which, as Woolf put it, 'human character changed') is still that the period produced no major women writers. Elaine Showalter wrote in 1991, 'after 1880, women novelists, while ever more numerous in the marketplace, entered a period of critical decline'. S.P. Rosenbaum, the chronicler of Bloomsbury's antecedents, affirmed, 'Nor were there any women novelists that could be read alongside Meredith, Hardy, Butler or James'. Yet many critics who lived and wrote during the *fin-de-siècle* tell a different story. In his influential 1904 study *The Feminine Note in Fiction*, W.L. Courtney declared, 'Whatever may have been true of preceding ages, it is an arguable thesis that the modern novel is written by women for women.' Recent critical attention to late Victorian and Edwardian writing has uncovered a history of eminent women producing not only New Woman novels but naturalist and Aesthetic literary experiments, to critical and popular acclaim.[9] Like all literary canons, the canon of writing that counts as major for the turn-of-the-century period was formed for the most part retroactively, by subsequent writers and critics during the modern and later periods, who had their own agendas for formulating and interpreting the precedents leading up to their own present moment. One of the most influential of these writers and critics was, of course, Virginia Woolf.

Most ironically, the great essay that enjoins us to look back through our mothers is part of a tradition of feminist theorising that it does not acknowledge. In reclaiming a literary matrilineage and taking seriously materialist explanations for an ostensible lack of 'great' women in creative enterprises, *A Room of One's Own* recapitulates arguments made in prior fiction and essays by Robins, Caird, May Sinclair, Willa Muir and the Viscontess Rhondda, among others: women ranging in age from the generation of Woolf's mother to the generation of Woolf herself.[10] In taking over an active public discussion on the subjects of women's status and women's writing without acknowledging any of the major participants, Woolf was in effect depopulating a room full of women in order to make it habitable for the solitary woman of genius.

The public woman and the feminist novel

The precedents are suggestive because of Woolf's equivocal attitude towards the maternal generation of feminists. For many women of that generation the suffrage movement motivated both non-fiction and fiction that dealt with women's potential equality and significance in the public sphere. In effect, the movement created an alternative value system in which women had the moral scope and advantage. Furthermore, it posited a collectivity, 'women', that suffered political oppression and could seek political power. These developments prompted late Victorian and Edwardian feminist writers to develop strategies for writing innovative narratives and essays, works that challenged and modified existing forms, sometimes in ways that anticipated modernism, sometimes in ways that provoked modernist reaction. Woolf both borrowed from and reacted against many of these foremothers.

The foremother with whom she had the most ambivalent relationship was Elizabeth Robins. Leonard Woolf described her at the age of 66, 'When young she must have been beautiful, very vivacious, a gleam of genius with that indescribably female charm which made her invincible to all men and most women.'[11]

Leonard's wording was characteristically careful. One woman for whom Robins clearly was not 'invincible' was Virginia Woolf, whose path crossed Robins' from her childhood until her suicide in 1941. The history of their intermittent contacts over Woolf's lifetime suggests less that the two women were soul mates or sisters in struggle than that Robins was in Woolf's face a great deal of the time – as a friend of her mother, an actress the young Stephen girls were taken to see, a fiction writer emblematic of the preceding generation, a fragile and ageing female body, a neighbour of the Woolfs in Sussex, and the adored mentor and partner of Octavia Wilberforce. As a political voice, a public presence, a writer of popular and critically esteemed fiction, and most of all an accessible and attractive but somehow self-contained female body who continually moved through the private as well as the public lives of the Stephens and later the Woolfs, Robins was both a model of strikingly public female behaviour and a social force of some power in Virginia's own world. In these respects she was the antithesis of the woman writer who can create only when she has the solitude and security of a room of her own.[12]

As a public figure, Robins was also a public author. She began writing novels in order to make extra money, and could play to a mass readership in the same way that as an actress she played to an audience.[13] Her two produced and published plays, *Alan's Wife* (1898), which sympathetically portrayed maternal infanticide, and *Votes for Women*, which turned on the hypocrisy of the sexual double standard and in 1907 played to sell-out crowds in the West End (with proceeds going to the Women's Social and Political Union), explicitly aimed to generate public debate. A number of her novels also provoked widespread discussion. They included *The Open Question* (with Florence Farrell, 1898), which presented eugenic suicide as a solution to the problem of hereditary insanity, *A Dark Lantern* (1905), which treated the infamous Weir Mitchell 'rest cure' as a 'rescuer' erotically mixing trauma, desire and masochism, and *My Little Sister* (1913), which represented forced child prostitution as a widely accepted perquisite of upper-class men.

Robins was thus an author on display, like the 'well known Mrs. Smith' whom Woolf caricatured in a draft of *A Room of One's Own* as the popular writer who appears frequently in newspaper photographs, is professionally obliged to 'cut a dash', and produces 'the book of the year', which is of course ephemeral by definition (*Women and Fiction* 188). As a public spectacle, she incarnated many of the problematic aspects of female fame that repelled Woolf in all her essays about women writers. She seemed often to invite hostile or shocked reactions. She was a subject of sexual speculation, not only because she wrote about women who were unabashedly embodied and desiring but also because her art as an actress involved using her body to produce effects onstage. And she turned her celebrity to political ends, sending letters to major newspapers criticising and correcting their coverage of suffrage events, writing articles for mainstream and suffrage journals in Britain and the US, writing fiction and plays that brought to popular audiences arguments for women's emancipation and information about the government's treatment of suffragettes, touring England and Scotland to speak on such topics as 'Should women work?' and participating in the mass demonstrations of 1908–12 wearing dresses that were the height of current fashion, made up in the suffrage colours of white, purple and green. Woolf's proposed antidote to the cult of the great man, 'Let us now praise unknown women', was the furthest remove from Elizabeth Robins, who was, above all, known.[14]

In many respects, then, Robins was Woolf's paradigmatic other, an Edwardian who embodied much of what the younger writer defined herself against. Predictably, Woolf claimed in a review that Robins was anachronistic, 'a pre-war writer', putting her into the same camp as Bennett, Wells and Galsworthy. But rather than the playful hyperbole of 'human character changed', which she had used in the manifestos attacking the male Edwardians, she seems to have felt obliged to spell out what the historical transition had to do with both the subjects and the emphases of 'Georgian' – and by implication her own – writing: 'our charge against Miss Robins is simply this – that, misled largely by her strong dramatic sense, she has backed certain human qualities which dropped out of the race and neglected others which are still running.' In this review, the 'human qualities which dropped out of the race' involved specific subject matters: 'In those days there were suffrage raids, and butlers, and haunted houses.'[15]

By grouping 'suffrage raids' with butlers and haunted houses as events gone the way of Victorian class rigidities and *fin-de-siècle* experiments with the gothic and occult, Woolf exposed her own ambivalence about the most important single accomplishment in the history of the British feminist movement. Ironically, her review did not mention the key story in Robins' collection, 'Under His Roof', in which all these elements combine in a black humour genre that might be called the feminist gothic. 'Under His Roof' is about the fundamental danger of female economic and legal dependency, even when a woman shelters under the most evidently solid of patriarchal structures, a theme to which Woolf herself would return in *The Years* and *Three Guineas* as well as in *A Room of One's Own.* Yet she did not acknowledge its contemporary relevance in her review, in her eagerness to place Robins outside the boundaries of significant modernist writing. One reason was doubtless Robins' use of sentimental and dramatic conventions, part of a heritage of formulaic, clumsy techniques that Woolf decried in claiming 'there was no English novelist living from whom [modern novelists] could learn their business' ('Character in Fiction' 427). Another reason was probably Robins' status as an author of best-sellers, whose works lay on the fault line between high and mass culture, which Woolf would deride later as middlebrow.[16] The most evident reason, however, is that Robins was a thoroughly public woman whose writing embraced and endorsed a democratic vision of public life. This vision, part of the ideology of the socialist wing of the suffrage movement, consistently stressed the public good, not the fostering of individual female talent.

We see this vision in Robins' best-selling novel, *The Convert* (1908), based on the wildly successful play *Votes for Women.* Both works centre on the plot, familiar to contemporary audiences from melodrama, of the woman who is seduced and abandoned and who reveals her story years later in order to bring about a climactic turn in the action. Onto this dramatic structure Robins mapped a second formulaic plot, this time of conversion, in which a protagonist becomes committed to a major change of belief. In its feminist version, as the suffrage story, the conversion narrative was by this time so conventional as to constitute a whole sub-genre.

In Robins' hands, however, the combination was original and powerful, both in the theatre and on the printed page. The two goals of the dramatic action – the revelation of a middle-class woman's sexual debasement and thus social vulnerability, and the eventual conversion of this woman to the cause of female suffrage – produce two kinds of action for the main character, Vida Levering. On the one hand, Vida moves towards increased identification with the working-class 'fallen' women who serve as reminders of the most potent threat posed by female self-reliance to 'respectable' women of her own class. Her past sexual exploitation by the central male character, who has risen to the position of Member of Parliament and likely future Cabinet member, emerges at the apex of a brilliantly realised scene of a street rally, in which men's heckling incites her to bring up the case of another seduced and abandoned woman, this one a servant who was tried for the murder of her infant.

> 'Why did men, when British justice was born – why did they so long ago insist on trial by 'a jury of their peers'? So that justice shouldn't miscarry – wasn't it? A man's peers would best understand his circumstances, his temptation, the degree of his guilt. Yet there's no such unlikeness between different classes of men as exists between man and woman. What man has the knowledge that makes him a fit judge of woman's deeds at that time of anguish – that hour that some woman struggled through to put each man here into the world. I noticed when a previous speaker quoted the Labour Party, you applauded. Some of you here, I gather, call yourselves Labour men. Every woman who has borne a child is a Labour woman. No man among you can judge what she goes through in her hour of darkness.' (268–9)

Playing on the double, gendered meanings of key verbs in the phrases 'when British justice was born' and '[s]o that justice shouldn't miscarry' – both of which anticipate a climactic pun on 'labour' – the speech visibly shames the MP. His young fiancée is jolted into awareness of the specific incident that Vita must be invoking, at the same time as Vita's choice of example emphasises the cross-class allegiances of militant feminism.

Votes for Women and *The Convert* emphasise the extent to which privileged women in the suffrage campaign learned theory, organisation and public speaking from working-class women, who are represented as the leaders and the backbone of the movement. In *The Convert* the crowd effectively performs the work of *Bildung* for Vida Levering, presenting the 'common people' as an incipient collective protagonist for which Vida, by the end of the novel, is a synecdoche.

If there is an implied collective protagonist in *The Convert*, however, it is less the common people than the common woman, broadly conceived as a woman of any class. Gender politics in this novel incorporates class, enabling analogies like the one Vida proposes between women as a group and labour, but concentrating on issues that arise because women are prohibited from meaningful participation in public life. The insistence on a public role for women leads to a very different treatment of female creativity than the one we find in *A Room of One's Own*. Nowhere is this difference more marked than when the perennial heckler's question arises about why there was no female Shakespeare –

by implication, no woman generally acknowledged to have produced artistic works of genius.

Virginia Woolf first responded publicly to this question in her 1920 *New Statesman* exchange with Desmond McCarthy on the subject of the intellectual status of women. In appealing to history for evidence confirming the importance of external considerations in women's writing, Woolf's argument looked forward to the more overtly materialist thesis of *A Room of One's Own*: 'a woman must have money and a room of her own to write fiction '. Her approach drew on other contemporary feminist responses to the question. In 1924, Elizabeth Robins published anonymously a book-length feminist manifesto, *Ancilla's Share: An Indictment of Sex Antagonism*, in which she also addressed the question of a presumptively missing female genius – 'why has the mind of her sex never yet flowered in terms of a Homer, a Shakespeare, a Leonardo, a Beethoven, an Edison?' Woolf in a response to McCarthy proposed the answer 'education and liberty'.[17] Robins invoked the same factors in somewhat more pragmatic language, 'training and opportunity'. Unlike Woolf, however, Robins discerned a gender and class bias in the way the question was framed: in the priority it placed on exceptional qualities of individuals. She saw the specifically feminist concern as with society as a whole, writing, 'But women, we find, are not primarily concerned about the genius of the exceptional woman ...' (*Ancilla's* 101–2). And in the crowd scene in *The Convert*, Vida Levering explicitly challenges the priority of individual genius that is assumed in questions about a female Shakespeare. In the process she establishes her connection to the collective political body that in the course of the narrative comes to replace her violated personal body. When a 'shabby art student' cries, '"The schools are full of them! ... Where's their Michael Angelo? They study music by thousands: where's their Beethoven? Where's their Plato? Where's the woman Shakespeare?"' Vida shoots back, '"Since when was human society held to exist for its handful of geniuses? How many Plato's [*sic*] are there here in this crowd?"' Having scored a point, she continues:

'Yet that doesn't keep you men off the register. How many Shakespeares are there in all England to-day? Not one. Yet the State doesn't tumble to pieces. Railroads and ships are built, homes are kept going, and babies are born. The world goes on' – she bent over the crowd with lit eyes – 'the world goes on *by virtue of its common people.*' (*Convert* 203–5)

Because her explicitly feminist works addressed women as public presences who ought to exercise public power, Robins shared with Woolf a concern for equality of means. But she did not likewise insist that the goal of these means was insuring privacy for the female artist.[18]

The woman of genius

For Woolf in *A Room of One's Own*, however, the aim of money and a private space is to guarantee the integrity of the creative process. Like the female body in eighteenth- and nineteenth-century versions of the heterosexual romance plot, the drawing room, the quintessential female room in the private house, is by definition subject to violation. By contrast, the hermetic room of one's own is under the complete control of the woman writer, who because of her financial security can lock out society, which is experienced primarily as the threat of interruption. Central to Woolf's formulation of her thesis is the premise that interruption can condition the quality of work the female artist produces as well as hindering or preventing its execution. The hostess is subject to the requirements of others and essentially concerned to please. Similarly, the writer without a room of her own is available on demand and dependent on outside approval. Because she is impeded in her creativity, her work suffers: she has not the 'freedom to think of things of themselves' that for Woolf is the prerequisite for achievements of genius (*Room* 39).

Woolf was expressly concerned with genius. In response to the question about a woman Shakespeare she proposed her famous thought experiment in which the life of the hypothetical Judith Shakespeare illustrates the insuperable obstacles that would have prevented female genius from being realized in the sixteenth century, obstacles that still function, albeit to a lesser degree, in the twentieth century. For Woolf, as for any theorist who accepts the notion of genius, the quality had an innate component. Judith Shakespeare had as a birthright the character of being 'wonderfully gifted', which is to say that in her inherent *potential* to write brilliant dramatic and lyric poetry she was the equal of her brother. But Woolf manipulated the assumption widely regarded as a corollary to arguments about female inferiority, that *all* aspects of genius are inborn. She had her narrator agree with a 'deceased bishop', 'it is unthinkable that any woman in Shakespeare's day should have had Shakespeare's genius', then lets this narrator elaborate an alternative construction of the proposition, which acquires irony as the word 'born' is repeated in increasingly incongruous contexts:

> For genius like Shakespeare's is not born among labouring, unedu-
> cated, servile people. It was not born in England among the Saxons
> and the Britons. It is not born today among the working classes.
> How, then, could it have been born among women whose work
> began, according to Professor Trevelyan, almost before they were
> out of the nursery, who were forced to it by their parents and held
> to it by all the power of law and custom?

In this explanation, genius is not 'born' if it cannot grow up. It exists in the world only when it becomes an achieved creation. As an unrealised potential for creation within an individual subject it is only genius 'of a sort', which 'never got itself on to paper' (50). Money and privacy are necessary to bring such genius into being. Tradition has a more equivocal role, at least in the final pages of the essay, which assert that the second 'birth' of Judith Shakespeare is what the entire exegesis was *for*. One of the prerequisites for bringing her into existence is a recognition not of community but of solitude: we must 'face the fact, for it is a fact, that there is no arm to cling to, but that we go alone and that our relation is to the world of reality and not only to the world of men and women ...' Yet it is 'we', this paradoxical community of solitaries, presumably solitary women writers, who prepare for her coming. 'Drawing her life from the lives of the unknown who were her forerunners, as her brother did before her, she will be born.' Or, in the more evocative metaphor that often replaces and in the process interprets the metaphor of birth, 'the dead poet who was Shakespeare's sister will put on the body which she has so often laid down' (118).

For Woolf's Judith Shakespeare, the body was the agent of betrayal: specifically, sexual betrayal. If the generalised requirements of an Elizabethan middle-class feminine role dictated that she should be married to the son of a wool-stapler rather than becoming a playwright, the force behind the prohibition came from the prospect of sexual danger – from the potential for ruin housed in her public, and therefore available, body. Later the narrator remarks on '[t]hat profoundly interesting subject, the value that men set upon women's chastity and its effect on their education' (67). In the story of Judith Shakespeare, that value kills. Pregnant with her mentor's child, she commits suicide, for 'who shall measure the heat and violence of the poet's heart when caught and tangled in a woman's body?' (50)

A similar heat and violence motivate Vida Levering in *The Convert*, but in this case the violated female body is the agent of conversion and thus regeneration. In the course of the narrative, Vida is incarnated as a woman with a mission, a woman whose life is fulfilling and meaningful in contrast to the lives of the cosseted, subservient upper-middle-class women who surrounded her. But then, Vida is not presented as an incipient genius. The emphasis Robins places on political rather than individual achievement allows her to use the premise of sexual exploitation as an instrument in creating a truly public female body, a body that can act in the public sphere. The understanding Vida displays of the external conditions provoking less privileged women to become prostitutes, infanticides or suicides is represented as a direct consequence of her own seduction, pregnancy and abortion. And significantly, this understanding becomes fully political when she interacts with 'the common people', the crowd at the street rally. The back-and-forth of heckling and response generates Vida's feminist position – and also generates Vida as a coherent public identity, a committed suffrage activist.[19]

Social interaction in *The Convert* is thus positive and creative. In contrast, in Woolf's story of Judith Shakespeare, the social is wholly destructive. In a sense, Judith Shakespeare is the ultimate victim of interruption, kept by the demands of men (her father and Nick Greene) from writing a word, and finally from surviving. In Woolf's formulation, these are demands on her body, and this gendered body is opposed to – indeed, the prison of – her 'poet's heart'. For a future Judith Shakespeare to 'put on the body which she has so often laid down', the female body must not entail the social consequences that have heretofore 'tangled and imprisoned' it. It must be a public body, but one that is not vulnerable to the penetration and annihilation, both metaphorical and literal, that have heretofore been regarded as its fate. To write well – indeed, to write anything, Judith Shakespeare must have five hundred pounds a year and a room of her own.

'Cramped and thwarted'

Despite the differences between Woolf and Robins the two writers shared some of their most important arguments – or, to put the matter in historical perspective, it is interesting how many of Robins' arguments anticipated Woolf's. Both Robins and Woolf took as a premise the ostensible strangeness of men's anger at women who stray from their defined roles, when the postulated 'fact' of gender inferiority should have cued only amusement or disdain. Both saw women's apparently unobjectionable writing of fiction as a case in which this anger would seem conspicuously irrelevant. With characteristic irony, Robins observed in *Ancilla's Share* 'the monotony with which men struck this note of antipathy' to women's writing and noted, 'A lady of the harem may write a book. A lady in Haworth Rectory or in St John's Wood or the backwoods may write – and publish under the cloak of a man's name. It can all be managed quite decently' (86). Both constructed primarily materialist arguments insisting on the importance of social and economic factors to the successful achievement of great art, with Robins in *Ancilla's Share* providing an encapsulation that could have been the thesis statement of *A Room of One's Own*: 'No man has a right to ask for more sustained and concentrated intellectual work from women, nor for evidence of its range and reach, till women have about them something comparable to those fostering influences that men of analogous class, whether gifted or commonplace, take as a matter of course' (167).

Both observed shrewdly that given the ideology and practice of separate spheres for men and women, the measuring instruments for masculine achievement cannot discern the particular value of feminine contributions (*Ancilla's* 152; *Room* 40, 89, 109), and both used metaphors of optical illusion to suggest how evaluations within the dominant system necessarily rely on distorted perceptions (*Ancilla's* 97; *Room* 35–6).[20] But both also saw in the historically enforced institution of sexual difference a fertile source of new subjects and even forms for women writers, and both linked these subjects and forms with questions of value, reversing dominant categories by suggesting that hitherto unrepresented characters and experiences present a range of revitalizing possibilities for literature.[21] Both called for a more inclusive history and more biographies of women, and both suggested that this work of historical reclamation is best performed by female scholars.

Perhaps most radically, both Robins and Woolf linked women's subordination to institutionalised class and race inequality, and both went on to suggest that the very desire for hierarchical distinctions is at once masculinist and infantile. Woolf wrote, 'All this pitting of sex against sex, of quality against quality; all this claiming of superiority and imputing of inferiority, belong to the private-school stage of human existence where there are "sides," and it is necessary for one side to beat another side, and of the utmost importance to walk up to a platform and receive from the hands of the Headmaster himself a highly ornamental pot' (110). Robins wrote, 'We cannot but feel in our hearts, that this question of the superiority of one sex over the other is childish, and would be irrelevant to practical discussion but for the fact of it being the excuse for thrusting assertions of inferiority into the field' (*Ancilla's* 139).

And both aligned the goal of non-competitive equality with the good of humanity as a whole: with progress and with the establishment of an as yet unrealised condition that both called 'civilisation'. Woolf's most poignant and direct statement on this subject was in the *New Statesman* exchange with Desmond McCarthy: 'Certainly I cannot doubt that if such opinions [as those voiced by Arnold Bennett and McCarthy] prevail in the future we shall remain in a condition of half-civilised barbarism. At least that is how I define an eternity of domination on the one hand and of servility on the other. For the degradation of being a slave is only equalled by the degradation of being a master' ('Intellectual Status' 59). Robins in *Ancilla's Share* agreed that 'the goal of human endeavour, is a combination of the educated efforts of women with the educated efforts of men for the creation of a civilised society', but that 'a truly civilised society has never yet been existence, some of the strongest upholders of barbarism being those who have had most of what is miscalled education' (47). Both viewed sex roles as functions of power relations rather than as intrinsic or essential. Robins concluded the suffrage essay 'Women's Secret', 'I would like to ask [men] to remember that if our parts had been reversed, if woman had been the dominant partner, men would have exercised precisely those arts of dissimulation and of long silence, alternated with brief outbursts of bitterness, that always characterise the unfree' (*Way Stations* 16).

Such 'arts of dissimulation and silence', which 'always characterise the unfree', were for both theorists the enemy of good writing as well as of anything meriting the name of civilisation. Both dwelt on the destructive effects to a female writer of wearing 'the aspect that shall have the best chance of pleasing her brothers', as Robins observed in 'Women's Secret' (*Way Stations* 6), and both seized on Robert Lewis Stevenson's conceit of having 'played the sedulous ape' to describe inferior women writers who imitated the prose styles of eminent male writers. Perhaps most important, both Robins and Woolf contrasted writing that aims to please with writing that reveals, and gave aesthetic as well as ontological pre-eminence to the second kind of writing: 'truth-telling', in Robins' phrase (*Way* 8), representations of 'things in themselves' in Woolf's (39).

But while Robins and Woolf agreed on the harm to writing when the writer is dependent and required to please, they differed significantly on where they located the worst of the damage. In *A Room of One's Own* Woolf marshalled adjectives of deformity and disfiguration to describe writing that responded to the experience of oppression. Judith Shakespeare's work, had any emerged, 'would have been twisted and deformed, issuing from a strained and morbid imagination' (52). The poetry of Lady Winchelsea and of Margaret, Duchess of Newcastle was 'disfigured and deformed' by virtue of having issued from minds 'disturbed by alien emotions like fear and hatred' (62, 61). And Charlotte Brontë, because of her 'rage' and her determination to write 'of herself where she would write of her characters', produced books that were 'deformed and twisted' and – the final aesthetic ignominy – herself died 'young, cramped and thwarted' (71–2).

The harshness of Woolf's judgements and the extraordinarily physical tropes – especially the 'twisted and deformed' writing of Charlotte Brontë that modulates by connotation into a 'cramped and thwarted' life and/or body and becomes the insinuated cause of Brontë's early death – have startled even readers who do not blink at the assertion that fear and hatred are 'alien emotions' for a writer. The judgements and language are the more startling when contrasted with Robins' remarks on women writers who resisted gender oppression, as opposed to women writers who acquiesced to established norms and prohibitions. Robins, too, used metaphors of physical deformity and injury, but she used them in the context of damage caused by external pressure. In *Ancilla's Share* it was female capacity in general that, 'maimed and dwindled', still 'survived men's sex antagonism' as evidence of 'a power which is killed before it can leave an authentic sign' (152). But as she had argued a decade earlier, women's writing suffers most *not* when the writer is 'at war with her lot', as in Woolf's version of Charlotte Brontë (73), but when the writer seems unaware that being at war with her lot is even a possibility. Robins was trenchant on the subject of the female precursor who, upon entering a field controlled by men, conceived as her task 'to imitate as nearly as possible the method, but above all the point of view, of man', rather than 'to proclaim her own or other women's actual thoughts and feelings'. Such a writer inevitably followed 'meekly in the steps of the forgotten Master, the first tribal story-teller, inventor of that chimera, "the man's woman"'. Her female characters were equally 'man's women', 'puppets as nearly as possible like those that had from the beginning found such favour in man's sight'. Such fawning and lying affected the truth-telling or revelatory capacity of her fiction, which was Robins' main concern. Because truth-telling and revelation are the last things served by the woman writer's adherence to existing literary standards, Robins was acutely aware of the conventional nature of the reigning fictional genre, realism. She wrote, 'Little as we can judge of those princes and nobles from the starving men of letters who licked their boots, hardly more can men discover to-day what women really think of them from the fairy-tales of feminine spinning, however much the spider "makes faces," as Stevenson would say, and pretends, "Now I am being Realistic!"' (*Way Stations* 5)

In Robins' account, however, a number of pioneering female novelists succeeded in 'proclaiming their own or other women's thoughts and feelings' against existing norms of realism. In *Ancilla's Share*, the case in point is Charlotte Brontë, hailed explicitly for her representations of women at war with their lot:

> If Charlotte Brontë's novels were not the first examples, they were the most unflinchingly faithful the world had seen of the woman's mind – her inner thoughts and experiences – as revealed in fiction.
>
> Naturally this revelation appealed most to women. It was conveyed in a language to which women had the key and men had not. Such power of saying what had hitherto had only been thought, such frankness, such passion, *were* 'splendid,' to those who recognised not only the truth of the accent but the further reverberation. (*Ancilla's* 89)

The 'power of saying what had hitherto only been thought' is a capacity that Robins acknowledged in other female novelists as well.[22] Her accolades tended to go to writers who broke rules about the representation of female characters by showing women who initiate action, aspire to achievement in the public life, and feel emotions ranging from humiliation to desperation to fury at encountering the limitations placed on them by existing norms of femininity.

In contrast, Woolf made Jane Austen her main example – indeed, in a strict sense, her sole example – of literary success among her female predecessors. According to her account, Austen wrote 'without hate, without bitterness, without fear, without protest, without preaching'. Woolf went on to comment, 'That was how Shakespeare wrote', in that 'the minds of both had consumed all impediments ...' In this assessment, hate, bitterness, fear and protest are self-evidently 'impediments' to good writing and the means by which the personality of the individual writer encroaches illicitly on the impersonal ground of fiction.

These passages reveal how completely Woolf in *A Room of One's Own* assumed that negative or resistant emotions or opinions are by definition those of the writer, not a narrator or character, and moreover are peculiar to the writer as an individual, not a member of a socially demarcated group. In Woolf's account, 'grudges and antipathies' (the phrase could be an unsympathetic description of protests against injustice or cruelty) reveal 'the writer' expressing a personal bias. By contrast, in 'Woman's Secret', Robins addressed directly the assumption that a female writer who voices discontent or passion is writing 'mere' autobiography – that is, simply recording her own experiences and reactions to no purpose beyond unburdening or glorifying herself. Robins observed, 'No view is more widely accepted than that every woman's book is but a naive attempt to extend her own little personality', and went on to describe what might be called the autobiographical fallacy, in which a woman who creates a believable character is then damned for merely 'verbatim reporting' of her own presumed experiences.[23]

Robins' observations thus help clarify a second aspect that is revealing in Woolf's treatment of the female literary tradition. According to Woolf, most women who published and sold their writing to an audience receptive enough to assure their survival in literary memory were not only tainted by virtue of being public personalities. When they depicted female characters who protested at the economic, legal and social limits attendant on being female, they were also by definition flawed or self-indulgent. Woolf's feminist argument could make no room for expressions of overt feminist resistance in women's literary writing.[24]

The situation is clearest in the version of *A Room of One's Own* published in the US as 'Women and Fiction'. In this shorter essay, Woolf identified nineteenth-century female precursors with a kind of autobiography characterised by special pleading, the articulation of a personal grievance: 'In the early nineteenth century, women's novels were largely autobiographical. One of the motives that led them to write was the desire to expose their own suffering, to plead their own cause' ('Women and Fiction' 199). In this account of the evolution of female aesthetic production, Woolf regarded autobiography as a blemish disqualifying work from greatness, an impediment to the achievement of art. In her account, however, it is clear that autobiography is inartistic inasmuch as it motivates women 'to expose their own suffering, to plead their own cause' – to make the novel, as the passage continues, 'a dumping-ground for the personal emotions'. The female writer's greatness accordingly lies '[i]n future', when 'literature will become, for women, as for men, an art to be studied' and '[w]omen's gift will be trained and strengthened' (199). Woolf lapsed into passive constructions at the culmination of her closing paragraph, not specifying *who* will make the woman's novel 'a work of art like any other', *who* will explore 'its resources and limitations'. Most readers will be willing to make a guess about the writer she had in mind. Less equivocally than *A Room of One's Own*, 'Women and Fiction' is concerned with Woolf's own relation to a female literary tradition.

Modernism and greatness

In calling for a training and strengthening of women's talents in order to take women's novels beyond their presumed status of 'dumping-ground for the personal emotions', Woolf again made impersonality a defining characteristic of great works of literature. When she conflated 'androgyny' with such impersonality in *A Room of One's Own*, moving immediately from 'It is fatal to be a man or woman pure and simple; one must be woman-manly or man-womanly' to 'It is fatal for a woman to lay the least stress on any grievance; to plead even with justice any cause' (108), she equated the gendered with the personal, at least when the 'personal emotions' in question were negative ones.[25] The end-product of a fully evolved female writing practice is a novel that is significant primarily as an aesthetic object, 'a work of art like any other'. Only as such an object can the work be evaluated in terms of its creator's genius. But why must the genius that produces a novel be prohibited from depicting explicit resistance or protest on the part of a socially defined group? And why *this* socially defined group?

Again, Robins' emphasis, framed within a similar set of concerns, points up some of the problems Woolf did not formulate. Unlike Woolf, Robins was inclined to praise famous women and even to grant them genius, especially in *Ancilla's Share*, where she was acerbic on the subject of anti-feminism after the First World War. Because she was relatively uninterested in genius as an absolute quality of human beings or their artistic productions, she was less concerned with evaluation and more concerned with reception than Woolf was – more apt to ask what *sort* of audience praised or condemned a given writer, and why. But Robins was aware that general acclaim was rare for a woman writer and that universal acclaim was probably impossible for any writer. 'We have never heard of a writer whom every reader liked,' she wrote, 'but where a work is genuinely praised by women and belittled by men the difference between them may indicate a difference deeper than taste. Women may be praising something whose truth and beauty they know, but which is a kind of truth and an aspect of beauty which men do not know' (88). The division of readers into men and women is overly simple, as Woolf's own example attests. But the idea that aesthetic evaluation, as well as aesthetic production, is conditioned by social and economic factors haunts *A Room of One's Own,* undermining the messianic anticipation of a reincarnated Judith Shakespeare with the intimation that genius may not be immediately or universally apprehended, especially if it occurs in a place and a form where aesthetic gatekeepers are unlikely to look for it.

Why in Woolf's argument does the presence of adversarial emotion restrict communication so completely that ethical and political concerns become merely personal, and a potentially universal audience becomes individual and idiosyncratic? Why does a woman writer 'at war with her lot' have to end up 'cramped and thwarted' – adjectives that suggest invasive incarceration, less the room of one's own than the enforced solitude of the 'rest cure', to which Woolf herself was several times subjected? Elizabeth Robins had argued that in a work 'women like and men hate, women may be praising something whose beauty and truth they know'. Woolf's feminist precursors Alice Meynell and May Sinclair also made this point – and all three, by the way, articulated it in passionate defence of Charlotte Brontë. But Virginia Woolf, who in *A Room of One's Own* called for writing about such gendered subjects as Chloe and Olivia, the lady with the pug dog, and the prostitute, did not go on to maintain that one man's 'personal grievance' might be another woman's 'truth and beauty'. One reason seems to be that she did not see a predominantly female audience as capable of decreeing that a given piece of writing was a work of genius. And of course in a purely pragmatic, social sense she was right.

To use her own ironic formulation, genius is not 'born' when it is not recognised by the custodians of official excellence – when it does not receive from the hands of the headmaster himself a highly ornamental pot. But putting the question of genius this way emphasises how ambivalent Woolf was about the role of audience in determining literary value. The idea of a heterogeneous, historically shifting readership was the originating condition for *A Room of One's Own.* At the same time, such a notion of readership jeopardised the absolute status of genius. The fact that a writer could be hailed as a genius in one era and disregarded in the next had implications contrary to her construction of literary history as an evolution, in which women writers, especially, climbed from the primal ooze of self-expression onto the solid ground of artistry. But a great number of the writers who were granted genius by their contemporaries, only to be denied it by their antecedents, were women.

As I suggested, Woolf herself participated in this denial of female predecessors – and, for that matter, contemporaries – by presenting in her most important modernist manifestos a canonical list of Edwardian and modernist writers whose titles (with the tacit exception of 'Mrs. Woolf') were all 'Mr'. But the sympathy she brings to her chronicles of ostensible failure indicate an unease and even an identification that complicates her evident desire to insert herself into a masculine canon. The rhetoric of 'cause' and 'personal grievance' names issues that were pressing in her own fiction, as feminist critics from the 1970s to the present have pointed out. Furthermore, her attack on hierarchy in *A Room of One's Own* implicitly calls into question the criteria of 'greatness' that she presents as unproblematic elsewhere in the same essay. Her ridicule in *A Room of One's Own* of judgements about superiority and inferiority expresses a central element of her thinking, one that she developed throughout her career. In *Three Guineas* she explicitly aligned such competition with oppression, Fascism and war.

Yet Woolf herself was extremely competitive and extremely anxious about her own status, not only among her peers but also in literary history. She was not above taking 'sides' against contemporaries whose success could call into question the absolute nature of her own yardstick for excellence. Too often she seemed to be vying for the position of greatest *female* writer, competing in a game in which the Headmaster had only one highly ornamental pot to bestow in the minor category of women's literary production.[26]

Her ambivalence enacts the classic problem facing both upholders and challengers of any sort of canon. If criteria of greatness are relative to audiences, and thus to conventions specific to historical periods, nations and social classes, then excellence is fundamentally a matter of pleasing a given public or elite. Not only is the acclaim of such audiences transitory and capricious, but the requirement of pleasing compromises the integrity of the artist's vision, a sacrifice that for Woolf 'is the most abject treachery' (*Room* 110). The only apparent appeal is to a transcendent standard of excellence that can judge a context-bound standard of taste and dismiss it.

Yet the claim of transcendent judgement has in practice worked to dismiss women writers' work – as uncritically autobiographical, as sentimental, as self-indulgent or as trivial. It is understandable that Woolf oscillates between the two positions in *A Room of One's Own*. Neither is sufficient, and each troubles the other. Her motivation for throwing in her lot with the male modernists, and even for obscuring that identification by archly leaving her own 'Mrs.' out of the sequence of 'Mr.'s, seems more urgent, and seems bound up with the shape her modernism was to take. In evading an overt identification as a female artist, she was making one of many moves to separate the newly successful woman of genius from that other emergent phenomenon the public woman. Although this woman undermined gendered distinctions, especially the distinction between public and private spheres, the public woman was publicly on view *as* a woman, a vulnerable sexual body liable to appropriation, violation and especially judgement.

Notes

1 Virginia Woolf, *A Room of One's Own* (New York: Harcourt Brace Jovanovich, 1957), p. 79; 'Mr. Bennett and Mrs. Brown'; I cite from the 1924 version titled 'Character in Fiction', *The Essays of Virginia Woolf, Volume Three, 1919–1924*, ed. Andrew McNeillie (New York: n.p., 1988), p. 431. Hermione Lee notes a similar ambivalence in Chapter 4, of her biography *Virginia Woolf* (New York: Alfred A. Knopf, 1997); her epigraph conjoins the 'we think back through our mothers' quotation with a passage from 'Professions for Women' about killing the Angel in the House (79). Other important studies on the the subject of Woolf's ambivalent relation to female precursors are Sandra M. Gilbert and Susan Gubar, '"Forward Into the Past": The Complex Female Affiliation Complex', in Jerome J. McGann, ed., *Historical Studies and Literary Criticism* (Madison, WI: University of Wisconsin Press, 1985), pp. 240–65; and Elizabeth Abel, *Virginia Woolf and the Fictions of Psychoanalysis* (Chicago and London: University of Chicago Press, 1989), esp. pp. 84–106.
2 'Before I begin I shd. say that when I speak of the Georgians I am speaking of such writers as Mr Joyce, Mr Lawrence, Mr Forster, Mr Strachey, Mr Eliot, Miss Sitwell, Miss Richardson ...'. 'Character in Fiction' 503.
3 Elizabeth Robins, *Ancilla's Share: An Indictment of Sex Antagonism* (1924; rpt. Westport, Conn.: Hyperion Press, Inc., 1976), p. 76; *Both Sides of the Curtain* (London: Heinemann, 1940); *Ibsen and the Actress* (London: Hogarth Essays, Second Series, 1928); *The Convert* (Leipzig: Bernhard Tauchnitz, vol. 2, 1908); rpt. ed. Jane Marcus (New York: Feminist Press, 1980); *Way Stations* (London: Hodder and Stoughton, 1913).
4 *Women and Fiction: The Manuscript Versions of 'A Room of One's Own'*, ed. S.P. Rosenbaum (Cambridge, Mass. and London: Shakespeare Head/Blackwell,

1992), p.188. 'The Lives of the Obscure' is a three-part biographical essay in the first *Common Reader*; it is reprinted in *The Essays of Virginia Woolf, Volume 4: 1925 to 1928*, ed. Andrew McNeillie (London: Hogarth, 1994), pp. 119–45.

For the feminist critical tradition placing Woolf in harmony with a female literary tradition, see especially Jane Marcus, 'Thinking back through Our Mothers,' *Art and Anger: Reading Like a Woman* (Columbus: Ohio State University Press, 1988), pp. 73–100.

5 'A Sketch of the Past', *Moments of Being: Unpublished Biographical Writings*, ed. Jeanne Schulkind (New York and London: Harcourt Brace Jovanovich, 1976): 129. I discuss Woolf's avoidance of the 'social' female body – the body whose behaviour always has social consequences – in 'Virginia Woolf's Two Bodies', *Genders* 31 (2000). http://www.genders.org/g31/g31_hite.html.

6 Virginia Woolf, *To the Lighthouse* (New York: Harcourt Brace Jovanovich, 1989), p. 92.

7 Virginia Woolf, 'Speech of January 21, 1931' (early draft of 'Professions for Women'), *The Pargiters: The Novel-Essay Portion of 'The Years'*, ed. Mitchell A. Leaska (New York: New York Public Library and Readex Books, 1977), p. xxxi. The speaker of this injunction is the Angel in the House.

8 Andreas Huyssen, 'Mass Culture as Woman: Modernism's Other', *After the Great Divide: Modernism, Mass Culture, Postmodernism* (Bloomington: Indiana University Press, 1986), p. 48. Marysa Demoor, "Not with a bang but a whimper': Lucy Clifford's Correspondence, 1919–1929', *Cambridge Quarterly*, 30, 3 (2001), 238–9.

9 Elaine Showalter, *Sexual Anarchy, Gender and Culture at the Fin de Siècle* (New York: Penguin, 1991), p. 17: S.P. Rosenbaum, *Victorian Bloomsbury: The Early Literary History of the Bloomsbury Group, Volume 1* (London: St. Martin's Press, 1987): 44. W.L. Courtney, *The Feminine Note in Fiction* (London: Chapman and Hall, 1904), p. xiv. Important reconsiderations include Jane Eldridge Miller, *Rebel Women: Feminism, Modernism and the Edwardian Novel* (London: Virago, 1994); Ann Ardis, *New Women, New Novels: Feminism and Early Modernism* (New Brunswick: Rutgers University Press, 1990); and Talia Shaffer, *The Forgotten Female Aesthetes: Literary Culture in Late-Victorian England* (Charlottesville: University Press of Virginia, 2000).

10 Mona Caird, *The Daughters of Danaus* (New York: The Feminist Press, 1989); May Sinclair, *The Creators: A Comedy* (New York: The Century Co., 1910); Willa Muir, *Women: An Inquiry* (London: Hogarth Press, 1925); and Margaret Mackworth Haig, the Viscountess Rhondda, *Leisured Women* (London: Hogarth Press, 1928).

11 Leonard Woolf, *The Journey Not the Arrival Matters: An Autobiography of the Years 1939–1969* (London: Hogarth, 1969), p. 84.

12 In a groundbreaking essay, 'Art and Anger: Elizabeth Robins and Virginia Woolf', Jane Marcus notes, 'Elizabeth Robins was one of those "mothers" of fiction we think back through' (*Art and Anger* 26). In my present context, the observation insinuates some of the complexity the question of mothers and thinking 'through' them posed for the ambitious and anxious daughter. In suggesting that the relationship involved some hostility on Woolf's part, I diverge from earlier considerations of the relation of Robins to Woolf. Marcus pointed out the numerous affinities between the political

positions of the two women and suggested that Robins' argument against 'sex antagonism', *Ancilla's Share*, was a source for many of the arguments, strategies and images in *Three Guineas*. Robins' two recent biographers, Joanne Gates and Angela John, both note the acquaintance and the shared feminist commitment, and Gates does a certain amount of comparison between fictional works. Both, however, represent the association as largely amicable. In addition, I differ from these three important critics in regarding Robins as an important, and to a certain degree aesthetically innovative novelist as well as an astute theorist of female subordination. Joanne E. Gates, *Elizabeth Robins, 1862–1952: Actress, Novelist, Feminist* (Tuscaloosa and London: University of Alabama Press, 1994); Angela V. John, *Elizabeth Robins: Staging a Life, 1862–1952* (London and New York: Routledge, 1995).

Woolf's irritation with Robins shows up in the tone of diary entries and letters. A 1928 diary entry plays on Robins' name – 'like a red breast, creeping out': the metaphor develops in a letter to Ottoline Morrell: 'E.R. however is a bird of a very different feather, something like a humming bird stuffed.' Later, noting Robins' 'intense, exacting, pernickety demands', Woolf again elaborated the metaphor: 'A small frozen humming bird – with rouged lips; intense blue eyes, very small, old; full of accents and intensities.' Still later she complained that Leonard 'was riddled & needled by Miss Robins for 2 hours'. Yet she apparently never said anything critical to Robins herself. Most poignantly, she seems to have developed a crush on Robins' long-time partner, the physician Octavia Wilberforce, who unsuccessfully treated her depression before her suicide. The memoir that Wilberforce wrote about that period shows her trying to foster a connection between Woolf and the ageing Robins – who was outspoken in her admiration of Woolf and clearly could not conceive that Woolf might resent her – while fending off an infatuation on the part of an increasingly depressed and desperate woman. *Octavia Wilberforce: The Autobiography of a Pioneer Woman Doctor*, ed. Pat Jalland (London: Cassell, 1989), pp. 160–87.

13 In order to put through law school her brilliant, if feckless, younger brother, later the diplomat and labour organizer Raymond Robins. For this fascinating part the Robins story, see Elizabeth Robins' third autobiography, *Raymond and I* (London: Hogarth Press, 1956).

14 John 141–72. Robins collected many of her most important articles on the suffrage campaign and supplied a historical narrative connecting them in the fascinating volume *Way Stations*.

15 '"The Mills of the Gods"', *The Times Literary Supplement*, 17 June 1920, rpt. *The Essays of Virginia Woolf, Volume Three: 1919–1924*, ed. Andrew McNeillie (New York: Harcourt Brace Jovanovich: 1988), pp. 228–9.

16 'Middlebrow', *Collected Essays by Virginia Woolf, Volume II* (New York: Harcourt Brace and World, Inc., 1967), pp. 196–203.

17 'The Intellectual Status of Women', *Virginia Woolf: Women and Writing*, ed. Michèle Barrett (New York: Harcourt Brace Jovanovich, 1979), p. 56.

18 In less explicitly feminist works, Robins manifested confusion and worry about the rights of an individual woman to claim time and energy for her own work; see, for example, *The Florentine Frame* (Leipzig: Bernhard Tauchnitz, 1909). For Robins, the emphasis on women in public life entailed prizing traditional private-sphere female virtues of altruism and

even self-sacrifice. For the fullest examination of this tendency, see Jane Marcus, 'Elizabeth Robins: A Biographical and Critical Study', thesis Northwestern University, 1973.

19 Vida's first name suggests both 'full' and 'life', while the surname Levering indicates the kind of power to move or open that she achieves.

20 'Looked at from another angle, the sex antagonism we have examined seems to have arisen from the failure to allow for that law in optics by which we see as most important the nearest object: This nearest object is, inevitably, oneself' (*Ancilla's* 97).

21 13. The representation of Chloe and Olivia 'will light a torch in that vast chamber where nobody has yet been'; Woolf celebrates difference without essentializing it when she observes 'It would be a thousand pities if women wrote like men, or lived like men, or looked like men, for if two sexes are quite inadequate, considering the vastness and variety of the world, how should we manage with one only?' (*Room* 88, 92). Robins observes that in a fictional representation 'women like and men hate, women may be praising something whose truth and beauty they know' and urges 'the most immediately urgent study of womankind is woman' (*Ancilla's* 88, 152).

22 Notably in her contemporaries Edith Wharton and Mary (Mrs Humphry) Ward. The latter was a particularly generous appraisal in view of the fact that Ward, a lifelong antifeminist, was one of Robins' most formidable political enemies.

23 'If a woman but attempts this honourable task [of creating a believable character] – an affair of strong self-control and of almost mathematical accuracy – if she happens to bring it off, her critics pat her on the back with an absent-minded air, while they look about for 'personal experience'.

    'Or they do not even look about. They are content to say: 'This is so like the real thing it must be a piece of verbatim reporting, done by a person whose merit is a retentive memory. These life-like scenes are autobiography. The heroine is naturally the writer's self, made to look as she thinks she looks, or as she wishes to heaven she might! ... Otherwise it must be that she has imagination, which is plainly preposterous' (*Way Stations* 7).

24 Woolf could, and did, leave room for humorously satirical treatments – Austen's novels are full of examples and *To the Lighthouse* is as witty as *A Room of One's Own* in its treatment of what Robins called sex antagonism. Moreover, most of Woolf's fiction, and all her novels, deal with explicitly feminist themes. In the novels up to *The Pargiters/The Years*, however, protagonists rarely articulate such themes directly, whereas characters who do articulate or embody such themes (Evelyn Murgatroyd in *The Voyage Out*, Mary Dachet in *Night and Day*, Doris Kilman in *Mrs. Dalloway*) are always presented as to some degree pretentious or hyperbolic because of their views.

25 The Lawrentian Mr A. of *A Room of One's Own*, whose ludicrously phallic 'I' blocks the view of any other character in his novel, has similarly damaged his writing through overemphasis on an authorial self identified with gender: 'The Suffrage campaign was no doubt to blame. It must have roused in men an extraordinary desire for self-assertion; it must have made them lay an emphasis upon their own sex and its characteristics which they would not have troubled to think about had they not been challenged'

(*Room* 103). But Mr A's work is less 'stunted' and 'deformed' than rendered incapable of progeny, sterile: 'the dominance of the letter "I" and the aridity, which like the giant beech tree, it casts within its shade. Nothing will grow there' [104]). Such a consequence is less serious than the invisibility of Anon or the mute ingloriousness of Judith Shakespeare, and as the ironic invocation of the Suffrage campaign suggests, it is a late reaction to a protest against the sexual status quo.

26 For instance, she wrote in her diary about a novel by Dorothy Richardson, 'I felt myself looking for faults; hoping for them. And they would have bent my pen, I know. There must be an instinct of self-preservation at work. If she's good then I'm not': 315 (28 November 1919). Of her friend Katherine Mansfield, whom she respected far more, she wrote, 'I must think her good, since I'm glad to hear her abused.' *Diary, Volume Two, 1920–1924*, ed. Anne Olivier Bell assisted by Andrew McNeillie (New York: Harcourt Brace Jovanovich, 1978), pp. 78–9 (12 December 1920).

Index

Academy, The, 34, 36, 135–6, 142,
150, 158
Adams, Henry, 16
advertising, 1, 15, 61, 62, 69, 81, 148,
150, 151, 169, 183
Alger, Horatio, 156
Anderson, Margaret, 199
androgyny, 115, 119, 227
Anesko, Michael, 12, 41, 52
Anstruther-Thompson, Kit, 116, 119,
128, 133–4
Archer, William, 146, 148, 156, 184,
208
Ardis, Ann, 7
Armstrong, Paul B., 44, 49, 53, 138,
151, 156
Arnold, Matthew, 4, 11, 12, 18–20,
38, 71, 81, 139, 156, 158, 162,
164, 166, 169, 172, 180, 181–3,
222
Athenaeum, The, 28, 39, 135, 146, 147,
156
Atlantic Monthly, The, 47, 136
Austen, Jane, 8, 36, 210, 225, 234
Author, The, 5
authorial performance, 12, 14, 50–1,
83
autobiography, 10, 13, 23, 45, 99,
102, 110, 179

Bagehot, Walter, 3, 71
Ball, Wilfrid, 147, 152
Balzac, Honoré de, 78, 80, 99, 109
Baring, Maurice, 117, 129, 132
Barrie, J.M., 144
Baudelaire, Charles, 99, 109, 142
Beach, Sylvia, 190, 198, 199, 200–3,
205
Beaverbrook, William Maxwell
Aitken, Lord, 180
Beerbohm, Max, 99, 208
'A Defence of Cosmetics', 96
Beja, Morris, 202

Bell, William Henry, 150
Bennett, Arnold, 6, 11, 12, 13, 19, 20,
139, 156–84, 222, 230
Clayhanger, 170
Hilda Lessways, 170
How to Live on 24 Hours a Day, 157,
163, 174–5, 180
How to Make the Best of Life, 163
Literary Taste: How to Form It, 163
Mental Efficiency, 160–1, 162–3, 167,
175, 177
Riceyman Steps, 165, 173, 180
Self and Self-Management, 163, 169
The Human Machine, 160, 163
The Truth About an Author, 165,
168–9, 175–6, 180
The Old Wives' Tale, 173, 176
Bennett, Dorothy Cheston, 164
Besant, Walter, 5
Bhabha, Homi, 10, 114, 115, 117–18,
132
Bishop, Edward, 14
Black, Barbara, 131
Blackmur, R.P., 40
Bland, Lucy, 56
Blind, Mathilde, 151
Bloom, Harold, 33
Boer War, the, 1
book market, 1–3, 11, 81, 96, 103
Borderland, 56, 72
Bourdieu, Pierre, 2, 9, 14, 17, 19, 134,
137, 156, 191, 192, 207
Bourget, Paul, 78
Bradley, Katherine. *See* Michael Field
Brake, Laurel, 12
Brandom, Robert, 111, 113
Brontë, Charlotte, 223–4
Brontë, Charlotte, Emily and Anne, 8
Brown, Curtis, 5
Budgen, Frank, 195–6, 207
Burckhardt, Jacob, 19
Burney, Charles, 126
Butler, Judith, 12, 14, 50, 51, 53, 211

Byron, George Gordon, Lord Byron, 134, 157

Caird, Mona, 212
Campbell, James Dykes, 151
Carey, John, 2, 17, 19
Cerf, Bennett, 190–1
Chap Book, The, 146
Chitty, Susan, 81
commodification of culture, 7, 10
Conrad, Joseph, 2, 16, 17, 19, 97, 178
Cooper, Edith. *See* Michael Field
Corelli, Marie, 1, 9, 17, 134, 135, 157
Cornhill Magazine, The, 64
Courtney, Janet Hogarth, 19, 76, 79, 81, 87, 95, 99, 212, 230–2
Courtney, W.L., 76, 211
Crary, Jonathan, 125, 126, 130, 132, 134
Culver, Stuart, 43

Daily Graphic, The, 139
Daily Mail, The, 1, 59, 61, 67, 69, 70, 74
Daily News, The, 65
Daily Paper, The, 54, 59, 61–3, 67–9, 72–4
Daudet, Alphonse, 78
Dellamora, Richard, 119, 132, 133, 134
Demoor, Marysa, 137, 146, 211
Dettmar, Kevin, 16
Dick, Susan, 100, 104, 105, 111, 113, 114, 148
Dickens, Charles, 3, 4, 19, 49, 75, 83, 87, 99, 122, 179
Dickens, Mary Angela, 74, 81
Dilke, Charles, 26
Dilke, Sir Charles Wentworth, 27, 29
Dilke, Emilia, 6, 8, 9, 15, 19–40
    Book of Spiritual Life, The, 20, 27
    Renaissance of Art in France, The, 22–3
    Shrine of Death, The, 25, 26
    Shrine of Love, The, 25
Dolman, Frederick, 79, 86

Edel, Leon, 38, 40, 53
Elfenbein, Andrew, 134, 157

Elgar, Edward, 150
Eliot, George, 4, 9, 20, 32, 35–6
    Middlemarch, 20
Eliot, T.S., 207
Ellmann, Richard, 190, 202, 207, 208
English Illustrated Magazine, The, 140, 144
English Review, The, 167
Evening News, The, 74

Fame, 1, 156
Fawcett, Millicent, 139
Federico, Annette, 9, 13, 134
Field, Michael, 17, 115, 116, 132, 156, 158
Flaubert, Gustave, 78, 99
Flint, Carl, 203
Flower, Newman, 180
Ford, Ford Madox, 167
Ford, James L., 79
Forster, E.M., 178
Forster's Education Act 1871, 2
Foucault, Michel, 6, 17, 170, 182
Fraser, Hilary, 10
Fraser's Magazine, 138
Frazier, Adrian, 99, 101, 103, 106, 108, 111–12
French literature, 78–80, 99, 109
Freud, Sigmund, 7, 15, 98, 101–3, 105, 114, 168
Furniss, Harry, 75

Galsworthy, John, 207–8
Gaskell, Elizabeth, 8
Gautier, Théophile, 78, 99, 109
Geddes, Patrick, 129, 130, 131
Genette, Gerard, 190
Gissing, George, 5, 11, 17
Goncourt, Edmond and Jules de, 99
Gonne, Maud, 139
Gosse, E.W., 106
    Father and Son, 106
Greenblatt, Stephen, 14, 15, 19, 20–2, 35–7
Gregory, Augusta, Lady Gregory, 14, 185
Grubgeld, Elizabeth, 99–100, 102, 103, 108, 110–12
Gunn, Peter, 116–19, 121, 133

Gunning, Tom, 126, 133
Gwynn, Stephen, 79, 80, 82, 94

Habegger, Alfred, 44
Hall, Stuart, 10, 114
Hardy, Thomas, 76, 97, 134, 157, 159, 211
Harper's Weekly, 76, 100, 136
Harris, Frank 99
Harrison, Mary St Leger Kingsley. *See* Lucas Malet
Harrison, William, 83
Hearst, W.R., 57, 65–8
Help. A Journal of Social Service, 56–7
Henley, W.E., 142–5, 150
historicism, 123
Hite, Molly, 10
Hogarth, Janet E., *See* Janet E. Hogarth Courtney
Holly, Carol, 44
Hollyer, Frederick, 140
Howells, William Dean, 42
Hughes, Linda K., 9, 82
Hugo, Victor, 79
Hunt, Violet, 75, 77
Hutcheon, Linda, 110, 112
Huysmans, Joris Karl, 80
Huyssen, Andreas, 8, 18, 211

Ibsen, Henrik, 14, 184–5, 193, 208–9
Illustrated London News, The, 142
Ingelow, Jean, 136, 140
investigative journalism, 68
irony, use of, 110–11
Israel, Kali, 36

Jackson, Holbrook, 99, 104
James, Henry, 6, 11, 16, 36, 40–53, 97, 208
    The American, 46–7
    'The Birthplace', 50
    'The Jolly Corner', 48
    Portrait of the Lady, The, 42, 47–8, 50
    The Princess Casamassima, 47–8
    'The Private Life', 41, 42, 51
    Roderick Hudson, 44, 46–8, 50
    The Spoils of Poynton, 49
    The Wings of the Dove, 47–8, 178
    What Maisie Knew, 49

Johnson, Samuel, 122
journalism, 1, 4, 54, 60, 61, 66, 69–73, 159, 160
Joyce, James, 6, 11, 13, 14, 20, 110, 112, 166, 179 184–207
    A Portrait of the Author as a Young Man, 185, 187, 188–9
    Chamber Music, 189
    Dubliners, 187, 189
    Exiles, 186, 188
    Finnegans Wake, 197
    Ulysses, 184, 189, 197
Kafka, Franz, 167
Kendall, May, 137
Kenner, Hugh, 204
Kernahan, Coulson, 138
Kimball, Roger, 15
Kingsley, Charles, 73, 82, 87, 89, 93, 96, 97, 99
Kingsley, Charles and Mary
    The Tutor's Story, 85
Kingsley, George, 74, 82
Kingsley, Henry, 74, 82
Kingsley, Mary, 74, 82–3
Kipling, Rudyard, 142

Landon, Laetitia, 138
Lane, John, 144, 147, 149, 152
Lang, Andrew, 136–8, 145
    How to Fail in Literature, 136
Langbauer, Laurie, 82
Larson, Jil, 13, 18, 96–8, 112
Lawrence, D.H., 16, 19, 20, 166, 179, 180, 189, 207, 230
Le Gallienne, Richard, 140, 151, 151, 158, 160
Lee, Vernon, 7, 8, 10, 20, 114–33, 157, 230
    Art and Man, 119
    Laurus Nobilis, 128
    Limbo, 122, 129
    Miss Brown, 119, 121
    The Spirit of Rome, 121, 123
    Studies of the Eighteenth Century in Italy, 120, 123, 125–6
    'The Tower of the Mirrors', 129
Lehmann, Lotte, 155
Leighton, Frederick, 27
Levy, Amy, 142

Liebowitz, Stan, 203, 206
literary agents, 6, 86
Little Review, The, 193, 195, 200, 201
Longman's Magazine, 136, 137
Loti, Pierre, 78
Lovelace, Maud Hart, 157, 159
   Emily of Deep Valley, 158–9
Lowell, James Russell, 138
Lund, Michael, 82
Lundberg, Patricia Lorimer, 94

MacIntyre, Alasdair, 96, 111–12
Maddox, Brenda, 202, 208
Malet, Lucas, 7, 8, 9, 20, 73–95, 208
   Adrian Savage, 76, 77, 80, 89
   The Carissima, 76
   Colonel Enderby's Wife, 76, 77, 89,
      92
   A Counsel of Perfection, 77, 89
   The Far Horizon, 76
   The Gateless Barrier, 76, 77, 91
   The History of Sir Richard Calmady,
      76, 89–92
   Little Peter, 81
   Mrs. Lorimer, 74, 83–4
   A Study in Black and White, 74
   The Wages of Sin, 73, 77, 89, 90, 91
Manet, Edouard, 99
Mansfield, Elizabeth, 9, 15
Mansfield, Katherine, 234
Marcus, Jane, 230
Margolis, Stephen, 205, 208
mass media, 15, 134
Mathews, T. Elkin, 144, 149, 186
Maupassant, Guy de, 78
McCarthy, Desmond, 217, 222
McDonald, Peter, 4, 11, 18, 160, 164,
   183
McWhirter, David, 40, 43, 49, 53, 54
Menand, Louis, 104,
Mercure de France, 201
Mermin, Dorothy, 138, 158
Meynell, Alice, 9, 140–2, 148–50, 151,
   208, 228
Michelet, Jules, 19
Mitchell, S. Weir, 24, 213
Moore, George, 11, 13, 20, 96–113,
   132, 180, 182
   Confessions of a Young Man, 98–103

Moore, Thomas Sturge, 188
More, Thomas, 35
Mudie's circulating library, 2, 103
Muir, Willa, 212

Nesbit, Edith, 140, 142
new journalism, 4
New Statesman, The, 217, 222
New York Daily Tribune, The, 75, 80
New York Edition of the Henry James
   novels, 12, 40, 42, 43, 48–52
New York Journal, 57, 65
New York Times, The, 80, 84, 196
Newman, John Henry, 22, 85
   Apologia Pro Vita Sua, 85
Nietzsche, Friedrich, 97, 98, 103,
   109–12
Norris, David, 202
Norris, Margot, 203
Northern Echo, The, 54, 59, 71, 74

Oliphant, Margaret, 82
Olney, James, 50–1, 54

Pacchierotti, Gasparo, 127
Pageant, The, 146
Paget, Violet. *See* Vernon Lee
Pall Mall Gazette, The, 13, 54, 58, 61,
   73, 135, 146
Pater, Walter, 32–4, 99, 106, 109, 112,
   113, 120, 133
   *Studies in the History of the
      Renaissance*, 33
Pattison, Mark, 9, 22–30, 36–8
Pearson, John, 12
periodical market, 3, 54, 73, 134
Phillips, Stephen, 149
Pinker, J.B., 5, 16, 20, 166
Portfolio, The, 20
Posnock, Ross, 43
Pound, Ezra, 187
Proust, Marcel, 98, 167
pseudonyms, use of, 9, 31, 73–9, 84,
   90–3, 108, 119, 136
Psomiades, Kathy, 16, 119
psychic research, 63

Quaritch, Bernard, 152
Queen, 139

Quiller-Couch, A.T., 150
Quin, John, 187

Rabaté, Jean-Michel, 202
Rainey, Laurence, 15
Reese, Lizette, 142
Rendall, Vernon, 147
Review of Reviews, The, 54, 56, 58–63,
    68–70
Rhondda, Viscontess, 212
Ribot, Théodule, 134
Richardson, Dorothy, 208
Ricoeur, Paul, 10, 18
Rimbaud, Arthur, 99
Robins, Elizabeth, 5, 63, 138, 139,
    158–9, 207–9, 212–18, 220–33
    Alan's Wife, 213
    Ancilla's Share, 217, 221
    The Convert, 216–17
    Votes for Women, 213, 215–16
Rorty, Richard, 13, 97, 98, 100–5, 107,
    110
Rosenbaum, S.P., 211
Rossetti, Christina, 136, 140
Rossetti, Dante Gabriel, 136
Rowe, John Carlos, 40, 54
Ruskin, John, 21, 25, 30–4, 36, 38, 40

Said, Edward, 91
Salmon, Richard, 16, 42
Sand, George, 79
Saturday Review, The, 28, 30, 32
Schaffer, Talia, 8, 9, 16
Scholnick, Robert, 142, 159
Schopenhauer, Arthur, 100, 103,
    111–12
Scots Observer, The, 71, 135
Scott, Cyril, 150
Scott, Walter, 49
Scribner's Magazine, 136
Sedgwick, Eve, 44–6, 49, 54, 88, 94,
    100
Shakespeare, William, 18, 35–6, 122,
    124, 217, 223, 225
Shaw, George Bernard, 4, 5, 6, 16,
    18–20, 117, 169, 208
Showalter, Elaine, 39, 115, 211, 231
Sigerson, Dora, 140
Sinclair, May, 81, 212

Sitwell, Edith, 208, 230
Smiles, Samuel, 156
Society of Authors, 5, 6
Speaker, The, 150
Spencer, Herbert, 170, 181
Squillace, Robert, 12
Srebrnik, Patricia, 75, 78, 80–1, 83,
    100
St. James's Gazette, The, 136
Star, The, 65, 71, 74, 152
Stead, William T., 4, 11–13, 16, 20,
    54–72
Stedman, E.C., 142, 152 159
Stevens, Wallace, 203
Stevenson, Robert Louis, 4, 49, 157,
    222
Strong, Francis. *See* Emilia Dilke
suffrage laws, 3, 29
Swinburne, Algernon Charles, 136,
    150
Sylvia's Journal, 144
Symonds, John Addington, 19
Symons, Arthur, 151

Tennyson, Alfred, Lord Tennyson, 3,
    19, 135
Thackeray, William Makepeace, 64
Thompson, Yates, 59
Time, 185, 195
Times, The, 1, 19, 59, 60, 67, 71, 72,
    76, 95, 96, 100, 101, 137, 232
Tomson, Arthur, 142
Tomson, Graham R.. *See* Rosamund
    Marriott Watson
translations, role of, 100, 110
Trollope, Anthony, 82, 94
Tynan, Katharine, 144, 148

Uccello, Paolo, 205
Unwin, T. Fisher, 133, 142, 143,
    148–9, 180

Vallings, Gabrielle, 77, 91, 93
Van Vechten, Carl, 143, 159
Veblen, Thorstein, 204
Verlaine, Paul, 100, 142
Vicinus, Martha, 119, 134
Victorian medical practice and
    women's enfranchisement, 24

Walkowitz, Judith, 56
Ward, Mary (Mrs Humphry Ward), 36, 81, 139
Watson, H.B. Marriott, 144
Watson, Rosamund Marriott, 7, 8, 9, 20, 73, 134–55
   After Sunset, 147
   'Ballad of the Bird-Bride', 150
   The Bird-Bride. A Volume of Ballads and Sonnets, 137
   A Summer Night, and Other Poems, 142
   Tares, 142
   Vespertilia and Other Verses, 147
Watson, William, 142
Watt, A.P., 5, 17, 20
Watt, Stephen, 16
Weaver, Harriet, 187, 189, 190, 193–6, 199, 200–3, 208
Webster, Augusta, 151
Weir, David, 24, 103–4, 107, 111
Wells, H.G., 2, 166, 167, 169, 178–9, 183, 198, 207, 214
Westminster Review, The, 28, 33, 36, 39, 40, 72
White, Gleeson, 137
Whitelock, William Wallace, 79
Whyte, Frederic, 59, 63, 73, 74
Wicke, Jennifer, 151
Wilberforce, Octavia, 213, 231

Wilde, Oscar, 6, 94, 96, 97, 99, 100, 104, 106, 118, 138, 139, 145, 151–2, 158, 160, 205, 208
   The Critic as Artist, 99
   The Decay of Lying, 96, 99
   The Importance of Being Earnest, 90–1
   De Profundis, 106
Williams, Raymond, 7
Woman, 139
Woman's World, 139, 151, 159, 160
women artists, 21, 27
women authors, 8, 9, 20, 138, 151, 215
women readers, 62, 63, 74
Woods, Margaret L., 148
Woolf, Leonard, 213
Woolf, Virginia, 6, 7, 8, 10, 19, 20, 89, 95, 101, 179, 207–34
   'Mr. Bennett and Mrs. Brown', 207–8
   A Room of One's Own, 207, 209, 212, 215, 226–9
   Three Guineas, 215
   The Years, 215
Wyld, James, 131

Yeats, W.B., 142, 186
Yellow Book, The, 146, 152, 169
Yonge, Charlotte, 82, 84

Zola, Emile, 78, 99

Printed in the United States
35601LVS00001B/166-171